without Borders

The International Pastime

EDITED BY GEORGE GMELCH

University of Nebraska Press | Lincoln + London

CHAPTER 3, "China: Silk Gowns and Gold Gloves"
by Joseph A. Reaves, was adapted and updated from
an article that originally appeared in *Nine* 7, no. 2
(Spring 1999) and from a chapter in the author's
Taking in a Game: A History of Baseball in Asia
(University of Nebraska Press, 2002).

CHAPTER 4, "Taiwan: Baseball, Colonialism, and
Nationalism," by Andrew Morris, was adapted
from an article "Baseball, History, the Local and the
Global in Taiwan," in *The Minor Arts of Daily Life:
Popular Culture in Taiwan* (Honolulu: University of
Hawai'i Press, 2004), eds. David K. Jordan, Andrew
D. Morris, and Marc L. Moskowitz.

CHAPTER 13, "Italy: No Hot Dogs in the Bleachers"
by Peter Carino, was adapted and updated from
an article titled "Baseball in Translation," which
originally appeared in *NINE* 7, no. 2 (Spring 1999).

Library of Congress Cataloging-in-Publication Data
Baseball without borders : the international pastime
/ edited by George Gmelch.
   p. cm.
ISBN-13: 978-0-8032-7125-8 (pbk. : alkaline paper)
ISBN-10: 0-8032-7125-5 (pbk. : alkaline paper)
1. Baseball. I. Gmelch, George.
GV867.B36 2006   796.357—dc22
2006007738

Designed and set in Adobe Minion by A. Shahan.

For **Bill Kirwin** and **Sharon Gmelch**

Contents

Illustrations

Acknowledgments

The idea for this book developed out of conversations with Bill Kirwin, the founder and editor of *Nine: A Journal of Baseball History and Culture.* I am also grateful to Ted Gilman, Dan Gordon, Bill Kelly, Alan Klein, Marty Kuehnert, Tim Wiles, Franklin Otto, Robert Whiting, and Rob Wilson, my colleagues in baseball scholarship, for their suggestions about the shape of the book and the selection of its contributors. I thank Sharon Gmelch, Dan Gordon, Jim Mann, Franklin Otto, Bill Kirwin, Alan Klein, and Lisa Quirk for their insightful comments on drafts of the manuscript.

I owe many thanks to the participants and the organizers of the Baseball and American Culture symposium in Cooperstown, New York, and the *Nine* Spring Training Conference held in Tucson, Arizona. These annual gatherings of baseball academics have helped incubate many ideas about baseball culture and history. I am indebted to the Freeman Foundation and to Union College's East Asian Studies program for a generous grant that enabled Ted Gilman and me to bring to our campus the leading scholars of baseball in Asia, three of whom became contributors to this volume.

Baseball Hall of Fame librarians Bill Francis and Tim Wiles were, as always, an immense help, as were Union College reference librarians Donna Burton, Bruce Connolly, Dave Gerhan, and Mary Cahill. For unstinting assistance in editing the essays, for ensuring their coherence, and for keeping the language accessible, I thank Union College Anthropology Department aides

Emily Laing, Sandra Vega, and Amy Bell. Their efforts have made this a much better book.

My agent, Robert Wilson, gave wise counsel and urged me to expunge all jargon and reach out to a broader audience. Special thanks go to Rob Taylor, editor at the University of Nebraska Press, for his support of the project and to others at the press for shepherding the manuscript through the publication process. Morgan Gmelch did a splendid job on the index. If I may single out a few of my academic colleagues, I have benefited from frequent discussions on all matters of sport and writing with David Baum, Ian Condry, Richard Felson, Sharon Gmelch, Walt and Paula Gmelch, Jerry Handler, Lisa Quirk, Teresa Meade, Richard Nelson, Derek Pardue, Andor Skotnes, and Kenji Tierney.

Of course, my appreciation goes to all of the authors in the volume for their responsiveness and commitment and for the quality of their contributions. Their essays have greatly changed my appreciation of baseball beyond U.S. borders.

Introduction

Around the Horn

A televised baseball game from Puerto Rico, Japan, or even Cuba looks much like the North American game. The players use the same gloves and bats, wear similar uniforms, and play by the same basic rules. But beneath the outward similarity there is usually a very different history, and a culture influencing the nuances of the sport. Even how players and their fans think about the game and what they value may not be the same. As Joseph Reaves notes about baseball in Asia, "It can look so similar and somehow feel so different."[1]

The essays in this collection explore such differences in fourteen baseball-playing nations. The essays are diverse not only in the cultures they describe, but also in the perspectives adopted by their authors who range from anthropologists to historians, from journalists to English professors, with a few independent scholars as well. The essays are also diverse because I placed few restrictions on what they chose to write about. I suggested some topics, such as the origins of baseball in their country, its development, and how local versions of the game differ from that played in the United States, but otherwise the contributors were free to write about whatever aspects of the sport they thought American baseball fans (the intended audience) would find interesting. Some of the essays deal exclusively with the professional game abroad while some, especially where there is not a strong professional league, also look at the amateur level.

I could have organized the essays in several ways. One way might have been by the level of baseball's development, such as tier one, two, and three countries, with tier one comprising nations like Japan and the Dominican Republic, where baseball is a major national sport and a well-established professional league exists; tier three would include countries where baseball is a minor sport with few followers and no professional league, such as Brazil. Ultimately, however, I felt it made more sense to group the essays by geography. Each region—Asia, the Americas, Europe, and the Pacific—share similarities in history and culture that have resulted in some parallels in the origins, development, and local versions of baseball found within them.

The collection begins with Asia, with two essays on the Japanese game. Baseball is not a postwar, General MacArthur–inspired American import as some American baseball fans believe; it was introduced in 1867 by a young American teaching at a Tokyo university. Baseball became popular among schoolboys and eventually won recognition from the government for its educational and health benefits. In the first essay, "Japan: Changing of the Guard in High School Baseball," Dan Gordon reveals the unique characteristics of Japanese high school baseball and the all-Japan national tournament at Kōshien. Far more than a mere sport, Japanese school ball is a philosophy and an educational tool. It is considered a spiritual discipline that teaches many of the values that define the Japanese *bushido* tradition of teamwork, dedication, discipline, and respect. Gordon also notes an unhealthy side to Japanese high school ball, including hazing, corporal punishment, and its sometimes excruciating and borderline abusive training methods—activities that would not be tolerated in an American high school.

Gordon's essay has personal significance for me in that his research on international baseball dates back to when he was a student at Union College, where I have taught for the past twenty-five years. I was on the Thomas J. Watson Fellowship Committee, which screened student applicants for a generous grant that enables a lucky few to travel abroad and explore a topic of their choice for one year after graduation. Dan came to my office to talk about the fellowship, and out of that conversation emerged the idea of looking at local versions of baseball in four cultures. Dan wrote a compelling proposal, won the fellowship, and a few days after graduation embarked on an eighteen-month global baseball odyssey to Japan, Nicaragua, Cuba, and the Dominican Republic.

Fifteen years later he returned to two of these countries for follow-up research and is the author of two essays in this volume.

In "Japan: The Hanshin Tigers and Japanese Professional Baseball," Yale University anthropologist William W. Kelly examines professional baseball and its place in Japanese society. American fans may be surprised to learn that Japan's professional league was created by private urban railroad companies which in the early part of the twentieth century built sports stadiums and other amusements to boost business on their trains. Vestiges of that are evident in the time limits on Japanese games (which can result in games ending in ties) so that commuting fans can catch the last train home.

While the Japanese have certainly transformed baseball to fit their own culture, Kelly is critical of the exaggerated and simplistic image in the West of the Japanese game as "samurai baseball"—that is, as a sport that turns play into pedagogy and a character-building enterprise. While Americans play baseball, the Japanese work baseball, goes the stereotype. The most common metaphor used to explain the national differences is the so-called Japanese propensity for playing "Little Ball," with its emphasis on sacrifice bunts, hit-and-run, slap hits, and getting the lead early, versus the American preference for "Big Ball," where hitters swing for the fences and managers play for the big inning until late in the game.

Ironically, some of the most exotic and outlandish aspects of Japanese baseball were borrowed from the early American game, such as the organized chanting and cheering of private fan clubs. This phenomenon originated with American university cheerleading squads, which the first Japanese college baseball teams, which toured the United States in the early twentieth century, observed. The Japanese were impressed and took notes, and upon their return to Japan trained their own student cheerleading squads, thus starting a tradition that was later adopted by the professional game. Discovering this in Kelly's essay was embarrassing for me; while teaching in Japan I had on occasion taken my American students to watch Japanese baseball games and had always drawn their attention to the organized cheering as something uniquely Japanese—an example of Japanese collectivism and group unity.

Kelly notes the many ways in which the Japanese game has diverged from the North American game. For example, baseball is Japan's dominant or "center" sport and does not get much competition from other sports. In the United States, Major League Baseball (MLB) must compete with the NFL and the NBA for fans. Infields in most Japanese stadiums are composed solely of dirt, the games are slower, players' careers are shorter, the salary range is more compressed (with a smaller income gap between superstars and journeymen), and the rosters are much larger because teams do not have much of a minor league system. It is this version of the game, and not the great American game, that has diffused across Asia.

In "China: Silk Gowns and Gold Gloves," journalist Joseph A. Reaves, who covered Asia for the *Chicago Tribune* for many years and who upon his return to the United States in 1992 reported on the Chicago Cubs for four seasons, charts the erratic history of baseball in China. Surprisingly, baseball was played in China as early as 1863, a decade before the first game in Japan. However, the game did not take root until much later. In nineteenth-century China, baseball was best known for the role it played in the cancellation of China's first and most ambitious educational exchange with the United States. Many of the 120 Chinese students sent to the United States in 1872 to learn the best of Western science and engineering developed a fondness for baseball, along with some other Western habits. When Chinese conservatives reported the students' transgressions back to the Imperial Court, the mission was canceled and the students were called home. Baseball then languished until the early 1900s, when many Chinese students began studying in Japan and became reacquainted with baseball, Japan's major collegiate sport. Baseball then gained a small following in China until the Cultural Revolution (1961–74), when the game was dismissed as a symbol of Western decadence. Across China zealous Red Guards ridiculed and sometimes persecuted players and coaches, and international competitions were no longer held. After the Cultural Revolution the game made a comeback and was even extolled by Chinese leaders for its benefits in military training (e.g., it teaches soldiers how to throw hand grenades more accurately). At times reviled, at times exalted, baseball survived these upheavals; today Chinese leaders are encouraging the development of baseball in anticipation of the 2008 Summer Olympics in Beijing.

Baseball arrived in Taiwan in 1897, shortly after the Japanese colonized the island. First played by Japanese youth, mostly at school, it was later adopted by Taiwanese boys and was an acceptable setting in which Taiwan's colonized population could interact and compete with the Japanese. "Taiwan: Baseball, Colonialism, and Nationalism" is by historian Andrew Morris, who lived two blocks from the baseball stadium in Taizhong while doing research for his doctoral dissertation on another topic. He became a die-hard fan of the President Lions, and eventually became interested in questions of colonialism, nationalism, and ethnic identity in Taiwan's national game, questions he addresses in his essay.

Many American readers will recall Taiwan's unparalleled Little League success (ten Little League World Series titles between 1969 and 1981 and sixteen altogether). Morris examines the role of these championships in developing national pride and promoting nationalism. Morris is particularly interested in the interplay between the local and international dimensions of Taiwanese baseball. The popularity of the Chinese Professional Baseball League (CPBL), for example, has depended on maintaining a balance between respect for local Chinese tradition and the international (e.g., allowing foreigners to play in its league). The league lost much of its fan support in the 1990s when it allowed so many foreign players (up to ten per team) in that they pushed all of the native Taiwanese players out of the starring roles.

In "Korea: Straw Sandals and Strong Arms," Reaves charts the development of Korean baseball. Like Taiwan, Korea was also a colony of Japan; both later became close allies of the United States. Although a U.S. missionary first introduced baseball to Korea in the 1870s, it was the Japanese occupiers who spread the game. The colonial authorities promoted baseball as part of their plan to indoctrinate Korean youth with Japanese ways. Much like in Taiwan, Koreans first adopted the game as a way to peacefully challenge their oppressors, but it later became a way to impress outsiders. Reaves also shows how a government, threatened by a restive population, used baseball as an opiate. Indeed, one of the primary objectives of the Korea Baseball Organization in the 1980s was to divert the public's attention from politics to sports—to find an outlet for its restless and often rebellious young men.

Part 2, made up of seven essays on baseball in the Americas, leads off with the Dominican Republic. Baseball in the Dominican Republic is sometimes described as "a national fever." Dominican children relate to baseball in the same way that American children respond to TV and video games. No other aspect of Dominican life, except perhaps merengue, has provided as much joi de vivre in this Caribbean country as has baseball.[2] As Alan Klein so ably documents in his book, *Sugarball: The American Game, the Dominican Dream*, the development of Dominican baseball is closely tied to sugarcane. Early on baseball became a diversion for cane workers during their breaks from the sugar fields, and many of the first leagues were organized by sugar factory managers. In "Dominican Republic: Forging an International Industry," Klein explores the Dominican Republic's rise to international baseball prominence. After a brief review of the early history of baseball in the country, Klein turns to the ways talented local youths are developed into professional prospects. These center on the baseball academies set up by MLB organizations to train Dominican youths, and the Dominican network of *buscónes* or amateur scouts who locate, nourish, instruct, and then link young prospects with a Major League organization (in exchange for a percentage of the prospect's signing bonus).

Klein also examines the transnational relationships between Dominican and American baseball. Where some observers have viewed the relationship in mostly exploitative terms (e.g., Arturo J. Marcano Guevara and David P. Fidler's *Stealing Lives: The Globalization of Baseball and the Tragic Story of Alexis Quiroz*), Klein shows that while North American interests dominated Dominican baseball in the 1950s and 1960s, severely crippling the local Dominican professional league, relations have become more reciprocal in recent years.

Baseball arrived in Cuba in the 1860s, introduced by students returning from the United States. Folklore credits Nemiso Guillo for bringing the game to Cuba, when he returned from Springfield College in Mobile, Alabama, with a bat and baseball in his trunk. American sailors helped spread the game by playing with locals in Cuban ports. Interest in the game also got a lift from visiting American barnstormers in the 1870s. Just as the Japanese were responsible for spreading the game through Asia, Cubans became the apostles of baseball in parts of the Caribbean. Tim Wendel, in "Cuba: Behind the Curtain," takes us on a personal journey across the island's baseball landscape. Along the way he examines the inflated claims that Fidel Castro was a genuine prospect (he wasn't) as well as the impact of the Cuban revolution on the island's national pastime (considerable). In Wendel's interactions with a baseball official and with fans we learn of their thirst for information about the North American Major Leagues, particularly what American baseball looks like—Cuba's fans have no access to TV or other images of American games and ballparks.

In the second essay on Cuba, "Cuba: Community, Fans, and Ballplayers," anthropologist Thomas Carter tells us more about the consequences of the revolution for Cuban baseball and then focuses on the relationship between Cuban fans and their baseball heroes. Carter, who went to Cuba to study other aspects of baseball for his doctoral dissertation, became enthralled with the easy, unrestricted relations fans have with Cuba's ballplayers, which is in stark contrast to the more distant relationship between fans and players in the United States.

In "Puerto Rico: A Major League Steppingstone," Thomas E. Van Hyning and Franklin Otto write from the perspective of fans who grew up on the island watching Puerto Rico Winter League (PRWL) baseball in its heyday. They survey the early development of Puerto Rican baseball and then turn to the PRWL, where so many fine U.S. and Caribbean Major League players spent their winters in the six-team league.[3] In operation since 1938, the PRWL was in danger of folding in the early 1990s, in part because many of the homegrown stars no longer wished to return home to play—as Major Leaguers they had large salaries and didn't need the money and their American teams didn't want them to risk injury. Today a new generation of Puerto Rican stars is playing in the PRWL, wanting to honor their country and let their fans, many of whom will never travel to the United States, see their heroes in person.

While the PRWL is making a popular and financial comeback, organized baseball in Nicaragua is not faring as well. In "Nicaragua: In Search of Diamonds," Dan Gordon describes the declining interest in the game that he observed when he returned to the war-torn country in 2003 after a fifteen-year absence. Baseball is losing ground to soccer among the nation's youth. In this desperately poor nation neither the central government, the local authorities, nor the traditional business sponsors have the resources to fund baseball adequately, as they once did. Fewer youths play the game, and some ball fields have been torn down to make room for new housing. The salaries in Nicaragua's one professional league are so depressed, Gordon reports, that some players have given up the game and have returned home to better-paying blue-collar jobs. Nonetheless, Nicaraguan ball fields still produce Major League prospects and there are now more than fifty Nicaraguans playing professionally in the United States, though nearly all are in the minor leagues.

Brazil is the southernmost nation in the Western Hemisphere to play baseball. But Brazilian baseball is not unique because of its geography but because of who plays it. Although introduced by visiting American workers in the early 1900s, baseball was actually developed by Japanese immigrants. It is the Japanese community today that embraces the sport, and the style of play is closer to the Japanese game than to the Latin or North American games. In "Brazil: Baseball Is Popular, and the Players Are Japanese!" Brazilians Carlos Azzoni and Tales Azzoni, economist and journalist, respectively, and American Wayne Patterson, a computer scientist and a provost at Howard University, examine this anomaly in baseball demography as well as baseball's place in a country much better known for its dominance in soccer.

Not all baseball-playing nations of the Western Hemisphere trace their roots to the United States. In "Canada: Internationalizing America's National Pastime," Colin Howell finds much evidence that baseball in Canada developed on its own without direct influence from the United States. But until World War II it was supported by Canada's Anglo-Saxon elites. Baseball's reputation for rowdiness, gambling, and drinking prior to that turned away the Anglo-Saxon upper class, whose class, race, and nativist prejudices caused them to prefer curling, cricket, tennis, and golf. In this volume Howell is the only one to discuss women's baseball. Canada had its own organized women's baseball leagues, and about 10 percent of the women who played in the United States in the All American Girls Professional League (1943–54), the wartime creation of P. K. Wrigley, were Canadian.

Part 3 contains three essays on Europe. Peter Carino, an American English professor, views the Italian game from the vantage of a fan in the stands in "Italy: No Hotdogs in the Bleachers." He doesn't have a lot of company, though, because, as elsewhere in Europe, Italian baseball is not popular outside its small coterie of devoted followers. Most regular season games draw fewer than one thousand spectators. Italy is considered the strongest European baseball country, though the Netherlands has won more European Championships. Carino reports that the gap between the strongest and the weakest teams and players is considerable. The team at the bottom, for example, can go an entire season without winning a single game, while league champion teams often win 80 percent of their contests.

In "Holland: An American Coaching *Honkbal*," Harvey Shapiro describes the baseball scene in the Netherlands from a perspective unique in this volume. Shapiro, an American college coach, was recruited to coach a club team in the Dutch National League (the Amstel Tigers), and later became the head coach of the Dutch National Team. Shapiro gives us a good sense of how Dutch amateur baseball games and players are different from those in the United States. In recounting his experiences as manager of the Dutch National Team, he reveals much about international competition, particularly the European and World Baseball Championships. In Britain, baseball must compete with its distant relative, cricket, for attention. In "Great Britain: Baseball's Battle for Respect in the Land of Cricket, Rugby, and Soccer," Josh Chetwynd charts the rocky development of the sport, beginning with Albert Spalding's 1888–89 World Tour. The tour did cause enough interest that a few teams were formed. Even more so than in Italy and Holland, baseball is still a minor sport in the UK, dismissed by many as a glorified American version of rounders. There have been several modest professional baseball leagues in Britain, but all have ended in financial disappointment.

Part 4, the Pacific, comprises a single essay, "Australia: Baseball Down Under," by historian Joseph Clark. As in Britain, baseball was initially accepted in the late-nineteenth century as an off-season sport for cricketers who wished to keep fit. From its beginnings as solely a winter sport, baseball eventually also became a summer game. Clark traces its early growth in popularity to the influence of visiting American sailors, minstrel groups, and Albert Spalding's World Tour (though it never gained mass appeal). Clark concludes his essay with the ill-fated attempts to organize a national baseball league in the 1990s. Clark's research was initially done for a doctoral dissertation—a ten-year odyssey undertaken while he taught history at a private secondary school in Sydney.

A few words are in order about how I came to edit this collection. As I am an anthropologist, I have spent a good deal of my career over the past thirty-five years living in other cultures; as a former baseball player who had devoted his youth and early adulthood to the game, I was naturally interested in knowing what other versions of baseball were like. In some of the countries in which I have taught or done research—Austria, Barbados, and Vietnam—there isn't any baseball to speak of, which in itself I found intriguing. Why in Vietnam, for example, where hundreds of thousands of U.S. troops had been deployed over nearly two decades, had baseball not caught on, at least in a few places? Or why in Barbados, where there had been a small U.S. naval station where Americans played baseball and softball, was the sport never taken up by local villagers? In other places I have lived, notably Japan, Ireland, Britain, and Australia, baseball has taken root, though with wildly varying levels of interest.

My interest in "foreign" baseball also stems from having spent several seasons playing in a professional league outside the United States—in the independent Quebec Provincial League. Even before that, while still a minor league first baseman in the Detroit Tigers farm system, I had fantasies, which I duly recorded in my journal, of someday playing in Japan. And once, after having been selected to play on a Canadian team that was to barnstorm in the Caribbean, I looked forward to the trip with much anticipation only to be dropped from the squad because I held a U.S. passport. Instead, I settled for watching Puerto Rico Winter League games on TV. Editing this collection has allowed me to explore what might have been.

Notes

1. See Joseph Reaves's fine history of baseball in Asia, *Taking in a Game: A History of Baseball in Asia* (Lincoln: University of Nebraska Press, 2002).
2. Rob Ruck, *The Tropic of Baseball: Baseball in the Dominican Republic* (Westport CT: Meckler, 1991).
3. The winner of the best-of-nine championship series joins the champions of the Dominican, Mexican, and Venezuelan leagues in the Caribbean World Series, which is played in early February.

Baseball without Borders

1 | Asia

1 | Japan

Changing of the Guard in High School Baseball

In October 2000 Astronaut Koichi Wakata's mission was to operate the space shuttle Discovery's fifty-foot robotic arm, lifting two segments from the orbiter's payload bay and position-
ing them on the thirteen-story International Space Station.
The charismatic thirty-seven-year-old from Omiya, Japan, had
become a hero in his own country for being the first Japanese
mission specialist in space four years earlier. On this flight, the
Japanese press was focusing on another milestone. The former
catcher from Saitama Prefectural Urawa High School baseball
team played the first game of catch with a baseball in space. The
ball and a royal blue high school baseball flag featuring a red letter "F," standing for "Fair Play, Friendship, and Fight," were on
loan from the Japan High School Baseball Federation. In a nationally televised conversation from orbit with Prime Minister
Yoshiro Mori, the main topic was not the mission but the accomplishments of the Miyake High School baseball squad, which appeared in the summer national high school baseball tournament
known as Kōshien, despite having to live and train in Tokyo after
a volcanic eruption ravaged Miyake Island a few months before.
"Many people were moved by your team's participation and the
spirited way that you played," Wakata told team captain Hide-
nori Tsumura, who joined the conversation by conference call. "I
hope you'll value the understanding of the importance of teamwork, concentration, and discernment you've cultivated through
baseball and apply them as you work toward your own goals."

The tight confines of the space shuttle limit what astronauts can bring along. Most carry items that are highly symbolic and personal; Israeli Ilan Ramon brought personal artifacts from Jewish concentration camps on the ill-fated Columbia mission in 2002. The fact that Wakata brought a high school pennant reflects the impact high school baseball had on him. When asked later why he made so many overtures to high school baseball from space, he explained,

Baseball has been my most favorite sport since I started playing it in Little League. I think that high school baseball in Japan, especially the national championship games at Kōshien field, demonstrates the wonderful spirit of sports and its relationship to school education. I remember that Mr. Junichi Nakajima, who was our team coach in high school, always encouraged us in playing baseball to learn to focus on achieving a goal, to have insight, and to cherish teamwork. All of these helped me throughout my life in achieving my goals.[1]

High school baseball in Japan is not so much a sport as it is a philosophy and a tool of education—not in the sense of molding boys into gentlemen like one might see at an English prep school but in building character and refining spirit. The spiritual underpinning of high school baseball is the same as in the martial arts. The philosophy plays out on the diamond in some of the most intense baseball I've ever had the privilege to watch.

In 1987 I traveled the globe on a Thomas J. Watson Fellowship, witnessing local versions of baseball. I spent about five months in Japan. And like most first-time spectators of Kōshien, I was enthralled by the unbridled pageantry and passion of the players and fans. I was fresh out of college and watched with a naïve pair of eyes. Even with the scant knowledge that I had of corporal punishment and militaristic training regimens, I found Kōshien unlike any baseball I had seen in my youth, whether on school diamonds or at Fenway Park. This was baseball played with guts and idealism.

The most-watched high school sporting events in the world—Kōshien and, in the last few decades, its invitation-only spring counterpart—have been producing heroes since the inception of a schoolboy national tournament in 1915. Every August when the do-or-die tournament begins at the start of the O-Bon holidays, the whole Japanese archipelago grinds to a halt. On any given day, millions of television viewers enjoy seesaw contests with sayonara home runs, squeeze play bunts, players sliding headfirst into first base even on sure outs, and losing players crying and scooping infield soil into Ziploc bags to carry off as keepsakes. Accompanied by a volunteer interpreter, Yoshihiko Sasai, who was taking time off from preparing for Japanese university entrance exams, I got a whirlwind look at Kōshien Stadium, which is considered a repository of Japanese spirit. With the stadium's ivy-covered walls and wailing siren, concessionaires speaking in earthy Osaka-ben selling noodles in broth, polite fans laughing tensely at their own team's defensive mistakes, marching bands playing "Popeye the Sailor Man" and "Mickey Mouse Club," female fans in the loge boxes fanning themselves with *uchiwa* (flat, nonfolding paper fans), elderly men in tank tops nursing beers and a scorecard, and fans of all ages propping *kachiwari* (packed ice) on their heads to combat the intense August heat, the Kōshien grandstand feels like a cross between Wembley and Wimbledon (the pinnacles of British soccer and tennis, respectively). Near the turnstiles, vendors sell inflatable seat cushions. In the cafeteria near the pressroom one can buy spicy curry with coffee, a popular fare at Kōshien. The pressroom looks like the newsroom of a major daily, with close to eighty reporters from the six national sports tabloids and the large dailies scurrying in and out or tuned to the action on television. A heroic performance at Kōshien earns a player instant stardom and typically assures him a spot in the Japanese pros. An appearance at Kōshien inspires hordes of female students to sneak baked goods to a team's dormitory late at night. Yoshihiko, my interpreter, shared with me that at Shizuoka High School, where he went to school, female students would often loan their handkerchiefs so players could wipe their brows, then the girls would display them, unwashed, on the walls of their bedrooms. Thousands of residents from the hometown of a team represented at Kōshien travel on overnight buses to attend the games. If the team wins the tournament, shopkeepers back home create window displays in festive colors and kick off sales. When Yokohama won the summer tournament in 1998, several thousand locals greeted the team at the train stop with a banzai salute.

I was first introduced to Japanese high school baseball at the semi-

1. *Players from Tokyo's Tokaidai Kofu High School line up, just after their elimination from the 86th Annual National High School Baseball Championship Tournament, at Kōshien Stadium near Osaka. 2004. (Photo by Projectile Arts / Jake Clennell, 2004.)*

finals of a tournament qualifier in 1987 in Osaka's Nissei Stadium. The nearly sellout crowd seemed blue collar and the vast majority were over forty, which I hadn't realized at the time was symptomatic of the decline in popularity of high school baseball among Japanese youth. The rain started to pour seconds after Yoshihiko and I arrived at our seats, and we hurried with fans into the furnace-like indoor corridors.

I had liked Yoshihiko from the moment I met him at a youth hostel in Osaka, and I quickly developed an immense trust in him as a cultural interpreter, undoubtedly biased by our mutual obsession with baseball. Although his English was shaky—like my Japanese—his status as a recent high school graduate worked to my favor because he seemed to know in detail the inner workings of the Japanese high school baseball scene.

From the top of the ramp we watched several hundred players, all with close-cropped hair, hoarsely singing and chanting, marching in place, and thrusting fists in unison in the downpour. A handful of boys in the front rows wore buzz cuts like the players. Yoshihiko said they were freshmen. Demonstrating enthusiasm was a prerequisite for obtaining a spot on next year's squad. The buzz cuts represented purity, the most popular attribute of high school players. "Professional baseball is amusement," he said, "but the high school baseball player thinks of nothing but baseball. He has no interest in money. He thinks only of the team. When a person looks into the eyes of the Japanese high school player he sees his earnest nature, fighting spirit, and Japanese purity."

After the final out the teams lined up at home plate, bowed to each other, and sprinted to their respective cheering sections where they bowed to the fans; then the winning team lined up again at home plate to hear their school song. As Yoshihiko and I left the stadium, winning players strutted out from an exit door carrying colorful origami chains. Yoshihiko explained this was a good luck charm called *senbazuru*, made from one thousand paper cranes constructed by female students. Teams hung the chains in their dugouts and lockers. In ancient Japan paper was believed to contain a spirit. Losing players filed out with tears streaking down their faces. Hundreds of sobbing schoolgirls swarmed around them.

I looked inquisitively at Yoshihiko. He said, "In Japan, tears are considered beautiful."

Purity

Shedding tears in Japan has traditionally represented shedding impurities. "Pureness is the symbol of Kōshien," says Mitsuyoshi Okazaki, senior editor at *Bungei Shunju.* "At Kōshien all the uniforms are white, the ball is white, the caps are white, and the infield soil is pure; it's a special blend of sand trucked in from Western Honshu. Purity is fundamental in Japan. It's the Japanese way of thinking."

Robert Whiting, a well-regarded author on Japanese baseball, defines purity as moral rightness and total sincerity toward your chosen sport—clarity of thought so one can concentrate:

It's not just in baseball, but in the martial arts. Judo athletes also wear white. Part of the whole package of learning judo and kendo was to learn how to be a better human being, to learn character and morality. In that sense, I think they talk of purity of heart: In any kind of judo and kendo, you don't violate the rules. You're not supposed to go around beating people up. When you come to practice, you bow as a sign of respect to the dojo. High school ballplayers do it. Even some pros do it.[2]

The purity ethic traces all the way back to Miyamoto Musashi, a seventeenth-century swordsman, who wrote about proper spirit, education, hard work, and state of mind—the idea you can exceed your physical limitations and overcome physical pain and injury through sheer force of will.

During the Meiji period (1868–1912), a wave of Western culture washed over Japan. Meiji rulers brought in American and European teachers, scientists, engineers, and professors as Japanese society changed from a system of feudalism to industrialization. A handful of American schoolteachers brought baseball equipment and an enthusiasm for sharing the game with Japanese youth. In a country emerging from three hundred years of self-imposed isolation, baseball was readily embraced because it pitted pitchers against batters in both physical and mental standoffs similar to traditional Japanese sports like sumo and the martial arts. The desire to return to traditional Japanese values such as purity were soon expressed through baseball and emerging martial arts such as judo and kendo.

The introduction of *koto gakko* (elite preparatory schools) in Japan was a countermeasure against the Western influence in Japanese society. These schools were crafted by Meiji educators to teach Confucian philosophy (Bun) and martial arts (Bu) to the prospective elite. Students at *koto gakko* embraced machismo, punishing physical training, and hazing rituals as a means of perfecting moral faculties. Ichiko (First Higher School of Tokyo), the most prestigious of the preparatory schools, approached baseball with the same rigid discipline as judo. Coaches started talking about "bloody urine." If you didn't urinate blood, you hadn't practiced hard enough. When Ichiko lost to bitter rival Meiji Gakuen, a school run by American Protestant missionaries, that symbolized to Japanese traditionalists the Western cultural invasion, and Ichiko stepped up excruciating training methods. Players were forbidden to use the word "ouch" in practice, although if they were in real pain they were allowed to use the word *kayui* ("it itches"). And players whose elbows were deformed from excessive throwing of curve balls would hang from trees to straighten out their arms. Ichiko went on to defeat a squad of American part-time ballplayers 3 games in a row, an accomplishment that drew national media attention and put baseball on the map in Japan.

Joseph A. Reaves, in his fine history of baseball in Asia, *Taking in a Game*, writes about the larger significance of these victories:

Baseball, from that moment, assumed a new sociopolitical role in Japan. No longer was baseball an instrument of cultural oppression—a symbol of the perceived social and military superiority of the United States. Baseball, it turned out, could be a great equalizer. It opened doors to new levels of self-worth and international respect. Schools across Japan began forming baseball teams. From that moment, baseball was on its way to becoming the Great Japanese Game in Asia.[3]

Samurai Style

A country already well attuned to amateur baseball showed phenomenal interest in the premiere of the national tournament in 1915. The *Asahi Shimbun* sponsored the tournament with the aim of "rearing youths with a healthy body and mind." By 1923 the capacity crowds at Naruo Stadium in Nishinomiya prompted construction of the 55,000-seat Kōshien Stadium, the largest stadium at that time in Asia. Suishu Tobita (1886–1965), the "Ring Lardner" of Japanese amateur baseball, embodied the samurai spirit of baseball as manager of Waseda University and in his extensive writings on baseball. In one of his most famous books, *Yakyu-do* (The path of baseball), he wrote that baseball is mostly about respecting the master, as in the martial arts. One has to respect others in order to be respected oneself.

This mental approach is regarded as Bun Bu Ryodo (pursuing both Bun and Bu), descended from Bushido, a code and way of life of a samurai. Bun Bu Ryodo is still widely embraced and is often used as a school motto by teams. Hironari Isoguchi, the coach at Iwakura High School, has his players shovel snow from the street of the neighborhood surrounding their dormitory and training ground, one hour away from their high school by train. The shoveling serves both as physical training and a gift of kindness to neighbors. On the field, players praise their opponents for fine defensive plays. The spirit of kindness also extends to the stands, where fans of a winning team at Kōshien shout "Come back again next year!" to the losing team.

The most famous public discussion on Bun Bu Ryodo in schoolboy baseball took place during New York Yankees outfielder Hideki Matsui's senior year at Seiryo High School. During a second-round game at the 1992 Kōshien summer tournament, the much-feared slugger was walked intentionally in all five plate appearances. After the fifth walk, supporters hurled garbage onto the field (virtually unheard of at Kōshien), and the following day the national media vilified the opposing manager's actions. "Five walks in a row was regarded as a violation of the justice and honesty ethic in Bushido spirit," explains Yukihiro Ueno, professor of sociology at Shizuoka University of Arts and Culture. "In high school baseball, honor can only be achieved through fair play."

Selfless Play

Leading off opening day of the 1987 Kōshien tourney, players marched lockstep around the diamond then took an oath to play ball "as purely as the ball is white and the sky is blue." After securing press passes, Yoshihiko and I entered the right-field grandstand and sat in front of the Ika High School cheering section, which was made up of several hundred students wearing blue cardboard rice-paddy hats chanting "Ika, Ika, let's go!" in unison through plastic megaphones. With 4 games per day and only minutes separating each game, the corner grandstands would often dramatically change colors, composition, and movement. A section brimming with fans snapping red handkerchiefs might give way to hundreds of fans rhythmically thrusting blue pompoms.

Yoshihiko enthusiastically shared with me that Okinawa Saison High School cheering sections were noted for whistling school songs. Ika High School has three songs, and a handful of the students, upbeat and enthusiastic although their team was losing 5–1 to Chuo High School, waved Japanese flags with prayers on them. A quieter, larger contingent of fans surrounded the student section. Many wore whites and straw hats to protect them from the sun. Even with all their protection, fans throughout the stadium often complained about the heat. Numerous fans held hand radios with headphones and were leaning forward

2. *A fan at Kōshien holding up a picture of his deceased son. (Photo by Dan Gordon.)*

in their seats, some softly predicting *sanshin* (strikeout) on two-strike counts. Standing on the staircase flanking the left side of the student formation, a man with a hand towel resting on the back of his neck held at shoulder height a framed photo of someone batting.

"Why is he doing that?" I asked Yoshihiko.

"Tradition. When a boy dies and does not play in Kōshien, a parent brings a picture to Kōshien for the son to see the game he might have played."

A man in the middle of the crowd stood up and shouted in a voice of desperation, and almost everyone in the section laughed. I turned quickly to Yoshihiko, "What did he say?"

"He says, 'Ganbatte. [Give your best.] Please listen to me! Ganbatte.' Everyone laughed because they think he is foolish."

Chuo increased its lead with a series of singles in the eighth inning. Fans surrounding us squirmed. Some women sobbed openly with palms on their faces. With his hands on his knees, Ika's right fielder yelled, "It all depends on me!" The crowd didn't react. Yoshihiko said, "He said that to the pitcher to make him relax."

Taking on the burden for the good of the team goes hand in hand with fighting spirit. Managers of high school squads have a long tradition of using their star pitchers every inning of every game in the tournaments. Stories abound of pitchers at Kōshien performing with injuries or heat stroke. It is no small wonder that many pitching heroes at Kōshien later go on to have short, uneventful careers in the pros. In August 2000 Marty Kuehnert described in his *Japan Times* column a pitcher collapsing from heat exhaustion on the mound during Kōshien, then returning to pitch six minutes after receiving fluids and a leg massage, only to wilt again, at which point the manager transferred the youth to right field, where he soon collapsed and had to be carried off the field. In a quarterfinal match at the 1998 summer tournament, Daisuke Matsuzaka hurled all eighteen innings of a scoreless tie, pitched all nine innings of a replay game the following day, played the outfield and pitched the ninth inning in the semifinal, and spun a no-hitter in the finals. Matsuzaka's performance catapulted him to superstardom. He threw all 200 pitches of the quarterfinal game, though it was only the day after the game in which everybody was concerned about his elbow and shoulder.

The teams also assume the burden for the mistakes of individuals. In his engaging autobiography, *Sadaharu Oh: A Zen Way of Baseball*, Japan's most prolific home run hitter explains the collective punishment when one of his freshman teammates hit out of turn or spoke out of line. His teammates were forced to line up in facing rows and punch each other. If the underclassmen watching the lesson deemed your punch soft, then you were forced to punch again. Oh looked back on the ritual with nostalgia.

It is not easy to acquire a sense of shared responsibility. People by nature look out for themselves first and for others second. But it is higher consciousness to learn to care for others, to acquire a sense of genuine responsibility for the actions — good or ill — of the team or group to which you belong. On a baseball team, there is simply no avoiding this demand. The lesson is painfully learned — but it is learned.[4]

Until the mid-1990s, team punishment was inflicted for player transgressions that might seem minor outside of high school baseball circles but were intolerable under the purity doctrine of Kōshien. If a player was caught smoking, drinking beer, or driving without a license, the school immediately withdrew from competition or the Japan High School Baseball Federation banned the school from play. Although team punishments are starting to be scaled back, players are still dropped from a team for smoking cigarettes. This is the opposite of what happens in American scholastic sports, where coaches and players often intervene to protect players from the consequences of their transgressions. "It's a difficult problem, but it's our duty to maintain the purity of high school baseball," explains Haruo Wakimura, chairman of the Japan High School Baseball Federation. "Because high school baseball is very popular, ballplayers are tempted to act differently from normal students in the school life. Our federation has a judicial committee to punish the school whose ballplayers engage in impure acts."[5]

Perhaps the most striking example of team before self is the absence of postgame recognition for individual players. There is no MVP and no award for best pitcher, because that would infer that individual superiority is more important than teamwork.

Shared responsibility also plays out on the diamond, where high school teams huddle between innings, bunts are more common than swings for the fences, and players carry injured teammates off the field piggyback style.

Maybe the best example in a nine-inning frame of loyalty to both team and school colors was a 122–0 drubbing in a preliminary round of the 1998 summer tournament. Too Gijuku High School scored 39 runs in the first inning. Down 93–0 in the seventh, Fukaura High School's coach suggested throwing in the towel but his players insisted on persevering. After the game, Fukaura's captain told the *Mainichi Daily News*, "Because the supporters were shouting for us, we decided to play on to the end of the game. I'm glad we continued."

Schoolboy baseball training reflects what takes place in public schools. For example, every student in Japan rises when a teacher enters the classroom, similar to how an American courtroom rises for a judge. Players also show deference toward the coach. "The high school coach is considered absolute in baseball," said Yoshihiku. "If a mug is white and the coach says it's black, it's black." Each day students spend a half hour cleaning their school—mopping floors, polishing school gates, scrubbing toilets, dusting, washing windows, and removing gum from under desks. The logic is that since students use the school they should clean it. Likewise, in school baseball, students meticulously rake the diamond and care for the outfield grass. High school students are also under tremendous pressure to succeed in college entrance exams, which parallel the "one shot only" single-elimination philosophy at Kōshien. Although the practice is now discouraged, Japanese teachers have routinely inflicted corporal punishment on students, and coaches have beaten players.

Striking Back

In May 2000 PL Gakuen second baseman Yuta Mo rino filed a lawsuit against the school, alleging that the upperclassmen he was assigned to pummeled him two to three times per week for acts such as forgetting to ask permission to go to the bathroom or failing to ask his "master" what time dinner was served. The school soon acknowledged that other underclassmen had also been slapped, punched, kicked in the chest, or hit with bats and metal chairs. According to Jim Allen, who writes a sports column for the English-language *Daily Yomiuri*, these beatings are an inseparable part of a ballplayer's education in Japan. In Allen's online column "The Hot Corner," Kenichi Yazawa, a former captain of Waseda University, described how freshmen were only allowed to say "yes" or "no" and upperclassmen enjoyed tricking players into responding otherwise, which resulted in brutal beatings. "You'd want to cry it hurt so bad," said Yazawa, who later became a star first baseman with the Chunichi Dragons. "But you didn't dare. If you did, it would mean even more punches."

Takami Miki, PL's principal, downplayed the seriousness of dormitory beatings, saying they merely want "to guide (the team members) properly and have them be absorbed in baseball." In a radical departure from how the Japan High School Baseball Federation usually addresses corporal violence, they banned the team from that summer's Kōshien tournament as well as the spring invitational.

Reports of other beatings and corporal punishment spread like wildfire in the Japanese media. In Yamaguchi Prefecture, Hagi High School's baseball squad boycotted their practice, refusing to return to the field until their abusive manager was fired. According to the *Mainichi Shimbun*, the coach had repeatedly punched players in the head during training and struck their backsides with a bat for "not showing enough fight." "It was a hard decision to make as we love playing baseball," said one of the ballplayers. "But our desire to kick out our coach was much stronger than anything." At Oku High School in Okayama Prefecture, a seventeen-year-old student bludgeoned four teammates on his baseball squad with a metal bat in alleged retaliation for being bullied, then killed his mother using the same bat so she wouldn't be shunned by neighbors. The youth later told authorities that his teammates, who suffered multiple injuries in the attack, had repeatedly harassed him for not wearing his hair close-cropped like his teammates. In a newspaper interview, Seattle Mariners superstar Ichirō Suzuki described the hazing he endured as a high school underclassman. Ichirō was not only required to cook and do laundry for the upperclassmen, but he was forced to kneel on the edge of a metal garbage can in a *seiza* (a prescribed zen meditation position) for a half hour for infractions ranging from talking out of turn to upperclassmen to leaving the dorm at night to buy ice cream.

There is a growing backlash against the more brutal forms of "educating players." For example, there are now fewer incidents of coaches slapping players in public. Parents no longer want their sons to undergo "death training" and might sue if their child is hurt by corporal punishment. Takahiro Horikawa, a baseball writer with the *Asahi Shimbun*, says the lesson of instilling hierarchy remains, however.

Parents never complained, because the coach wasn't doing it to be mean. He was doing it just to educate or guide the players. But it's not like that anymore. People stopped thinking that way. They still have some high schools that practice this in the countryside. The only thing is to a senior player, you don't talk back. You listen to them when they tell you to go take the garbage out. Senior players come around, you move over to the side, so they can go first in the line. Little things like that always exist and still will exist.[6]

In the late 1990s Japan discovered the American art of the lawsuit. In response the Japanese government plans to triple the number of licenses issued to lawyers by 2010. One group of parents even sued a high school because the baseball coach did not provide their sons with enough baseballs during practice.

The Future of Japanese High School Baseball

In recent years attendance has declined at Kōshien because of the rise of professional soccer in Japan and changing attitudes among Japanese youth. The average age of people who watch high school baseball has been increasing each year. For Japanese youths, soccer is to baseball what Calvin Klein was to kimonos. Japanese youths seem to respond better to free-spirited play and the funky, dyed hairdos of J. League (soccer) players. When superstar J. Leaguer Hidetoshi Nakata shocked the nation by refusing to sing the Japanese national anthem (which praises the emperor's reign) before a match, he caught so much flak that he left Japan to play in Rome; many Japanese youth, however, found the act of self-expression and rebellion refreshing. (Part of soccer's newfound popularity is a result of kids no longer tolerating the militaristic aspects of baseball.) "Soccer is more about self in space," said Mitsuyoshi Okazaki. "But baseball is more instructive. Youths want to move away from that. Instead of hearing, 'Do this, do that, do this,' they don't want anything to do with that torture." "Soccer arose in Japan only recently and is based on the professional game elsewhere," explains Masayuki Tamaki, an independent sports journalist. "Therefore it is not stalled in the rigidity of the past. Baseball models itself after tradition, while soccer took shape from the game in Europe."

Japanese high school students are becoming more like high school students in the West, and high school baseball officials are making cautious efforts to attract these youths back to the game. In the mid-1990s the Japan High School Baseball Federation formed a committee, called Looking Forward to the 21st Century, to consider reform. Scholars, businessmen, sportswriters, broadcasters, and former players were brought together to brainstorm. The committee's 1997 report called for seminars to reeducate coaches, focusing on how to treat players and encourage enjoyment instead of obsessing about purity and the education of youth. The report fell on deaf ears, says journalist Marty Kuehnert, a committee member. Among his suggestions to the committee was a lifting of the requirement that Kōshien players sport close-cropped hair, which he felt suppressed individual expression. "Most people laughed at that suggestion," says Kuehnert, "the thinking being that it is an unwritten rule and tradition against which they can't mandate."

Still, the report paved the way for more flexible training and an easing of the year-round, seven-days-per-week training that was widespread among high school baseball teams. (It was not uncommon to see players in knee-high boots practicing in the snow with orange baseballs.) At some of the more competitive schools, the practice schedule contracted incrementally from 365 days per year to 355, and coaches afforded players the freedom to develop individual training regimens outside of formal practice. "Today's young players are different," said Motonori Watanabe, Yokohama High School baseball coach. "It's important to talk to them and to encourage them to stand on their own two feet."

"Coaches are trying to change to give people individual identity, which is good," says Yusuke Abe, a sports editor. "Because that's the reason they're losing a lot of good players to American teams. Because American players are more interested in individuality. Japan is too much dictatorship and not enough individuality."

More players are trash-talking opponents. In 1995 Kōshien star pitcher for powerhouse Moriokadai Fuzoku, Kiyotaka Koishizawa, nicknamed "Big Mouth" by the media for his brash statements, boasted that nobody could touch his fastball. While such showmanship would raise few eyebrows in the United States, where cocky young athletes are more prevalent, it was a highly unconventional statement in Japan that got lots of press.

A scout for the Orix Blue Wave expressed his dismay: "Kids today are taking in entirely too much instant food. They won't even eat *jako* (small fish) any more. When we were young, we were hungry, and we ate anything. One of the key points scouts always look for in players is whether or not they're hungry, especially in psychological terms. No one ever makes it in the pros without this kind of outlook." "Players want to enjoy training and win, and they don't like rigidity," says sociologist Satoshi Shimizu. "They want to profit more and more. And now they sometimes want to profit without endurance. It's not only in the sports worlds, but in the Japanese way of life."[7]

The blazing success in Seattle of Ichirō Suzuki, who was already an established superstar in Japan, has inspired a whole new generation of ballplayers. Children who had been playing less baseball and more GameBoy returned to the game, sparking record enrollment in youth leagues at the turn of the century. Japanese youth also began dressing in "Ichicazi," the rapper-style clothing worn by Ichirō. Before the dream was to play professional baseball in Japan, especially for the Tokyo Giants. Now schoolboy ballplayers yearn to play in the American Major Leagues.

When Hideo Nomo brought his effective tornado-style pitching delivery to the Los Angeles Dodgers, helping to lift American fans out of the post-strike doldrums, Major League teams started eyeing Japanese high school players (along with Japanese professional players, who could declare free agency after ten years) as a source of younger and cheaper talent. Major League teams have thus far only landed a few lesser-known high school players, although former Dodgers manager Tommy Lasorda made a special trip to Japan to watch high school hurler Hayato Terehara, who raised eyebrows at Kōshien with his 95 MPH fastball. The largest obstacle for Major League teams is that they are prohibited from signing high school players unless they resign from their team, which many of the best players are reluctant to do for an uncertain future in a foreign country.

Satellite television has exposed Japanese youth to the American style of baseball, and the Japanese high school game is gradually changing as a result. As Robert Whiting notes, "Japanese youth really got to see the difference in the game—how free-wheeling and free-spirited the Americans were. And they really got a look at what the strengths and weaknesses are on both sides of the Pacific."[8]

Medical science is also penetrating Japanese high school baseball. The Japanese used to believe that Japanese arms were more elastic than those of Americans and therefore could endure pitching several days in a row. But now coaches are beginning to understand that a high school player's shoulder is not fully developed. Orthopedic surgeons are doing shoulder and elbow checks on all pitchers who participate in Kōshien, and in March 1994 an x-ray room was added to Kōshien Stadium. But the full benefits of these x-ray room programs are questionable because most of the exams take place only after the pitchers are overused.

Critics worry that the advanced age of the federation leadership leaves them less likely to implement deeper reform. When Naotaka Makino stepped down in 2002 he was ninety-two. His successor, Haruo Wakimura, took over at age seventy. "For almost fifty years nothing changed under Naotaka Makino because he did not want to change anything," says Yusuke Abe. "The new leader is from the same generation of thinking. At his age, how much change can he make?" "The problem is not with the federation," says Marty Kuehnert. "It is that coaches, particularly from the countryside, can't stop themselves from embracing the traditional approach to baseball that they have known all their lives."

"Japanese newspapers still give more coverage to baseball than to soccer, but that might change in the next five years," says Mitsuyoshi Okazaki. "Right now small children are playing soccer. In the next five years they'll be big players, and that's why baseball is going to have to do something. Otherwise baseball will be pushed out by soccer."

Events such as Koichi Wakata's overtures to high school baseball from space reflect that high school baseball still holds a place in the hearts and minds of many Japanese. After returning from orbit, Wakata threw out the ceremonial first pitch at the 2001 summer Kōshien tournament using the ball he'd taken into space. In another symbolic gesture, Wakata watched the opening game with the living descendants of the late American schoolteacher Horace Wilson, whom some historians credit with introducing baseball to Japan in 1873. "Baseball is a symbol of the friendship between Japan and the United States," explained Wakata. "An

American introduced it to Japan and 127 years later I was able to introduce playing baseball in space onboard an American spacecraft. I think there are many young people who learn from baseball how to work toward achieving their goals and dreams."

Notes

1. Koichi Wakata, e-mail interview by the author, December 26, 2002.
2. Robert Whiting, telephone interview by the author, December 21, 2002.
3. Reaves, *Taking in a Game.*
4. Oh and Faulkner, *Sadaharu Oh*, 37.
5. Haruo Wakimura, telephone interview by the author, January 14, 2003.
6. Takahiro Horikawa, telephone interview by the author, January 13, 2003.
7. "Kōshien Still Inspires," p. 11; Satoshi Shimizu, e-mail interview by the author, December 24, 2002.
8. Whiting interview.

Bibliography

Allen, Jim. "The Beat Goes On in Japanese Schools." *Daily Yomiuri*, September 20, 2001, http://www2.gol.com/users/jallen/column/20010920.html.

"Aomori High School Sets Baseball Record." *Mainichi Daily News*, July 20, 1998.

Ikei, Masaru. *Baseball and the Japanese People.* Tokyo: Maruzen, 1991.

"Kōshien Still Inspires Blood, Sweat, Tears, But Who Cares?" *Mainichi Daily News*, August 25, 1996.

Kuehnert, Marty. *On the Keen Edge.* "Kōshien Horror Stories—Stop This Madness Now!" *Japan Times Online*, August 20, 2000.

Oh, Sadaharu, and David Faulkner. *Sadaharu Oh: A Zen Way of Baseball.* Tokyo: Kodansha, 1984.

"Players Thumb Noses at Traditionalist School Baseball." *Mainichi Daily News Interactive*, May 5, 2001.

"PL Gakuen Denied Entry into Osaka Tourney over Assaults." *Japan Economic Newswire*, June 29, 2001.

Reaves, Joseph A. *Taking in a Game: A History of Baseball in Asia.* Lincoln: University of Nebraska Press, 2002.

Roden, Donald T. "Baseball and the Quest for National Dignity." *American His-*

torical Review 85, no. 3 (June 1980): 511–34.

———. *Schooldays in Imperial Japan: A Study in the Culture of a Student Elite.* Berkeley: University of California Press, 1980.

Shimizu, Satoshi. *Kōshien Baseball Archaeology.* Tokyo: Shinkolon, 2002.

Whiting, Robert. *You Gotta Have Wa: When Two Cultures Collide on the Baseball Diamond.* New York: Macmillan, 1989.

2 | Japan

The Hanshin Tigers & Japanese Professional Baseball

As Dan Gordon's chapter describes, Kōshien Stadium's opening in 1924 as Japan's first full-dimension baseball park was sponsored by the Asahi Newspaper Company as the new venue for the national schoolboy tournament that the newspaper had inaugurated in 1915 and had so rapidly gained popularity. But the prime mover in the stadium's construction, and then its owner and operator, was the Hanshin Electric Railroad Company. Why a railroad firm?

Particularly in Osaka and Tokyo but also in other growing Japanese cities, this was an era of fierce competition between private urban railroad companies to build terminals and commuter rail lines through the metropolitan regions, vying for riders, for customers at the department stores and other retail businesses built around their terminals and stations, and for residential land they bought and resold along their rail lines to ensure a steady ridership. Building tennis courts, swimming pools, amusement parks, and athletic stadiums were additional projects to induce riders, and this fueled a boom in recreational and spectator sports in the 1910s and 1920s. In the Osaka-Kobe-Kyoto metropolis, five major rail companies crisscrossed the region with rival lines, and four of them built sports stadiums that featured baseball. Amateur baseball at this time moved from being a purely school sport to becoming urban entertainment.

Companies began to sponsor employee teams around this time, and there were a few attempts at fully professional clubs, but it was not until the mid-1930s that a professional league of six teams was established. The main force was the Tokyo-based Yomiuri Newspaper Company and its powerful owner, Shōriki Matsutarō, who had sponsored several visits by U.S. All-Stars (including Babe Ruth in 1934) and was stunned by the huge welcome and attention given the series. He then sent a group of Japanese players on an extended exhibition tour of the United States in 1935. The core of that team returned to become the Tokyo Yomiuri Giants. Several other newspaper and railroad companies joined in sponsoring teams that began tournament play in 1936. Among these was the Hanshin Railroad Company, which immediately recognized the opportunity to find more commercial use for its Kōshien Stadium and formed a team, the Hanshin Tigers.

The small league shifted from tournament to league format in 1938 and played into the wartime years before ceasing at the end of the 1943 season. Its revival was encouraged in 1947 by General Douglas MacArthur as a means of fostering an American spirit in occupied Japan. A two-league structure was inaugurated in 1950 in part because MacArthur believed it was a more democratic format than the original single league. The Hanshin Tigers chose to remain in the Central League with the Yomiuri Giants while other Osaka-area railroad teams (Hankyū, Kintetsu, and Nankai) joined the new Pacific League. After some fluctuation, eventually there were six teams in each league, with the league champions meeting in a postseason best-of-seven-games Japan Series. Japan Professional Baseball (JPB) has remained at twelve teams and never expanded as MLB did through the second half of the twentieth century.

Thus, before and after the national high school tournaments in April and August, for a season that now runs from early spring through late fall, Kōshien is home to another level of baseball, the professional game. And the team that calls the stadium home, the Hanshin Tigers, evokes the same intense media attention and fan feelings that Gordon has described for the schoolboy tournaments. There are few stadiums in the global baseball world like Kōshien that are so powerfully central to the parallel worlds of amateur and professional baseball.

The difference is the national sentimentality that has made Kōshien the country's mecca of high school baseball and the schoolboy athletic spirit versus the local and heavily partisan passions that Hanshin fans throughout the region invest in a team that is deeply beloved but seldom successful. The team, many have observed, is the Boston Red Sox or the Chicago Cubs of Japanese professional baseball. In particular, because it chose to remain in the Central League with the powerful Tokyo-based Yomiuri Giants, Hanshin has come to bear the burden of Osakans' rivalry with the national capital in what remains the country's predominant spectator sport. The Giants have always been Japan's most popular and prestigious team, by success and by clout. Yomiuri had the first private television network in the 1950s and used to broadcast its team to the far corners of the country and then used that popularity and revenue to assemble an overwhelming team that ran through nine straight Japan championships from 1965 to 1973, consolidating Yomiuri control of the baseball world and hold on the national spectatorship.

Thus the Giants-Tigers rivalry is one of intensity rather than balance. In the fifty-four years since the two-league system, the Giants have won the Central League pennant thirty-one times and have been Japan Champions twenty times. In the same period, Hanshin has won the league title but four times and has taken only a single Japan Series. In the eighteen seasons since its sole 1985 championship, Hanshin finished in last place ten times and next-to-last three times. Its stunning league championship in 2003, under a manager brought in from the outside, was the most electrifying regional event of recent years. In 2004 it fell back to a distant fourth-place finish.

In this chapter I want to use Kōshien's other team, the Tigers, to fill out the reader's view of Japan's most venerable stadium and to sketch some of the more general features of professional baseball in Japan and its importance to Japanese society. There is some danger in relying on a single team—and a team as singular as the Tigers—and I shall try to distinguish its unique elements from its more generic characteristics.

Club Organization

One of the first things a visitor to Kōshien's other team will notice is its name—not that of a city but of a company. Professional baseball is big business in Japan as well as in the United States, but MLB teams have generally been owned and operated by wealthy business individuals or partners. Only recently have corporations begun to own and operate clubs. In Japan, however, the teams have always been owned by major companies and run as subsidiaries. Public information about club balance sheets is as scarce in Japan as it is in the United States, but it is widely believed that most JPB clubs have always run deficits. They serve instead as publicity vehicles for the owning company and thus bear the names of their corporate owners, not the cities in which they play—the Hanshin Tigers and not the Osaka Tigers, the Chūnichi Dragons, not the Nagoya Dragons, and so forth.[1]

Another distinctive feature of JPB is that the clubs themselves are very large organizations. JPB has never developed a tiered minor league system as in the United States, and the twelve clubs maintain large rosters. Presently each can have seventy players under contract and most are close to or at that maximum (in 2004 Hanshin had sixty-eight). The seventy players are divided into two squads, a first team and a second team. The first team is the actual Major League team, with a roster limit of twenty-eight players. The remainder are registered to the "farm" team, which plays a short season of games against the farm teams of the other clubs.[2] Injuries and performances result in much up and down movement between the first and second teams during a season (in 2004 fifty-three of the Hanshin players appeared in a Major League game, including twenty-five different pitchers).

Such team sizes have several consequences, one of which is a need for an extensive coaching staff. Hanshin's first and second squads each have a manager, ten coaches, three trainers, and several batting practice pitchers and catchers. The Tigers' second team practices and plays at a facility named Tiger Den, several miles from Kōshien; the ballpark there has been laid out in the exact dimensions of the parent park. Tiger Den also has a modern dormitory for bachelor players, which used to be mandatory but is now optional—and not particularly popular.

And because the seventy players range from the most talented stars to raw rookies, the Hanshin staff must devote a lot more time to teaching fundamentals than they would for a MLB club (which depends on its largely independent farm system to prepare and winnow young players). This is not just drill time but also coordination—there are constant structured practices and it takes detailed scheduling to coordinate the drills of a hundred players and staff. In this regard, JPB resembles less

MLB than the NFL, with its large staffs, highly orchestrated practices, and often dominant head coaches.

Above those on the field is the Hanshin "front office," the club's management and support staff (whose offices are actually underneath the center- and left-field bleachers at Kōshien). The large team size requires a large front office; Hanshin's sixty-five employees compose a much larger organization than a typical MLB club, with positions ranging from administration to accounting, marketing, player development, and press relations. Like other clubs, the Hanshin front office is organized in a corporate hierarchy of divisions, departments, and small sections that would be familiar to any Japanese office worker. In effect, then, to get nine players on the field to start each Major League game, the Tigers baseball club has become an organization of over 160 employees.

The Hanshin Tigers club is embedded in an even larger corporate nexus. In Japanese business shorthand, the club is a "child company" or wholly owned subsidiary of the Hanshin Electric Railroad Corporation. The parent company preserves its original business, but it now controls a family of businesses, including department stores, travel agencies, air transport companies, land development companies, taxi companies, and leisure park operations in addition to the railroad. Even baseball-related operations are distributed among a set of subsidiaries—the Tigers ball team of course, but also a stadium management company, a horticulture and grounds-keeping company, a security company, and a goods and concessions company—all under the control of the parent corporation. Each club has a designated "owner" who is usually the chief executive officer or chairman of the board of the parent company. It is the owner who represents the club in all executive dealings with the league and the Commissioner's Office. In the case of Hanshin, Kuma Shunjirō served imperiously as owner for twenty years, from 1984 until his resignation in late 2004; he was replaced by the company's CEO.

Thus, the business of Japanese baseball is more corporate than entrepreneurial, but this elaborate organization does not ensure harmony despite notions that Japanese prefer supportive collectivism. Indeed, the Hanshin organization is rife with friction and infighting—between the parent headquarters and the child club, within the front office (especially between those who are dispatched by the main company and the permanent employees of the club), and between the "suits" of the front office (claiming educational credentials and corporate seniority) and the "uniforms," the field manager and coaches who claim baseball expertise and public recognition.

All clubs encounter these difficulties, although Hanshin is especially liable to these tensions because the club has always been the tail that wags the dog. Although Hanshin was the earliest of the surviving electric rail companies in Kansai, it lost out in the race to expand; it found itself with but a single twenty-mile east-west rail line from Osaka to Kobe, boxed in by the sea to the south and the powerful Hankyū Railroad to the north. Its most valuable corporate assets are Kōshien and the Tigers, and the club and its finances loom much larger than they do with other companies. The club's fortunes very much determine those of its owner.

The Baseball Season

The rhythms of the professional baseball season in Japan would be familiar to any fan of U.S. baseball, although Japanese baseball has several distinctive features. Spring training is in the "south"—Okinawa and the southern island of Kyushu are current favored locations—and month-long camps open on February 1. Preseason exhibition games are played from late February through March. The 140-game regular season begins around April 1 and continues into mid-October. The best-of-seven Japan Series usually overlaps with the World Series. Most clubs have a postseason camp and rookie leagues in October and November. The off-season is busy with personnel issues: the player draft, free agent and team trades, and player salary negotiations.

The short distances between ballparks, the country's single time zone, and the high-speed train network in Japan make travel less of a determinant than in MLB. For several decades, almost all regular season games have been evening games (starting time at Kōshien is 6:00 p.m.), and there are no doubleheaders. Teams play three-game series twice a week (Tuesday-Wednesday-Thursday and Friday-Saturday-Sunday), with Monday as a travel day. Given the six-team leagues, each team faces its five opponents twenty-six times, which gives an intensity and frequency to the five league rivals that is largely lost in MLB.

It is frequently said that Japanese players put in many more hours of practice than MLB players. This is generally so, although as with other aspects of the global game we should not exaggerate the differences and we should be clear about the reasons. In both countries through the 1960s at least, the off-season was just that, and many players needed other jobs to augment their modest baseball earnings. (Alternatively, the Caribbean and Central American winter leagues provided income and playing exposure for Caribbeans and North Americans alike.) Only more recently have rising salaries permitted and competition demanded a full-year commitment by players to practice and training. In America, though, most of the off-season effort is beyond public notice because MLB vies for media exposure with two other powerful professional leagues, the NBA and the NFL.

In Japan—indeed in most places—the situation is fundamentally different. The U.S. sports world is unusual in having three dominant spectator sports. In most countries there is a single "center sport" and other secondary sports. As with baseball in Cuba and the Dominican Republic, with hockey in Canada, and with soccer in many European and South American countries, baseball in Japan is the center sport. Sumo, soccer, golf, horse racing, and other sports fit around and within the baseball calendar.

What this means is that JPB keeps itself in front of the public eye as much as possible—and it must do this to retain its media preeminence. The clubs' owners want maximum exposure for their corporate name; the media, which have invested resources in baseball reporting, need to generate nonstop news; and the players themselves, even those on the lowest rungs of the second squad, are playing for the club. The pressures—and the profits—for keeping the operations of baseball before the public even in the off-season (and even during breaks in the regular season) are enormous and go a long way toward explaining the distinctiveness of the pro ball work year.

The Game

Sports are by definition rather tight sets of formal rules, basic equipment, and set strategies, and their modern history has been one of local games being standardized across wider regions, then being nationalized and eventually "transnationalized" across societies. The earliest Japanese baseball organized itself around American rules, and the regulations and patterns of game play have changed in tandem with the American game. The JPB rulebook remains largely identical to the MLB rulebook; the innovation of a designated hitter by the American League was copied by the Pacific League in Japan. Equipment is also much the same; for instance, as in the United States, amateur associations allow metal bats, and learning to hit with the required wooden bats in the pros in both countries is a difficult transition.

Kōshien itself, as Gordon describes in his chapter, could easily find a place among America's green cathedrals with its dimensions, grand ivy-covered exterior, and interior layout of covered stands and bleachers. Nonetheless, any visitor to a Hanshin Tigers game will notice small differences, some with important implications. Like most fields in Japan, the Kōshien infield is all dirt and this makes for slightly slower infield play.[3] And while the MLB Commissioner's Office designates a single manufacturer's baseball to be used by all teams, in Japan, each team can choose among three manufacturers' balls. Managers select slightly livelier or deader baseballs according to their teams' strengths.[4]

JPB games have a reputation for taking a long time and for ending in ties. Games do tend to run longer because many pitchers prefer to work the count, batters take more elaborate set-up time, and Japanese umpires are more indulgent toward coaches and managers who want meetings on the mound. However, you will rarely see a tie game at Kōshien or elsewhere; they are possible within the rules, which limit the number of extra-inning games, but they are statistically insignificant (about 3 percent of all JPB games in the last fifty-four years). It is the time limits, of course, which offend the sensibilities of MLB purists for whom the sport is limitless: the foul lines continue out into infinity and the game continues as long as required to produce a winner.[5]

But JPB has constraints. As with most stadiums, Kōshien is in the city, and almost all fans come by public transportation—indeed, largely by Hanshin railroads and buses. Almost all games are evening games, urban transit shuts down late at night, and the clubs cannot risk inconveniencing tens of thousands of spectators of extra-inning games that extend into the early morning.[6]

The Players

The life of a professional athlete is not Hobbesian—nasty, brutish, and short—but it is often ruthlessly competitive, unpredictable, and short. This is certainly true for baseball players in Japan, despite our preconceived images that Japanese sports professionals working for Japanese organizations must be securely enmeshed in a familiar nexus of long-term loyalty and mutual commitment. Not so. As with aspects of rules and game conditions, the contractual status of players and the course of their careers have broad similarities to MLB players, in part because JPB has tended to borrow such features of the U.S. model.

For instance, like MLB, Japanese players (and coaches) are independent contractors. This is a legal status in Japan; it means that players are not legally members of their club in December and January and every year must negotiate their salaries with the club. And as independent contractors, they have no pension or other company benefits.[7] Loyalty and commitment must be revalidated each year in November and December.

However, player vulnerability is not matched by club exposure. Through a reserve clause similar to but longer than that of MLB, Japanese clubs have exclusive rights to all players on their roster for nine years, which is an effective hold over most players for their entire professional career. There is less player movement among Japanese teams than in the American Major Leagues, but there is more than one might think. In 1998 eleven of the Hanshin Tigers' sixty-nine players were traded or otherwise signed from other Japanese teams, and with new foreign players and rookies, twenty-one of the sixty-nine were on the roster for the first time.

In general, compared with MLB, salaries are lower at the high end and higher at the low end of the player spectrum. Star players earn far less than those at the top of the MLB pyramid. In 2004 several JPB players broke through the 50-million-yen threshold (about $4.55 million), although the highest Hanshin salary was $2.7 million. At the other end of the scale, though, players are drafted with higher average salaries than MLB draftees. There is a much smaller pool of professional-level players in Japan, and each club signs only four to eight rookies each year out of high school, college, and industrial leagues (the average U.S. professional club drafts forty-five to fifty players a year). Fierce competition has led to a salary structure that pays exorbitant signing bonuses of $1–$1.5 million to untried teenagers.

What pro baseball shares everywhere, though, is a relatively short career path. Few players ever last beyond their early thirties. The average age of the Tiger roster hovers around 26–27, and there were only five older than 35 in 2004. Only fourteen of the sixty-eight players on the 2004 opening day roster had ten or more years in the pros; forty players had five years or fewer.

Even salaries controvert the standard Japanese corporate model of steady upward increments. Automatic steps in pay have no relevance in the baseball world, whose dense statistical indicators exactingly measure player performance as the basis for annual adjustments of salaries. In tracking the reported salaries of Hanshin players over the last ten years, I have calculated that fewer than half of the annual re-signings have been for salary increases (from 5 percent to 250 percent); about one-third of the players were forced to accept salary reductions (of 5 percent to 40 percent) and another quarter of the players were renewed at the same salary as the previous year.

The salaries themselves range widely across the sixty-eight-player roster. In 2004 a quarter of the players, those starting out or permanently stuck on the farm team, made $40,000 to $90,000; most made between $100,000 and $1,000,000, and only ten players exceeded the $1 million mark. But 36 percent of the club's total payroll of about $30 million encompassed the top five salaries.

The top salary in 2004 went not to Hanshin's outstanding thirteen-year veteran All-Star outfielder, Kanemoto Tomoaki; his $2.36 million was second to the $2.7 million paid to infielder George Arias, whose résumé included only three undistinguished years in MLB before heading for Japan. This draws attention to the pivotal but controversial place of foreign nationals in JPB. Professional baseball is multi-ethnic almost everywhere (except in Castro's Cuba), but the deployment and treatment of foreign players varies. In the early years of Japanese baseball little was made of Japanese Americans, White Russians, Taiwanese, and Korean Japanese who were often prominent on the rosters, but by the early

1970s the rush to hire aging stars from MLB and other pressures created a category of "hired bats" brought over with large salaries, special perks, and separate treatment. At present, about seventy-five of the eight hundred players in JPB are foreign nationals. In 2003 the Hanshin roster had six (from the United States, the Dominican Republic, and Australia), which is about average. Only three of them may be registered on the major team roster at any one time; the others keep in shape, sometimes impatiently, on the farm. All were given luxurious condominium housing, interpreters, separate hotels on road trips, and the freedom to follow their own training routines.

All but one of the Hanshin foreign players were released during or after the season (including Arias). Mercenaries are well compensated, but patience is short, adjustment is difficult, and their time is brief. A few find what it takes to succeed but most are rarely re-signed for a second year, and their experiences often end in mutual bafflement and bitterness.

The Media

If you arrive at Kōshien early on a game day to watch batting practice and warmups, you will immediately notice a huge media contingent lounging in the dugouts, staked out along the sidelines, and standing behind the batting cages. Baseball clubs in major U.S. markets face intense media coverage, but not even the Yankees are scrutinized as intensely as the Hanshin Tigers. On any day in the season all three national newspapers, the five major sports dailies, two local dailies, the two major news agencies, three radio networks, and three television networks send reporters, photographers, announcers, and commentators to the ballpark. Such attention is welcome but also problematic for the club. The Yomiuri Corporation, which runs the rival Giants, owns its own television network (Japan's first and largest private system), the largest-circulation daily newspaper in the world, and one of the major daily sports newspapers. Not surprisingly, the Giants are relentlessly featured in Yomiuri publications. Other media are often a step behind and sometimes heavy-handedly sanctioned for being too critical. The Hanshin Group by contrast owns no media and finds itself at the center of (and often at the mercy of) an intensely competitive Kansai region media whose dominant yearlong subject is the team fortunes of the Tigers. It needs the media but it fears them at the same time. It is an anxious and uneasy balance of courting and controlling.

Walking from the Hanshin train station the several hundred yards to the stadium and passing the Babe Ruth plaque to the right of the main ticket office, one comes upon the one entrance that is not open to ordinary visitors. This is the *kankeisha iriguchi* (official persons' entrance) for players, team officials, and the media, all of whom are funneled into a single guarded door that leads directly under the infield bleachers. Straight ahead lies the runway to the field dugout and officials' rooms behind home plate. A stairway to the left leads to the second-floor team rooms and to the press box.

Throughout the year, the media pack waits in the pressroom of the club offices and hangs out in a low-hanging, crowded room of old desks and chairs that is euphemistically called the press club room; they fill the field sidelines and dugouts during practices and game warmups. During the game itself, they are packed into a center section behind the backstop—literally a press "box" with folding chairs and rickety wood boards for tables, open to the surrounding spectators and stadium noise, unchanged for seventy-five years.[8] However, as with all stadiums in Japan, they are banned from the team locker room and manager's office, and thus they keep watch in the runway to the field and in the hallways outside the team dressing rooms to catch players and coaches for a comment.[9]

Professional baseball's popularity rose with the increasing prominence of national media, and it became the national sport through television in the 1960s and 1970s. Of all the media, those which have come to drive the gathering and reporting of Tiger news are the daily sports newspapers, an important feature of other countries like Italy, France, Brazil, and Mexico, although not the United States.[10] There are five national sports dailies, four of which date from the late 1940s, although the big jump in their circulation and notoriety occurred in the 1960s. Their circulations are in the millions, and they depend almost entirely on spot sales at street and station news kiosks and in convenience stores, not through subscriptions. Thus, to catch the eye of the passerby, they borrow from Japanese comic art and graphic design so that every front page is a garish, full-page, multicolor spread about a single story. Professional baseball tends to dominate the papers' daily front pages, total coverage, and staff assignments. For the Kansai editions of the sports papers this means the Tigers; the other teams are relegated to a few stories on the inside pages. The previous day's game if in season, front office conflicts, draft plans, contract signings, spring camp—whatever the moment in the baseball year, the sports dailies will find a Hanshin topic to foreground, and Osaka commuters, whether they buy the papers or not, will glimpse the florid front-page spreads as they pass the newspaper kiosks throughout the region.

The Fans

Equally conspicuous to anyone arriving early for a Kōshien game are the people who begin to fill the right-field bleachers, dressed in yellow-and-black jackets (the Tiger team colors), busily at work attaching banners to the railings of the walkways, assembling large flags, and testing trumpets and drums. These are the officers of the many fan clubs, who are based in the right-field stands but spill over into adjacent outfield and infield sections and who give a distinctive flavor and sound to Kōshien games. Indeed, no doubt the most striking difference that a fan from another baseball culture will notice at Kōshien is the level and form of cheering—it is loud, constant, and coordinated. From start to finish, the stadium pulsates with the frenzied chanting of the fans, driven by the percussive beat of drums and thumping clackers, accompanied by blaring trumpets and huge flags.

Significantly, though, they are not coordinated by either official cheerleaders or the stadium announcer. Rather, the energies of the crowd are directed by an elaborate organization of private fan clubs, several hundred in all, organized into several broad associations and all centered in the right-field bleachers. From there, whistles and hand signals communicate downward from a single association field chief, who sits in the lower far right corner of the bleachers, to a hierarchy of subordinates stationed throughout adjacent sections. There are anthems, marches, and chants for individual players (when first announced and when coming to bat) and for specific moments in the game (at the start, at pitching changes, for home runs, at the end of each victory, and so forth), all of which are composed and copyrighted by the lead association, not by Hanshin.

In this, too, the chanting and cheering parallels the support given the school teams in the spring and summer tournaments, and indeed there is a historical connection that leads back to the early days of U.S. college football. When the first Japanese college baseball teams toured the United States in the opening decade of the twentieth century, they studied the baseball they encountered, but they were even more impressed with the cheerleading squads of the college football teams and the enthusiasm with which they could engage the student spectators. They took careful notes, which they used on their return to train student cheerleading squads, which were immediately popular. It was this tradition of organized cheering that baseball fans later brought to the professional game.

And certainly Kōshien rocks in ways alien to any U.S. baseball game and at a level far surpassing even the exuberant fans at Caribbean and Mexican games. Visiting American baseball fans sometimes complain that the cheering disrupts the concentration and decorum necessary to properly appreciate the game, but this has always seemed to be hypocritical provincialism. Spectator participation at Japanese baseball games is perhaps most similar to that seen in soccer stadiums in Europe, Africa, and South America, where there are also highly organized fan clubs to motivate and orchestrate the crowds. In both cases, spectatorship is active, indeed proactive, trying to create with collective voices and frenetic movement an emotional charge and a sensory atmosphere that will motivate their team. It is the fan as "tenth player," trying to intervene energetically.

Yet the discerning visitor will note one further aspect of Kōshien cheering: it is only done for half the game, that is, for the half of each inning when one's team is at bat. For the defensive half of an inning, the fans relax—and schmooze. The key to appreciating the Kōshien fan club organizations is that they serve not only to orchestrate a colorful outpouring of emotional support for the Tigers, but also to provide opportunities for socializing among friends, fellow workers, business associates, and others who are drawn together by this network. It is where Osakans go to cheer on their Tigers but also to cheer up one another through the spring, summer, and fall evenings after long days in factories, offices, and homes.

"Samurai with Bats": Sporting Style in a Transnational Sportscape

Large player forces mobilized around a stern and commanding manager and panoply of coaches, engaged in extended seasons of coordinated and arduous training, deployed in contests that are drawn out by methodical probing for tactical advantage, egged on by coordinated cheering of the passionate spectators—all of this may well convince the spectator that s/he has come upon a sporting battlefield of "samurai with bats." Indeed, the dominant image of Japanese baseball is that of a society that has actively and forcefully reshaped baseball's original forms and spirit to fit a set of purposes that turn play into pedagogy, that subordinate the excitement of the contest to the demands of character building. We play baseball; they work baseball—and they are worse for it.

This is a powerful image, especially in the transnational world of baseball, because it is a vividly oppositional metaphor (setting the Japanese East against the U.S. West) that clarifies the often confusing task of sorting out what is common and what is different. That is, as a singular image and a universal label for baseball in Japan, it allows us to ignore important and intriguing differences across teams, across levels of play, and across history (that is, the differences and changes that fans often find most absorbing about the sport in their own society). It is also conveniently all-purpose. In one simple opposition (group work versus individual play), it purports to describe Japanese baseball (this is how they play it over there), to explain it (they play it that way because they're samurai), and to judge it (usually negatively, because although we idealize cowboys, we castigate samurai). This is sport reduced to eternal, essential national character.

So what are we to make of such imagery? To what extent should we look out on the Kōshien field and see figurative warriors giving their all for the team? As our most perceptive writer on Japanese baseball, Robert Whiting, has shown, samurai baseball may be a stereotype, but it is one with real grounding in Japanese baseball. In part, this is due to historical legacy—Japanese baseball was an amateur school game for fifty years before turning pro. In this regard, it is less like baseball in the United States and more like soccer and rugby in Great Britain and like football in the United States. All of these sports came out of elite schools in the late nineteenth century, a place and time that bred an ethic whereby games playing inspired virtue, formed character, and developed manliness. Sports were used to cultivate loyalty and obedience as well as the confidence to lead, and to channel men's military spirit toward service to the state. To make itself palatable and profitable with a public warmed toward sports as character building, pro baseball in the 1930s tried to adopt some of this amateur spirit into its own image. Famous managers, famous teams, and famous players all have appealed to reputed samurai qualities to explain themselves, to exhort others, and to distinguish themselves from the foreigners who fall outside this noble heritage.

But we must keep in mind three aspects of all this samurai talk over the decades. First is the amount of deliberate fabrication in modern Japanese notions of their "samurai," not unlike the selective amnesia that modern Americans have given to cowboy types. The samurai images that coaches and commentators hold up to their players as examples to follow bear about as much resemblance to warriors of the past as the Marlboro Man does to the original "cowboy" ranch hands of the 1870s and 1880s. To be sure, loyalty to the point of sacrifice to one's superior, the single virtue promulgated by samurai baseball, was central to the codes by which warriors lived in epochs past, but what is conveniently forgotten are the many forms that could take and the other virtues ennobled in the warrior's code, including overweening pride, moral purity, and sheer opportunism.

Second, loyalty itself has been redefined over baseball's history to suit the times. The "original" baseball samurai were the boys at the most elite prep school in the new nation, the First Higher School of Tokyo, celebrated for their victories over resident American teams in the late 1890s. However, this was a proudly self-run school club, free of adult authority—and soon replaced by a new orthodoxy of an autocratic adult-manager of college teams and early pro teams. This remains the high school model (where often a single adult coach must direct up to seventy aspiring high school kids), but the pro ranks have corporatized player standards; loyalty now is demanded to the impersonal authority of a large organization. If today's pro player is a samurai, his bat is more a briefcase than a sword.

Third, we must note—because most Japanese inside and outside the baseball world certainly do note—the difficulties of actually coaching and performing "samurai" baseball, especially at the pro level. For every legendary example of 1,000-fungo drills, of pitchers' overextending their innings, and of unwavering obedience to managerial whims, there are undercurrents and counterexamples of petulance, irreverence, and outright resistance to these practices and demands. As is often the case with moral injunctions, the frequency with which they are demanded is a clue to the difficulties of eliciting acceptance.[11]

This is where the Hanshin Tigers offer an instructive and entertaining angle. A number of its outward features—the overt hierarchies and proud inbreeding—are those idealized as virtues of Japanese-style baseball. But they have long coexisted with factional infighting, inept management, and disgruntled players, to which the media have devoted equal attention. The game at Kōshien is not samurai baseball as farce, but it does reveal samurai baseball as futility. And much of the allure of the Tigers for its long-suffering fans—especially the millions of Kansai residents into whose daily lives the team's fortunes and foibles percolate even when they are not paying attention—is in savoring and in hand-wringing over the constant efforts and inevitable failures to perform baseball as noble "samurai" sportsmen.

The Future

Kōshien Stadium is aging. The years have taken their toll on its physical condition, and as with the few classic grounds that remain in the United States, what is endearing tradition to some is an obstacle to modern comfort to others. A debate rages in Osaka about whether the stadium should be renovated or replaced, much like the controversial reconstruction talk about Fenway Park in Boston. For the near term, neither is likely because the Hanshin Group, the stadium's sole owner, lacks the capital for any major project.

But even more broadly, Japanese professional baseball is in turmoil. We must be careful about such inflammatory claims because crying wolf about crisis and impending doom is common—and useful—rhetoric across most professional sports. But there are three reasons to believe that several years into the future we may look back on 2004 as a watershed.

The first is the continuing "bright flight" to professional baseball in the United States. The increasing success of prominent stars, from Nomo and Ichirō to Matsui, only enhances the allure of MLB to Japanese players and to Japanese fans, who follow the games on ever-widening television coverage in Japan. And though the numbers are still small, another migration is perhaps even more portentous—that of young Japanese amateur players coming out of high school and college who are avoiding JPB altogether for rookie contracts and free agent tryouts with U.S. organizations. There are currently thirty-five Japanese playing in the United States; only a dozen or so are on Major League rosters and the rest are riding the buses and living off of meal money in the minor leagues. The Japanese clubs are understandably unhappy about this trend but are relatively impotent to slow the migration; the JPB agreement with MLB is a stopgap measure to regulate the sale of players under contract.

Second, this external threat only exacerbates the longstanding financial difficulties of most of the corporate owners, including Hanshin. Large deficits, and parent company misgivings about them, are not new, but in 2004, after more than a decade of national economic stasis and corporate doldrums, several companies finally decided to throw in the towel. In February 2004 the two other Kansai-area teams, the Orix Blue Wave of Kobe and the Osaka Kintetsu Buffalo (both in the Pacific League), announced their intention to merge, and this precipitated months of warnings, proposals, and debates about further club sales, relocations, and mergers, about league realignments and retrenchment to a single-league format, and about the reorganization of baseball administration. Owners fought owners, the players union charged the owners with malfeasance and called the first strike in Japanese professional baseball history—a two-day walkout in September—and fans across the country organized in support of the players and against the owners.

When the 2005 season started, the two-league structure was intact, but little has been settled. The two clubs did merge to become the Orix Buffalos, and a new club, the Rakuten Eagles, was admitted to the Pacific League as its sixth team. Rakuten is sponsored by a new software company and will play out of the northern city of Sendai. Meanwhile, the beleaguered Daiei retail chain sold its Fukuoka Hawks, winners of two of the last three Japan Series, to Softbank. Change will likely not end there, as other companies are trying to dump their teams and key owners are resisting approving new companies who want to buy in. A schedule of interleague games has been added to the 2005 regular season schedule, but there are still many demands and proposals under discussion (lowering the free agency requirement, renegotiating the agreement with MLB, strengthening the Commissioner's Office by consolidating some broadcast rights contracts, and so forth). Already the changes are having particular consequences for Hanshin because Orix and Kintetsu were the other two Kansai teams. Whether this will strengthen or threaten Hanshin's local preeminence and loyalty is uncertain.

As if American baseball and the Japanese economy don't offer sufficient dangers, a third factor that now faces JPB is a renewed threat from professional soccer. The opening of J. League professional soccer in 1991 scared the baseball world, which mobilized to minimize the soccer challenge by dissuading corporate support, keeping J. League teams out of major stadiums, and limiting soccer's access to television and press coverage. It worked, and the initial "new product" effect of J. League wore off by the late 1990s. Soccer interests hoped that Japan's cohosting of the World Cup in 2002 would fuel a second soccer boom, but this did not happen despite the publicity, the initial success of the Japan national team (soon outshined by the South Korea team), and the construction of soccer stadiums across the country.

Now, however, the 2006 World Cup in Germany and the 2008 Beijing Olympics loom. The enormous investment of resources and national prestige that China is making to strengthen its sports teams, in the context of its explosive economic growth (and Japan's continued weakness), has already inflamed the passions of the region's sports fans. And soccer will be a much more popular sports venue for East Asian rivalries than will baseball, still undeveloped in China. Combined with the effects of the issues above, this may be the moment when soccer is finally able to challenge and dismantle the hold baseball has had on Japan for more than a century.

All of these factors have precipitated heated debates in baseball circles, in the press, and among fans. Issues that have percolated for years are coming to the surface again—including the reform of free agency and the player draft, salary caps, interleague play, reorganizing front offices, instituting general manager positions, strengthening the Commissioner's Office, and consolidating television rights and branding. Watching Japanese pro baseball try to reassert and reinvent itself over the next few years will be fascinating, and these arguments will be as consequential as the players' contests on the fields themselves.

Notes

1. When professional J. League soccer began in 1991, it emphasized naming its teams for their home cities, which proved popular with fans. Some JPB clubs have now added their city to the team name (thus, Fukuoka Daiei Hawks for a team based in Fukuoka and owned by the Daiei retail chain).
2. The farm teams of the twelve clubs are organized into two leagues, Eastern and Western, which are geographically determined and thus do not coincide with the Central and Pacific League composition.
3. The reason for the all-dirt infield is improved drainage for the rainy season that runs from June through early July. Tarpaulins are not spread over the infield during rain, as they are in the United States.
4. All manufacturers must meet the common specifications of the Commissioner's Office, but small differences are possible. A team can only use balls from three manufacturers during a single season and must use those of a single manufacturer per series, and samples must be given in advance to the opponent.
5. Of course such commentators fail to recognize the hypocrisy of complaining about time limits on game length while also bemoaning the time taken by long counts, mound meetings, and other ways of taking advantage of the very time limitlessness that they invoke as the essence of the sport's purity.
6. For many clubs, neighborhood complaints (and lawsuits) about the disruptions of noise, stadium lighting, and large crowds are also constraining.
7. The club does provide medical treatment and insurance for job-related injuries.
8. Most stadiums in Japan have enclosed and air-conditioned press boxes, but Kōshien's facilities remain unchanged. This is largely at the insistence of the

Asahi Newspaper Company, which wants to preserve the old-fashioned atmosphere of the schoolboy tournament.

9. In part this is because the locker rooms of older facilities like Kōshien are barely big enough for the players, who are packed into a room of hooks, baskets, and open lockers that is less well-appointed than my old high school gym.

10. The United States and Canada are notable exceptions, for reasons that include the expansion of sports news desks within the regular urban and now metropolitan and national papers, the early development of television sports journalism, and the near disappearance of public transportation for commuting to work. Sports dailies in Japan are designed to be read on the rail and bus commute to work and on breaks at work.

11. Japan's all-time greatest catcher and later successful manager, Nomura Katsunori, has opined that the during the 1960s, the era when the Yomiuri Giants were held up as a model of "samurai baseball" to the country and the world, the most important job of most managers was keeping their players out of jail.

Bibliography

Cromartie, Warren. *Slugging It Out in Japan: An American Major Leaguer in the Tokyo Outfield.* Tokyo and New York: Kodansha International, 1991.

Guttmann, Allen, and Lee Thompson. *Japanese Sport: A History.* Honolulu: University of Hawaii Press, 2001.

Kelly, William W. "Sense and Sensibility at the Ballpark: What Fans Make of Professional Baseball in Modern Japan." In *Fanning the Flames: Fans and Consumer Culture in Contemporary Japan*, ed. William W. Kelly, 79–106. Albany: State University of New York Press, 2004.

Roden, Donald F. "Baseball and the Quest for National Dignity in Meiji Japan." *American Historical Review* 85, no. 3 (1980): 511–34.

Whiting, Robert. *The Meaning of Ichiro: The New Wave from Japan and the Transformation of Our National Pastime.* New York: Macmillan, 2004.

———. *You Gotta Have Wa: When Two Cultures Collide on the Baseball Diamond.* New York: Macmillan, 1989.

3 | China

Silk Gowns and Gold Gloves

In the spring of 2003, a strange new disease swept through much of Asia. More than 800 people died and nearly 9,000 were infected with Severe Acute Respiratory Syndrome, or SARS. The fast-spreading sickness caught health experts by surprise. Worried they were on the verge of a worldwide pandemic, officials of the World Health Organization issued a series of unprecedented warnings against travel to Hong Kong, Taiwan, and large parts of mainland China. Later, Toronto was added to the list of places to avoid. Fears that traveling athletes would circulate the disease forced organizers to cancel or move scores of international sporting events, including the women's World Cup soccer tournament in China and the badminton world championships in Birmingham, England.

By midsummer SARS was in check, and the travel warnings were gradually lifted. Quarantine precautions were eased, and tourism agencies across the globe were touting the wonders of visiting exotic Asia again. The surest sign of a return to normalcy came when twenty-five-year-old catcher Ren Min of the Tianjin Lions took the field at his home stadium for the first Chinese Baseball League All-Star Game. Tianjin was a military fortress during the Yuan Dynasty in the fourteenth century and today is one of China's biggest industrial and port cities. It is the closest seaport to the capital, Beijing, and sits astride the Bohai Sea. Tianjin also long has been a hotbed of baseball in China. In 1986, when Deng Xiaoping was in the early days of reopening his nation to the West after decades of isolation and internal turmoil,

Los Angeles Dodgers president Peter O'Malley wanted to make a gesture of friendship from the people of the United States. He did it by financing the construction of a baseball stadium in Tianjin.

Nearly two decades later Tianjin was one of four cities chosen to field teams in China's first professional baseball league. The simply named Chinese Baseball League (CBL) was established with the blessing of China's top governmental leaders, who announced unabashedly that their goal was to upgrade the quality of baseball to make "a historical breakthrough at the 2008 Olympic Games in Beijing."[1]

The Tianjin Lions, Beijing Tigers, Shanghai Eagles, and Guangzhou Leopards played a five-week, trial-run season in April and May 2002, with Tianjin defeating Beijing 6–4 in the championship game. The next spring, the league was settling into its first full, four-month season when SARS hit and panicked authorities imposed severe restrictions on travel and public gatherings. Baseball in China seemed to be the last thing on anyone's mind, and it may have been for a few frightening weeks as SARS spread out of control. But as soon as the international medical community seemed to get the spread of the sickness under control, China's top leaders looked to the game long hailed as "America's pastime" to send an important political signal to the rest of the world. The first public event they allowed after months of SARS-imposed quarantine was the first Chinese Baseball League All-Star Game at Dodger Stadium.

Baseball has a long, mostly forgotten history in China, spanning all of one century and parts of two other centuries. The sport was played at the Shanghai Base Ball Club as early as 1863—more than a decade before the first game in Japan. It was instrumental in bringing a premature end to one of the most ambitious educational exchanges of all time in the late nineteenth century. University baseball clubs served as a cover to help Sun Yat-sen's revolutionaries overthrow the Chinese emperor, and the game was hailed by generals of the People's Liberation Army who claimed it helped their soldiers learn how to throw hand grenades. Baseball was played in prisoner-of-war camps across China during the ghastly Sino-Japanese War and was a passionate diversion for Gen. Claire L. Chenault's Flying Tigers during breaks in their spectacular job providing air cover for the Burma Road and protecting the city of Chongqing when it was the capital of China. Chinese players fielded teams in secret in the countryside during the Cultural Revolution and, when the chaos finally ended, became regulars in international tournaments across Asia.

Time and again, from the late-nineteenth century to the early years of the third millennium, China played an important role in the globalization of baseball.

Gold Glovers in Silk Gowns

The Imperial Court of the late Qing Dynasty (1644–1911) realized things had gone too far when word got back to Beijing about the games of "bat ball." China's proudest students were smitten by the strange sport. One hundred twenty mandarins of the future had been shipped to the United States to learn the secrets of Meiguo, "the beautiful country," in the hope that they could use the foreigners' scientific knowledge to make China strong again. Instead of absorbing the best of the West, the students seemed to be embracing the worst. Beijing's spies reported a litany of sins. The students had become undisciplined, had squandered precious funds on personal vacations, formed themselves into secret societies, and ignored their Chinese teachers. Many were attending church and Sunday school, and a few even were planning to convert to Christianity.

Then there was the problem of sports. Physical exercise was considered beneath the dignity of a Confucian scholar. The concept of team games was virtually unknown in China. Yet, these scholars—the very elite upon whom the dying Qing Dynasty placed its greatest hope for the future—were spellbound by sports. "Within a few months, they were on the best of terms with their American schoolmates and were competing for honors both in their classes and on the baseball diamond."[2]

The students went to the United States in 1872 under an ambitious scheme devised by Rong Hong, an 1854 graduate of Yale who had become a naturalized U.S. citizen in 1852 and married an American woman, Mary Louise Kellogg of Avon, Connecticut, in 1875. Rong Hong returned to his homeland soon after graduating from Yale and spent the rest of his life professing his "undying love for China" the best way he knew how—by relentlessly advocating "reformation and regeneration" for her. His efforts reaped amazing rewards for China. The students he fought so hard to send to the United States returned home and introduced, among other things, a modern navy and sophisticated shipbuilding techniques, the long-distance telegraph, specialized mining skills, and the Beijing-to-Mongolia railway, an engineering marvel that Western experts said was impossible to build without foreign help.

The students might well have contributed much more, had not their love of all things American—particularly baseball—given Rong Hong's imperial enemies the ammunition needed to scuttle the Chinese Educational Mission prematurely.

Under a memorial approved by the emperor in the spring of 1871, the Chinese Educational Mission was to be composed of 120 handpicked students who would travel to the United States in groups of thirty per year for four years. The students, generally aged twelve to sixteen, would be accompanied by a retinue of Chinese teachers, translators, and attendants, and were to be supervised by two government commissioners. They were to study in the United States for fifteen years, concentrating on scientific, engineering, and military fields where the West was more advanced. At the end of fifteen years the students would be allowed to travel for two years to gain practical experience before returning to China to spend the rest of their lives in government service.

The first group of 30 students from the Chinese Educational Mission arrived in San Francisco on September 12, 1872. By 1875 all four "detachments" were in the United States and so thoroughly assimilated into their new culture that a conservative corps of Chinese officials began calling for an end to the daring experiment. The conservatives saw the educational mission as nothing more than "bowing down to the power of the hated foreigners." They warned the Imperial Court that if the students remained in the United States "they would soon lose their love of their own country" and "would be good for nothing or worse than nothing."[3] Two arguments the conservatives cited were intertwined: the students' newfound love of sports, particularly American baseball; and their disdain for traditional Chinese clothing, culture, and accoutrements.

The students had arrived in the United States wearing magnificent ankle-length brocaded silk gowns, known as *chang pao*, which were emblematic of Confucian scholars. Their hair was braided into long queues that symbolized their loyalty to the Manchu regime. Neither fashion was particularly practical nor welcome on the school grounds of nineteenth-century New England. "At first they were required to wear their long Chinese gowns and plaited cues [*sic*]," wrote one observer. "It made them look like girls and their fellow American students took great delight in teasing them and calling them Chinese girls. These taunts led to many blows and black eyes and a determination on the part of the Chinese lads to abandon their Chinese dress for American trousers and coats."[4]

A quasi-official history of Chinese baseball, published more than a hundred years after the Chinese Educational Mission, drew a direct link between the students' disdain for traditional clothing and their love of baseball—and claimed the two helped bring a premature end to the exchange program.

After this group of students was sent to America by the Qing Dynasty, they still wore the chang pao and ma kwa [long pants] and fox skin hats, from which stuck out very long queues of hair. Wherever they went, people gawked at them. At that time in America, baseball was already very popular in elementary and high schools, so a lot of Chinese students gradually participated in this sports activity. But the long gowns and queues brought them all kinds of inconveniences while playing baseball. In some ways, psychologically, they began to dislike the way they dressed. ... Because of all this, these students went out and cut off their queues and started dressing like American students. But who could have known this affair would cause great dissatisfaction within the Qing government? In 1881, the government sent an order by telegram and told them to return home.[5]

That version of events, however, appears somewhat misleading. Not all students cropped their hair. In fact, during the first few years of the mission, anyone cutting his queue was shipped home immediately. But by the spring of 1881, when the government abruptly canceled the program, most students had so embraced the American lifestyle that they had cut their queues and wore Western clothing exclusively.

Photographs of the students taken during their stay in New England clearly show their cultural confusion and conversion. Early in the mission, young members can be seen dressed in the traditional clothing their Qing sponsors supplied so they would "present a dignified appearance." As the students matured and became increasingly comfortable in a new world, their attire changed dramatically. Most adopted Western dress. Many even qualified as "dandies," sporting golf attire, natty derbies, classy frockcoats, and cravats. By 1878, three years after the last group arrived in the United States and three years before the program summarily ended, a photograph shows nine students looking considerably more like future Major Leaguers than mandarins.

The nine students in the 1878 photograph gained a measure of fame, both individually and as a team, in the United States as well as in China. Two of the nine died young, but the seven others played significant roles in China's future. The most politically prominent was Liang Dunyan, also known as Liang Tun Yen. He was one of the last foreign ministers of the Qing Dynasty and served as minister of communication in the first Republican government after the revolution of 1911. Under Liang's guidance, China negotiated a treaty with the United States that provided funds for the founding in 1911 of a new university on the outskirts of Beijing. Tsing Hua College, now known as National Qinghua University, specialized in preparing young men to study abroad, specifically in the United States. Consequently, the school's curriculum reflected a strong U.S. influence. English was the medium of instruction and physical education was emphasized. Not surprisingly, baseball was the most important and popular sport in the school program.

Zhan Tianyou, a star pitcher of the "Orientals" baseball club, also known as Tien Yow Jeme and Jeme Tien Yau, came to be "honored by all Chinese as China's first railway builder." Zhan studied engineering at Yale and graduated with honors from the university's Sheffield Scientific School in 1881, just weeks before the Chinese Educational Mission was recalled. He was one of only two members of the ambitious mission to return home with a degree from a U.S. university.

Both Liang and Zhan played starring roles in what probably was the most important and certainly the most memorable Chinese baseball game of the nineteenth or twentieth century. The game took place in Oakland, California, as the Chinese Educational Mission was making its way back to Shanghai. Members of the mission left Hartford, Connecticut, in July 1881 and were in San Francisco waiting for the steamer that would take them home when a baseball team from Oakland chal-lenged the Orientals to a match. A rousing account of the game was left by Wen Bingzhong, a member of the second group of Chinese students to arrive in 1873, who later became one of China's foremost engineers.

The Chinese nine had a twirler that played for Yale, and could do some wonderful curves with the ball, although in those days it was underhand pitching. Before the game began, the Oakland men imagined they were going to have a walk-over. . . . But the Oakland nine got the shock of their lives as soon as they attempted to con-nect with the deliveries of the Chinese pitcher; the fans were equally surprised at the strange phenomenon—Chinese playing their national ball game and showing the Yankees some of the thrills in the game. Unimaginable! All the same, the Chinese walloped them, to the great rejoicing of their comrades and fellow countrymen.[6]

As important as baseball appears to have been to some members of the Chinese Educational Mission while they were in the United States, and as rousing as the unexpected victory in Oakland must have been on the eve of their departure, there is little to indicate the sport played a prominent role in the lives of the students once they returned to China. In truth, baseball never gained widespread acceptance in China during the nineteenth or twentieth century. But the game did have a small fol-lowing. More importantly, baseball was played in China far earlier than heretofore widely believed—perhaps earlier than anywhere in Asia.

Shanghai Base Ball Club: A Decade Before Japan

As in other Asian countries, missionaries are credited with introduc-ing baseball to China. Foreign missionaries were known, though hardly plentiful, in the Middle Kingdom in the early years of the nineteenth century. However, they began moving into China in significant num-bers after the Treaty of Nanjing ended the first Opium War in 1842. That was the year the Knickerbocker Base Ball Club of New York gathered for its first organized games in the United States. Clearly it would have been some years, at least, before baseball made its way to China, even as a novelty. But by 1861, in the wake of another humiliating defeat for the Chinese in the Arrow War (1856–60), there was a growing willingness to accept Western ideas as part of a new "self-strengthening movement."

The ideological champion of the self-strengthening movement was

Feng Guifen, a scholar and official who came into frequent contact with Westerners in Shanghai and developed a grudging appreciation for their abilities. He urged his countrymen to adopt the "barbarians' superior techniques to control the barbarians"—a philosophy that indirectly led to the Chinese Educational Mission of 1872–81, the influx of missionaries to China, the spread of Western-style schools, and the arrival of baseball.

A book published by the American University Club of Shanghai in 1936 deals extensively with foreign influences on the modernization of China and reveals the early existence of baseball.[7] Only 1,001 copies of the book were printed. The text was composed of thirteen essays by separate writers. In a chapter titled "The Missionary and Philanthropic Sphere," author Charles E. Patton, a Princeton graduate, deals with the life of Henry William Boone, a medical missionary, who was born in Java in 1839 and was one of only four foreign children in Shanghai when his parents brought him there in 1845. According to Patton, "As a charter member of the first rowing and baseball clubs in Shanghai and in the Masonic brotherhood, Master of the Ancient Landmark Chapter, [Boone] was prominent in the Shanghai of the 'sixties.'"[8]

There is more proof baseball existed in China as early as the 1860s. The activities of the Shanghai Base Ball Club and the Rowing Club of Shanghai were closely related. The rowing club was founded on May 1, 1863. Its original rules, published on May 27, 1863, still exist. And details about a loan the club took out that year make it clear the Shanghai Base Ball Club was in existence already—a full decade before the date generally accepted for the first baseball game in Japan.

Bat Ball and the White House

The Chinese word for baseball is *bangqiu*, which translates literally to "bat ball" or "stick ball." American missionaries were taught to call the game *P'ai-ch'iu* or *paiqui*, which means "line ball"—*pai* being the term for a line, as in a file or a rank. Today, *paiqui* refers to volleyball.

Toward the end of the nineteenth century and through the years preceding World War II, baseball often was known as *yeqiu*, or "field ball," a term closely related to the Korean term *yagoo* and the Japanese term *yakyu*. The lexical connection is no coincidence. It mirrors the game's

3. Kan Yen, catcher for the Chinese team. Date unknown. (Photo courtesy of the National Baseball Hall of Fame.)

strong historical ties within Asia—distinct from its U.S. roots.

In 1895 Japan emerged as a major world power when it defeated China in the first Sino-Japanese War. Japan's swift victory humiliated China, exposed the weaknesses of the dying Qing Dynasty, and bore testament to the merits of modernization. Although the climate in China at the time remained distinctly antiforeign—indeed, the Boxer Rebellion was only four years away—the lingering impact of the self-strengthening movement and the recent lessons learned from Japan "spawned an interest in physical training in a very small number of Western-oriented Chinese schools." Three such schools—St. John's University of Shanghai, Tongzhou College of Beijing, and Huiwen College of Beijing—established baseball teams in 1895. That same year, the first YMCA opened in China at Tianjin and its staff promoted sports "as a useful front for its principal mission of Christian indoctrination."[9]

Sport long was considered an important teaching tool among Christian missionaries who struggled to change the traditional thinking of Chinese students toward physical exercise. An early convert to the promise of athletics was Liang Pixu, also known as Liang Cheng, who was twelve years old when he arrived in the United States with the final detachment of the Chinese Educational Mission in 1875. Liang Cheng went on to play baseball for Andover Academy in Massachusetts and was the hitting star of a dramatic Andover win against bitter rival Exeter Academy just weeks before the Chinese Educational Mission was recalled.

Liang Cheng went into government service after his return to China and was knighted in 1897 while serving in London as secretary to the Special Chinese Embassy to Queen Victoria's Diamond Jubilee Celebrations. From then on he was known as Sir Chentung Liang Cheng and went by that title in 1903 when he was named China's minister to Washington.

Sir Chentung had always been proud of his baseball experience and believed his proficiency at such an intrinsically American game helped his diplomatic career in Washington. Once, shortly after taking his post, Sir Chentung met President Theodore Roosevelt, who said an old friend had recently told him he thought the new Chinese minister played baseball for Andover and helped win a championship with a key hit in the 1880s. Sir Chentung happily confirmed the story and Roosevelt asked who had been the best player on that Andover team. The new minister temporarily abandoned his Chinese manners and diplomatic reserve and replied that it had been he. "From that moment the relations between President Roosevelt and myself became ten-fold stronger and closer," Liang Cheng said.[10]

Curve Balls and Hand Grenades

The Russo-Japanese War, which ended in 1905, gave Chinese baseball a boost. The Japanese had taken on and beaten Russia—one of the "Great Western" powers. Chinese students flocked to Japan to learn how a once-humble Asian land had grown so mighty. In 1905 the number of Chinese studying in Japan was estimated at twenty thousand. Within a few years, that grew to thirty thousand. They studied at Japanese institutions where, already, in 1905 "intercollegiate baseball was the country's major sport." Some absorbed baseball as thoroughly as their other subjects, bringing the game back with them far more openly and extensively than the students of the Chinese Educational Mission had done a generation earlier. One student who learned baseball overseas and put the game to practical use in his political life was the famed revolutionary Sun Yat-sen.

Sun was born in southern Guangdong Province but traveled to Hawaii in 1879 at age twelve to join his brother, who had emigrated earlier as a laborer. By 1883 Sun Yat-sen was back in China, but not before he picked up the sport of baseball. Just how enamored Sun was with the game and how often he played is unknown. But years later, on the eve of the 1911 Republican Revolution in China, Sun saw baseball as a convenient revolutionary tool. His party, the Tongmenghui (United League), formed a baseball club in Changsha, the capital of Hunan Province, which was a hotbed of unrest for nearly a century. The Changsha Yeqiu Hui (Changsha Field Ball Society) "took in young students to learn baseball techniques to improve their physical qualities . . . and to unite everybody." Essentially, the baseball team was a cover for Sun Yat-sen's anti-imperialist revolutionary activities in Changsha. "Part of the stated purpose of the association was that teaching baseball to young men also gave them practice in throwing hand grenades." "They are drilled to learn the basic skills of throwing hand grenades and tactical skills for armed insurrection."[11]

The idea of using baseball for military training, specifically to prepare soldiers and revolutionaries for throwing hand grenades, recurs frequently in Chinese history. It is difficult to say with accuracy whether the notion is fact or folklore. The authors of *Zhongguo Bangqui Yun-*

don Shi treat it with credence, as do numerous Western newspaper and magazine stories.[12] Others sources are more critical.

The most famous and most repeated tale about baseball and military training centers on Marshal He Long, an illiterate peasant who rose to fame when he formed one of the early units of the People's Liberation Army equipped only with vegetable knives. Every man in the unit was ordered to use his knife to kill a Nationalist soldier and steal a rifle. The daring tactics worked. Marshal He became one of China's most revered revolutionaries and was rewarded after the establishment of the People's Republic in 1949 by being named head of the Physical Culture and Sports Commission. While in that post through the 1950s he actively promoted baseball—particularly among military units—and the old stories about hand grenades and baseball were resurrected. In a 1981 article in the Asian Wall Street Journal, reporter Adi Ignatius, later editor of Time magazine in Asia, gave the clearest evidence that Marshal He, indeed, thought baseball had a role to play in training China's modern warriors. Ignatius seems skeptical at first, referring to the story as "legend," but then goes on to give specifics. "Marshal He pushed baseball because the Chinese lacked any sport which involved throwing an object about the size of a grenade," Ignatius wrote. "As the soldiers became skilled at throwing a baseball, the Marshal reasoned, their skills at throwing grenades would improve as well."[13]

Whether baseball was or ever could be an effective infantry training regimen remains questionable. But the game clearly served, on a small strategic level, the political interests of Chinese leaders as diverse as Sun Yat-sen and Marshal He Long. And in doing so, the "Great American Game" played at least trifling roles in both the revolution that brought down the Qing Dynasty in China and the modernization of the People's Liberation Army.

Glory Days and War

In the early years after Sun Yat-sen's revolution, baseball began to show signs of catching on in China, certainly not with the speed or general acceptance it enjoyed in Japan and other Asian countries, but more widely than is generally acknowledged by historians and baseball enthusiasts nine decades later. In April 1912, *Leslie's Weekly*, a popular illustrated magazine in the United States, ran a feature hailing the amazing rise of baseball in China.

Out in China, a baseball race just finished, concerned more people than did the overturning of the monarch. This year there will be an eight-club league in Shanghai. Last year, when the league had only four clubs, the games played there were very successful. Baseball promises to sweep through the coast cities of China with the same force that carried the Philippines and Japan.[14]

The article was written by former Major League baseball player Arthur "Tillie" Shafer, whose personal passions and pride perhaps led him to embellish the popularity of baseball in China. But there can be little doubt the sport was steadily gaining acceptance, particularly in Shanghai, where foreign influence was strong. The famed Hunter All-Americans featuring future Hall of Famers Casey Stengel and Waite Hoyt toured Shanghai in 1922. More than a decade later, Babe Ruth and Lou Gehrig played an exhibition game in Shanghai after their final triumphant prewar tour of Japan.

Communist revolutionaries played baseball throughout the 1930s and 1940s. A photograph published in *Zhongguo Bangqiu Yundong Shi* shows peasants and workers in Yenan, the communist stronghold, playing baseball some time during the Sino-Japanese War (1937–45). Another photograph shows members of a baseball team formed by the "511 Unit" of the People's Liberation Army in 1949, the year of the communist victory. A cut line with the second picture says, "Baseball is one of the most-loved sporting activities of the People's Liberation Army. In the past, baseball was known as 'Junqiu,' or army ball."

Some historians have assumed that baseball was dormant in China from 1937 to 1949 when the Chinese were busy fighting the Japanese and each other. Broadly speaking, that is true. But military units on all sides kept the game alive and even fostered its development. Baseball was most popular in areas where U.S. troops were stationed during the later years of the war against Japan and the final years of the civil war between Chiang Kai-shek's Nationalists and Mao Zedong's communists.

One U.S. veteran, Major Roger B. Doulens, came home in 1946 and wrote a glowing account of baseball's past and its promise in China for the *Sporting News*. He was cheered by a recent announcement that U.S.

troops would remain in China for at least another eighteen months to help rebuild the Chinese Army and felt it meant "the American national pastime will take on a definite Oriental flavor."[15]

Somewhat surprisingly, baseball prospered in China even after U.S. troops left and Mao's communists won the civil war. For more than a decade after the founding of the People's Republic in October 1949, baseball was played across China. Both baseball and softball were included in the first postrevolution National Games held in 1956. The winning baseball team, from Shanghai, was coached by Liang Fuchu, the "grandfather of Chinese baseball," who had been recruited by Marshal He to teach the game to soldiers. Three years later, baseball was popular enough to attract more than thirty provincial, military, and city teams to the first New China Baseball Tournament.

During Marshal He's reign as sports commissioner, tens of thousands of soldiers played baseball. The dominant team of the time was known as the Fighting Sports Brigade, and its star player was staff sergeant Du Kehe, who served as assistant coach of China's national baseball team. Du was a lifelong admirer of Marshal He, although Du admitted the man he called simply "my marshal" was "not much of a player himself." Du learned the game during the war and believed in its benefits long after. "My first coach was a Japanese POW," he told a reporter in 1991. "And my marshal used to say: 'Baseball and sports are the pillars of national defense and development.' [Baseball] made better soldiers, and our pitchers could toss a grenade faster and farther than anyone else . . . and with a curve on it."[16]

Both baseball and Marshal He fell from grace in the 1960s. From 1961 to 1974, baseball disappeared from regular national competition. Some say the game was banned, but Xie Chaoquan, deputy secretary of the Chinese Baseball and Softball Federation in the late 1970s and early 1980s, blamed baseball's disappearance from national sports competition in the early 1960s on economic problems caused by the disastrous Great Leap Forward. The game was still played in many large urban areas until the outbreak of the Cultural Revolution in 1966 and, rarely, during the Cultural Revolution. "Some of us still played in secret in the countryside," said Du Kehe. "We posted guards to whistle if someone came. Then we hid the bats and gloves and pretended to be doing exercises."[17]

Marshal He was denounced during the early days of the Cultural Revolution for criticizing Mao Zedong's economic errors. He was imprisoned in a remote country camp where he reportedly starved to death in 1968 after gnawing through the padding of his old military overcoat. Zealous Red Guards across China impeached sport in general, and baseball in particular, as an unwanted extravagance of Western decadence. Coaches were ridiculed and persecuted, sometimes by their own players. "My own coach was 'struggled' to death by the Guards," said Du Kehe, referring to a common practice of the Cultural Revolution where someone deemed to be an enemy of the people was beaten, spat upon, and harassed in public—often to the point of death.

The Cultural Revolution nominally ended in 1969, but baseball was not officially "rehabilitated" until 1975, when China built a Major League–sized stadium on the outskirts of Beijing and organized a series of exhibition games between a newly formed national team and players from Japan. As with most other things after the upheaval of the Cultural Revolution, the history of baseball had to be rewritten to fit new realities. A particularly propagandized book put out by the official government printing house in 1978 waxed eloquently about the political correctness of baseball: "Opposing the counter-revolutionary revisionist line [of the Cultural Revolution], Chairman Mao Zedong's revolutionary sports line deeply penetrated the people's hearts. The baseball movement generally progressed. Through urban workers, peasants and students, baseball organizations were developed." Baseball, the book declared, could help "build the [Communist] party" by promoting the "diligent study of Marxism, Leninism, and Mao Zedong Thought."[18]

What the post–Cultural Revolution Chinese leadership really wanted was to use baseball in much the same way they used other sports to promote friendship and gain credence and acceptance from other countries. The oft-touted policy of "Friendship First; Competition Second" was applied to baseball in the 1980s and 1990s as it had been earlier to Ping-Pong, soccer, basketball, and other sports. The fact that the breakaway province of Taiwan, still known as the Republic of China, emerged in the late 1960s as the dominant power in world Little League baseball clearly had an impact on the Chinese rulers in Beijing. In 1988, after years of slowly cultivating baseball, the People's Republic of China hosted its first official international baseball tournament, the Beijing International, for eleven- and twelve-year-old boys.

As late as the early 1990s, the specter of the Cultural Revolution still haunted baseball in China. The headquarters of the Chinese national baseball team, as it prepared for the 1991 national tournament, was a gymnasium at the Institute of Sports Technology in Lucheng, an isolated rural village southwest of Beijing. A poster in the gymnasium urged players to "Learn from Lei Feng"—hero of the people. Lei Feng was a legendary—probably mythical—young soldier who became a propaganda hero during the Cultural Revolution for countless elaborate, selfless acts supposedly performed out of love for the Communist Party and China. Almost all these acts led to his death, so Lei Feng literally died a thousand deaths for the party.

Knowing the Communist Party's penchant for fabricating wonderful stories, and seeing the motivational banner at the training grounds, a Western reporter asked one of the coaches of the Chinese national team about Lei Feng's baseball career. The coach smiled wryly and said, "Lei Feng didn't play baseball, but we will learn from his spirit of serving the people."

"We Adapt from the Japanese Style of Baseball"

By the late 1990s baseball again was played openly and regularly across China, including in the new Special Administrative Region of Hong Kong where Laurence Lee, district chief of the Hong Kong Little League, said the game had become "Asia-fied" since it made its way across the Pacific Ocean more than a century earlier. "We adapt from the Japanese style of baseball," said Lee. "We learn from them. We cannot learn from the Americans because the Americans do not practice all the time. They just warm up about a half hour before the game. We cannot learn from them like we can learn from the Japanese."[19]

Much as the United States had done a century earlier, Japan showed signs of using baseball as a tool of diplomacy in its dealings with China in the late 1990s. Baseball exchanges were frequent, including the first-ever tour by Japanese professional players to China in the fall of 1996.

The United States, too, renewed overtures to China through baseball.

Coaches were sent on goodwill missions beginning in the 1980s, and the stadium Peter O'Malley built in Tianjin in 1986 remains a symbol of baseball's rebirth in China.

Beijing 2008—China's World Series

If baseball ever becomes widely popular in China, historians will look back on 2003 as the year it all began. One-hundred and forty years after the Shanghai Base Ball Club was founded, and five years before Beijing was scheduled to host the games of the XXIX Olympiad, China's top leaders took a series of major steps to raise both the profile and quality of baseball in the country. They approved the first real full season of the fledgling four-team professional league. Then they decided to use the league's All-Star Game as the premier event to welcome the Chinese people back to public gatherings after the long and frightening SARS-imposed quarantine. In a land long accustomed to political symbolism, few failed to understand the blessings that bestowed on baseball. It was a clear indication China's leaders were ready to "play ball."

In the fall of 2003, the China Baseball Association (CBA) showed just how serious it was about trying to field a top-flight team for the 2008 Olympics. The CBA hired two former Major League stars to coach a Chinese national team that seemed to have promising potential, but pathetically little experience. Jim Lefebvre, a former National League Rookie of the Year with the Los Angeles Dodgers and manager of the Milwaukee Brewers, Seattle Mariners, and Chicago Cubs, was brought in to coach the national team. Hired to help him was Bruce Hurst, who pitched for four teams in a fifteen-year big league career and was a member of the 1987 American League All-Star team with the Boston Red Sox. Lefebvre and Hurst did a masterful job, training in Arizona for three weeks before heading to the Asia Games in Sapporo, Japan, where the Chinese National Team won its three opening-round games against the Philippines, Indonesia, and Pakistan by a combined score of 41–1. In the finals, though, China was overmatched against perennial Asia powerhouses Japan, Korea, and Taiwan. The Chinese scored only three runs in three games but did themselves credit with a tough 3–1 loss to Taiwan in the last game of the tournament.

The Chinese National Team continued to make progress under Lefebvre and Hurst over the next few seasons. In 2004 the squad competed against teams from the Arizona Fall League, an increasingly influential showcase for MLB's top prospects. The Chinese won four games against the U.S. professionals and took another important step toward becoming even more competitive by hiring former world champion decathlete Dan O'Brien to run a rigorous physical training program.

Shortly after the 2003 Asia Games, MLB and the CBA announced an agreement to promote the game. The agreement called for top Chinese coaches to travel to the United States to work with Major League clubs, training sessions for Chinese umpires, the establishment of youth development programs in China, and permission for U.S. scouts to begin scouring China for talent.

Jim Small, MLB's tireless vice president of international market development, could hardly contain his enthusiasm for the agreement. "Baseball was born in America. Now it belongs to the world," Small said in Beijing. "If baseball is truly to be considered a global sport, it needs to be played in some key countries—and China is at the top of that list."[20]

An indication that baseball was catching on in the run-up to the 2008 Olympics came in 2005 when the increasingly popular China Baseball League expanded to six teams and increased its season to 90 games. That was up from a 72-game schedule in 2004 and just 48 games in 2002. Joining the Beijing Tigers, Tianjin Lions, Guangdong Leopards, and Shanghai Eagles were the Sichuan Dragons and a team called the China Hope Stars. The Hope Stars were made up of top college and amateur prospects. To make up for their relative lack of experience, the Hope Stars were allowed to bring in six professional players from outside Japan. All six were Korean professionals in the Hope Stars' inaugural season. The other five teams in the league were allowed up to three foreign professionals. Guangdong used its slots to bring in two Dominican players on loan from the Hiroshima Carp of Japan's Central League. The Sichuan Dragons had one Japanese player who came to China, asked the club for a tryout, and made the roster.

By the time the first pitch was thrown in 2005, five of the six teams in the China Baseball League had working agreements with Japanese professional baseball teams. And, in a sure sign of the steady globalization of baseball, the Hope Stars signed deals with both the Chibe Lotte

Marines of Japan's Pacific League and the Lotte Giants of the Korean Baseball Organization.

Jim Small was right: baseball may have been born in the United States, but it increasingly belongs to the world.

Long Live Bat Ball

The Boxer Rebellion, the collapse of the Qing Dynasty, the Japanese invasion of Manchuria, World War II, the civil war between the Communists and Nationalists, and the upheavals of the Great Leap Forward and Cultural Revolution all hampered the development of sports, particularly foreign sports, in China during much of the twentieth century. But baseball somehow survived. It survived not because China's leaders ever sought to emulate the United States or its culture. Baseball survived because there was something practical to be gained by keeping it alive. In the early days of the People's Republic, Marshal He believed baseball made better soldiers—or, at least, better grenade throwers. In the late 1990s and early twenty-first century, China's leaders clearly saw new, practical benefits to baseball. China was awakening. During the final two decades of the twentieth century, China's leaders did what Rong Hong and the Chinese Educational Mission set out to do more than a century ago. They reached outside the Middle Kingdom, seeking the knowledge of foreigners to make China strong again. No one would argue that baseball played a leading role in China's modernization. But baseball has proven to be an important tool of diplomacy as China returns to its long-abandoned role as a global leader. The Chinese Baseball League is proof of that, as are Jim Lefebvre, Bruce Hurst, and the Chinese National Team as they gear up for the games of their lives in Beijing in 2008.

Notes

1. "CBBA Signs Development Agreement with Major League Baseball," available at http://en.olympic.cn/08beijing/towards/2003-11-24/130577.html.
2. LaFargue, *China's First Hundred*, 35.
3. Yung, *My Life in China and America*, 204.
4. LaFargue, *China's First Hundred*, 38.

5. Chen, Liang, and Du, *Zhongguo Bangqiu Yundong Shi*, 6–7.

6. LaFargue, *China's First Hundred*, 53.

7. American University Club of Shanghai, *American University Men in China*.

8. Patton, "Missionary and Philanthropic Sphere," 49.

9. Kolatch, *Is the Moon in China Just as Round?* 165.

10. Whitehill, *Portrait of a Chinese Diplomat*, 14.

11. Wilson, "Chinese History," 17; Chen, Liang, and Du, *Zhongguo Bangqiu Yundong Shi*, 8.

12. Chen, Liang, and Du, *Zhongguo Bangqiu Yundong Shi*, 6–7.

13. Ignatius, "Baseball in China."

14. Arthur Shafer, "Baseball All around the World," *Leslie's Weekly*, April 4, 1912, 408.

15. Doulens, "Chinese Grabbing Chance to Learn Game."

16. Schmetzer, "Chinese Baseball Hangs in There."

17. Schmetzer, "Chinese Baseball Hangs in There."

18. American University Club of Shanghai, *Bangqiu*, 1.

19. Laurence Lee, interview by the author, April 26, 1997, Hong Kong.

20. Quoted in a story by Ted Anthony of the Associated Press from Beijing: "Major League Baseball, China, Unite to Push U.S. National Pastime to the Mainland's Masses," distributed by Associated Press Worldstream, November 23, 2003.

Bibliography

American University Club of Shanghai. *American University Men in China.* Shanghai: Comacrib, 1936.

———. *Bangqiu* (Baseball). Beijing: People's Sports, 1978.

Boorman, Howard L. *Biographical Dictionary of Republican China.* New York: Columbia University Press, 1967.

Butterfield, Fox. "Baseball Achieving Popularity in China." *New York Times*, October 3, 1979, D19.

———. "'Play Ball!' Is the Cry in Peking." *New York Times*, August 27, 1975, C6.

———. "Taiwan Little Leaguers Stun Japan." *New York Times*, August 3, 1969, E4.

Chan, Kim Man. "Mandarins in America: The Early Chinese Ministers to the United States, 1878–1907." PhD diss., University of Hawaii, 1981.

Chen Yi Ming, Liang Youde, and Du Kehe. *Zhongguo Bangqiu Yundong Shi* (A history of Chinese baseball). Wuhan, China: Wuhan, 1990.

Chentung Liang Cheng. "Chinese Boy at an American School." *The Youth's Companion*, October 26, 1905, 535.

Doulens, Maj. Roger B. "Chinese Grabbing Chance to Learn Game." *Sporting News*, March 14, 1946, 13.

Harris, N.M.W. "Sampan Pidgin" (Being a History of the Shanghai Rowing Club). Shanghai: Mercantile, 1938.

Hummel, Arthur W., ed. *Eminent Chinese of the Ch'ing Period (1644–1912)*. Washington DC: GPO, 1943.

Ignatius, Adi. "Baseball in China Makes a Pitch to Be Re-established." *Asian Wall Street Journal*, February 8, 1981, op-ed page.

Knuttgen, Howard G., Ma Qiwei, and Wu Zhongyuan, eds. *Sport in China*. Champaign IL: Human Kinetics, 1990.

Kolatch, Jonathan. *Is the Moon in China Just as Round? Sporting Life & Sundry Scenes*. New York: Jonathan David, 1992.

LaFargue, Thomas E. *China's First Hundred*. Pullman: State College of Washington Press, 1942.

Lamberton, Mary. *St. John's University Shanghai, 1879–1951*. New York: United Board for Christian Colleges in China, 1955.

Lang, H. *Shanghai Considered Socially: A Lecture by H. Lang*. 2nd ed. Shanghai: American Presbyterian Mission, 1875.

Lunt, Carroll, ed. *The China Who's Who 1925 (Foreign)*. Shanghai: Kelly & Walsh, 1925.

Martin, Bernard. *Strange Vigour: A Biography of Sun Yat-sen*. London: William Heinemann, 1967.

Mateer, A. H. *New Terms for New Ideas: A Study of the Chinese Newspaper*. Shanghai: Methodist Publishing, 1915.

Mogridge, George. *The Celestial Empire; or Points and Pickings of Information about China and the Chinese*. London: Grant and Griffith, 1844.

Moore, Glenn. "The Great Baseball Tour of 1888–89: A Tale of Image-Making, Intrigue, and Labour Relations in the Gilded Age." *International Journal of the History of Sport* 11, no. 3 (December 1994): 431–56.

Nance, W. B. *Soochow University*. New York: United Board for Christian Colleges in China, 1956.

Patton, Charles E. "The Missionary and Philanthropic Sphere." In *American University Men in Shanghai*. Shanghai, 1936.

Pollock, John. *A Foreign Devil in China: The Story of Dr. L. Nelson Bell, a Surgeon in China*. London: Hodder and Staughton, 1972.

Robyn, Chris. "Building the Bridge: The Chinese Educational Mission to the United States. A Sino-American Historico-Cultural Synthesis, 1872–1881." M.Phil diss., Chinese University of Hong Kong, 1996.

Schiffrin, Harold Z. *Sun Yat-sen and the Origins of the Chinese Revolution.* Berkeley: University of California Press, 1968.

Schmetzer, Uli. "Chinese Baseball Hangs in There." *Chicago Tribune,* May 3, 1991, sec. 4, 6.

Sharman, Lyon. *Sun Yat-sen: His Life and Its Meaning, a Critical Biography.* Stanford: Stanford University Press, 1934.

Wei, Betty Peh-T'i. *Old Shanghai.* New York: Oxford University Press, 1993.

Whitehill, Walter Muir. *Portrait of a Chinese Diplomat: Sir Chentung Liang Cheng.* Boston: Boston Atheneum, 1974.

Willing, Richard. "Baseball Ends Long Home Run from China." *Detroit News,* April 6, 1989, A1, 15.

Wilson, Jeffrey. "Chinese History, Even in Baseball, Stretches Back Far in Time." *International Baseball Rundown* 5, no. 7 (August 1996): 16–17.

Yung Wing [Rong Hong]. *My Life in China and America.* New York: Henry Holt, 1909.

4 | Taiwan

Baseball, Colonialism, and Nationalism

On March 25, 2000, Chen Shui-bian chose a special engagement
for his first public appearance as Taiwan's president-elect, speaking at the Taiwan Major League's opening game. Before the contest between the Taizhong Robots and the Gaoxiong-Pingdong
Thunder Gods began, the capacity crowd heard the president-
elect describe baseball as a "symbol of the Taiwanese spirit" in
announcing that he would name 2001 "Taiwan Baseball Year" and
consider officially designating baseball as Taiwan's national sport.
In his customary self-deprecating fashion, Chen confessed to a
childhood fascination with baseball and joked that he only decided to be president after he realized he was not athletic enough
to succeed in baseball.

President Chen's attention to the game marks only the latest
chapter in the history of Taiwanese baseball, a game that has become much more than just a sport. It is a colonial legacy that was
planted and sunk deep roots during the fifty-year Japanese occupation of the island from 1895 to 1945. The professional version
of the game in Taiwan is a reminder of the profound influence
of transnational capitalism on Taiwan.

Taiwan's complicated history has given rise to the need to present and understand Taiwan as part of the world community in
its own right, *not* as part of the People's Republic of China (PRC).
Much of contemporary Taiwanese culture, thus, emphasizes both
the global and the local, and the blending of the two. Professional
baseball in Taiwan is a perfect example of this self-conscious,
ideological combination of the cosmopolitan and the provincial,

the international and the Taiwanese. The history of professional baseball in Taiwan, in many ways, is nothing more or less than the history of the effort to create a "baseball culture" that could speak to both of these striking and complementary aspects of Taiwanese life.

Baseball in the Japanese Colonial Era

Baseball in Taiwan, introduced by the Japanese colonial regime, has never thoroughly shed its Japanese heritage. From the name of the game, still called by many in Taiwanese *yagyu* (from the Japanese *yakyû*, and not the Mandarin *bangqiu*), to the Taiwanese-Japanese-English playground calls of "stu-rii-ku" and "out-tow," baseball's Japanese "origins" are still an important part of Taiwanese heritage. The sport, which was well developed in Japanese schools by the 1890s, was imported to the colony of Taiwan around 1897, just two years after its incorporation into the Japanese Empire. Initially played by colonial bureaucrats, bankers, and their sons in Taihoku (Taibei), baseball spread to southern Taiwan by 1910. In 1915 the colonial government formed the Taiwan Baseball Federation made up of fifteen (all-Japanese) school teams playing the quickly growing sport.

It was not long before Taiwanese youth joined in this new fun. In the early 1910s, Taiwan governor-general Sakuma Samata encouraged the development of baseball among Taiwanese youth. As he explained it, this was his humble way of repaying the local Taiwanese deity Mazu, who had appeared to his ailing wife in a dream and miraculously cured her. In 1921 Hualian native Lin Guixing formed a team of boys of the Ami aborigine tribe. They became known as the Nôkô Baseball Team, named for a nearby mountain, and achieved great fame when they traveled to Japan in the summer of 1925 and won four of nine games against Japanese school teams.

The most famous of all Taiwanese baseball traditions was that born at the Jiayi Agriculture and Forestry Institute (abbreviated Kanô) in the late 1920s. Under the guidance of Manager Kondô Hyôtarô, a former standout player who had toured the United States with his high school team, Kanô dominated Taiwan baseball in the decade before the Pacific War. What made the Kanô team special was its tri-ethnic composition; in 1931 its starting nine was made up of two Han Taiwanese, four

Taiwan aborigines, and three Japanese players. Kanô won the Taiwan championship, earning the right to play in the hallowed Kōshien High School Baseball Tournament, held near Osaka, five times between 1931 and 1936. The best of these, the 1931 squad, was the first team ever to qualify for Kōshien with Taiwanese (aborigine or Han) players on its roster.[1] Kanô placed second in the twenty-three-team tournament that year, their skills and intensity winning the hearts of the Japanese public, and remaining a popular nostalgic symbol even today in Japan. This team of Han, Aboriginal, and Japanese players "proved" to nationally minded Japanese the colonial myth of "assimilation" (*dôka*)—that both Han and aborigine Taiwanese were willing and able to take part alongside Japanese in the cultural rituals of the Japanese state. Of course, the irony is that the six Taiwanese players on the starting roster probably also saw their victories as a statement of Taiwanese (Han or aborigine) will and skill that could no longer be dismissed by the Japanese colonizing power.

The southern town of Jiayi cemented its reputation as the baseball capital of Taiwan when several of its sons went on to star in baseball in Japan. The greatest of these was Wu Bo, who starred on Kanô's 1935 and 1936 championship teams, signed with the proud Tokyo Giants in 1937, and played for the Giants for seven years. In 1943, under the nationalistic pressures of wartime, Wu took the Japanese name Kure Masayuki. However, the next year he reminded the Japanese baseball community of his ethnic Chinese identity when he refused to travel to Manchuria with the Giants to rouse Japanese troops stationed there. Wu left the Giants outright, but went on to play for thirteen more years with the Hanshin Tigers and Mainichi Orions, and in 1995 he became the first Taiwanese player selected to the Japanese Baseball Hall of Fame.

Taiwan did not just produce an elite class of standout baseball players. The sport became popular at all levels, making baseball as dominant a sport in the colony as it was in the home islands of Japan. Peng Ming-min would later trade his baseball mitt for the pen, enduring much sacrifice as he led the struggle for Taiwanese self-determination and independence during the Chinese Nationalist era. But as a boy in Gaoxiong in the 1930s, young Peng was a typical Taiwanese schoolboy obsessed with baseball. In a conversation with me in 1999, Peng fondly

4. *Three members of the 1931 Kanô (Tainan District Jiayi Agriculture and Forestry Institute) baseball team. Kanô placed second in the empire-wide Kōshien tournament and became famous for its triracial composition of Han, aborigine, and Japanese players.* (Photo courtesy of Andrew Morris.)

remembered huddling around the radio to listen to broadcasts of the Japanese high school championships at Kōshien every spring. In his memoir, *A Taste of Freedom*, Peng recalls,

I was an ardent baseball fan. When Babe Ruth visited Japan I boldly wrote a letter to him and in return received his autograph, which became my treasure. . . . [I] reserved my greatest enthusiasm for baseball. Our school masters took baseball very seriously, treating it almost as if it were a military training program. Although I was a poor batter, I was an excellent fielder, and played on our team when it won a citywide championship. Needless to say, my Babe Ruth autograph gave me great prestige among my classmates.[2]

The enthusiasm of millions of young people like Peng, who played and paid feverish attention to this Japanese institution, is what made baseball Taiwan's "national game" some seventy years before President Chen's remarks in 2000.

This Taiwanese excellence in baseball, the sport of the colonizing metropolis, reflects an important aspect of the experience of almost any colonized people. In Taiwan baseball was one way in which the colonized population sought to negotiate their relationship with the Japanese colonizing power on terms that the Japanese had to accept. Japanese exclusion of Taiwanese baseball teams or players would have given the lie to Japan's entire colonial enterprise.

Participation in Japan's "national game" allowed Taiwanese people to prove and live their acculturation into the colonial order at the very moment that Taiwanese baseball successes worked to subvert it. Taiwanese subjects, both ethnic Chinese and aborigine, could use baseball skills and customs taught by the Japanese to appeal for equal treatment within the national framework that baseball represented in so many ways. The Taiwanese baseball community, through its many triumphs, was able to use this arena to offer the final proof, in a "national" language that the Japanese had to understand, that the colonial enterprise was bound to fail.

Baseball in Guomindang Taiwan, 1945–1980s

When the Guomindang (Chinese Nationalist Party), or GMD, took the reins of Taiwan's government in late 1945, the government enforced policies of "de-Taiwanization," officially degrading distinctively Taiwanese cultures or customs in order to cut the colonial ties to Japan. At the same time, however, the GMD also realized what a valuable exception baseball could be to the erasing of all colonial remnants. The party had promoted physical culture in planning the construction of a strong and healthy Chinese populace and state on the mainland for two decades.

Official endorsement of baseball soon became one method of officially "Sinicizing" a cultural realm that still represented a Pandora's box of colonial thinking and customs. Baseball was included at the First Taiwan Provincial Games, held in October 1946 at Taiwan National University; twenty counties, cities, colleges, and government organizations sent baseball teams to this meet overseen by Chiang Kai-shek.

A baseball tournament was held in Taiwan in August 1947, even as government "anticommunist" forces continued their massacres, begun in March, of thousands of Taiwanese elites who were seen as a threat to Chiang's regime. It is telling that the baseball world was not able to escape this horror. Lin Guixing, coach of the great Hualian Nôkô teams of the 1920s, was killed on August 1, 1947, during the violent and sustained aftermath of what was called the "February 28 Incident." Fudan University and Shanghai Pandas teams also came to play against teams from Taibei, Taizhong, Taiwan Power, Taiwan Sugar, and Taiwan Charcoal, as if all was well that bloody summer. In 1949 a Taiwan Province Baseball Committee was formed, organizing annual provincial baseball tournaments at all levels of play.

What is interesting about the Guomindang efforts to promote baseball in Taiwan in the immediate postwar period is that Taiwan was the only region of the Republic of China (ROC) with any baseball tradition whatsoever; they could hardly promote baseball as a "Chinese" custom. Thus, their work to hijack the game's unique popularity in Taiwan for their own uses still had to be in explicitly Taiwanese terms. Baseball remained an arena where Taiwanese people could successfully, and without any fear of reprisal, challenge the Guomindang's policies of "de-Taiwanization" and claims to represent a true Chinese culture.

Baseball, then, is also central to the story of Taiwan's rapid and traumatic transition from wartime to decolonization to a new oppression delivered in the rhetoric of "retrocession" to Chinese rule. Original support for Chinese rule in Taiwan was dashed violently and unmercifully by the actions of tens of thousands of carpetbagging Guomindang troops, bureaucrats, and hangers-on. Relieved and enthusiastic searching for a "Chinese" Taiwan, among Taiwanese, thus quickly gave way to a yearning for cultural artifacts from the good old colonial days.

Yet the vagaries of decolonization and retrocession do not provide the full extent of this history. The Taiwanese people now had to contend with the reality of an invigorated American cold war imperialism in Taiwan and Asia as a whole. Taiwan's baseball history offers a look at this process as well. In 1951 the first All-Taiwan baseball team was organized for a series of games against Filipino teams in Manila. The Manila sporting public fell in love with the All-Taiwanese, especially the astounding home run hitting of Hong Taishan. But the young team from Taiwan made an even deeper impression when team members "volunteered" to give blood to American soldiers recuperating in Manila hospitals from casualties sustained in the Korean War. This episode, though anecdotal, provides a profound metaphor to describe life in small Asian nations during the depths of the cold war. In the end, the greatest triumphs that could be won were in activities (like baseball) that were defined and approved by the United States, in locales dependent on and exposed to American beneficence and greed, and in ways that figuratively sucked life from these locales as they were integrated into America's new postwar empire.

This incredible tightrope-walk between Japanese colonialist legacies and Guomindang-U.S. hegemony in Taiwan continued into, and was in many ways exemplified by, the international success of Taiwanese Little League baseball teams beginning in the late 1960s. In a tremendous run perhaps unmatched in the history of international sport, Taiwanese teams won ten Little League World Series titles between 1969 and 1981, and sixteen in the twenty-seven-year period from 1969 to 1995. This success brought desperately needed attention to Taiwan on the world stage and allowed the playing-out of a complicated jumble of national and racial tensions in Taiwan.

Taiwan's Little League success began in August 1968, with two great victories by the Maple Leaf (Hongye) Elementary School team over a visiting team from Wakayama, Japan. The Hongye Village team, made up of Bunun aborigine youth representing their tiny Taidong County school of just one hundred students, earned the right to play Wakayama after winning the island-wide Students' Cup tournament held in Taibei. They became superstars after their victories over Wakayama at the Taibei Municipal Stadium. The 20,000 fans who managed to get tickets for these historic games were joined by an island-wide television audience treated to more than thirteen hours of Taiwan Television broadcasts on the first game alone. The overall significance in Taiwan of the Maple Leaf boys' success is hard to measure. Virtually all of Taiwanese society was energized in a way that has few parallels in American history; the Olympic triumphs of Jesse Owens and the 1980 hockey team are perhaps the closest examples. To this day the 1968 Maple Leaf victories against Wakayama are cited as a defining moment in the history of Taiwanese nationalism.[3]

The next year, 1969, was Taiwan's first foray into the Little League World Series in Williamsport, Pennsylvania. The youth of Taiwan spared no time in making this tournament an almost yearly blowout of any and all challengers. The Taizhong Golden Dragons, Taiwan's 1969 champions, swept opponents from Ontario, Ohio, and California to take the world title. An impressed, if politically incorrect, *Sporting News* described the skill and infectious enthusiasm of "the Orientals":

Thousands of gong-clanging, cheering fans in the stands at Williamsport adopted the Chinese as their favorite team.

[Chen Zhiyuan] captured the fans' imagination when, after every out, he'd turn around and shout to his fielders, raising the ball above his head. In return they yell in Chinese the American equivalent of, "Go men!"[4]

The players' confidence was also boosted by the presence at their games of thousands of delirious Taiwanese and Chinese flag-waving fans who would make these yearly baseball pilgrimages to Williamsport for decades to come.

Fans at home in Taiwan were even more jubilant, glued to their radios into the wee hours of that humid summer night. One radio DJ remembered thirty years later how "the Taipei night nearly boiled over. When the game finished at 3 a.m., the streets of the city erupted with the constant banging of firecrackers, as ordinary citizens opened their windows and yelled out to the night sky, 'Long live the Republic of China!'"[5] At a time when Taiwan's standing in the international community was becoming less and less stable this, like the Maple Leaf triumphs the year before, was a satisfying victory indeed.

Yet this championship, unfortunately, was plagued by irregularities. It was common knowledge in Taiwan that the 1969 world champions, technically a school team from Taizhong in central Taiwan, had actually been recruited as a national All-Star team, a fact that clearly violated the Williamsport charter. Only two of the team's fourteen players were from Taizhong, while nine of the starting players were from Jiayi and Tainan in the south of the island.[6]

Yet these geographical technicalities mattered little to the Taiwanese public at the time. In 1971, when the Tainan Giants won the Williamsport championship, some ten million people in Taiwan—two-thirds of the island's population—watched the game on television, from 2:00 to 5:00 a.m. Baseball stardom became an almost universal aspiration among the boys and young men of Taiwan. Li Kunzhe, who starred professionally for the China Trust Whales in the late 1990s, remembers,

I grew up watching baseball. . . . I remember the days when everyone would wake up in the middle of the night to watch our national teams perform in the international competitions. They were national heroes. We all wanted to represent our country and be a hero.[7]

These triumphs were especially thrilling for Taiwanese people, but the humbled Americans were reduced to booing the Taiwanese youngsters (when the Tainan Giants won again in 1973, on their third consecutive no-hitter) and eventually even banning all foreign teams for a year in 1975 in order to guarantee an American "winner."

Success in this Taiwanese (and not mainland Chinese) sport of baseball also invigorated dissidents and critics of the Chiang Kai-shek regime, who were thirsting for tangible measures of uniquely Taiwanese accomplishment. Williamsport soon became a "new battlefield" for Taiwanese dissidents and independence activists. In 1969 frenzied Taiwanese fans shouted upon the Golden Dragons' victory, "The players are all Taiwanese! Taiwan has stood up!" Taiwanese supporters soon raised the stakes in this implicit protest against the Guomindang government. In 1971, as the Tainan Giants swept to a world championship, Taiwanese independence activists at Williamsport hired an airplane to fly over the stadium towing a bilingual banner reading, "Long Live Taiwan Independence, Go Go Taiwan." The Taiwan teams' games attracted fans from all points of the political spectrum, so each Taiwan independence flag or banner was matched by pro-Nationalist fans waving flags and cheering for the "Chinese" team. The pro-state fans had an advantage, however, in the dozens of New York Chinatown thugs hired by the Guomindang to identify and rough up Taiwan independence activists at the games. The 1971 championship game was interrupted when a dozen of these toughs ran across the field to rip down a banner reading in English and Chinese, "Team of Taiwan, Go Taiwan."

In 1972, when the Taibei Braves challenged for the world title, the Guomindang was better prepared, renting every single commercial aircraft for miles around to keep the Taiwan independence crowd from repeating their coup. Some seventy to eighty ROC military cadets training in the United States were also recruited to Williamsport to, as they shouted while beating Taiwanese male and female supporters with wooden clubs, "Kill the traitors!" One wonders what American fans at Williamsport thought of all this violence, but these concerns did not stop either side from carrying out their battles. In 1975, at the Senior Little League Championships in Gary, Indiana, Taiwanese activists floated a balloon bearing the message "Long Live Taiwan Independence." Thanks to the generous and curious ABC cameramen on the scene, this sky-high subversion flashed across millions of Taiwan television screens for the first time in history. Thus, through the manipulation of satellite technology and the tweaking of the connection between sports and nationalism that the Guomindang itself had tried to disseminate in Taiwan, Little League baseball became one of the most effective and joyous ways of challenging Chinese Nationalist hegemony in Taiwan.

The many jumbled and precarious directions along which Taiwanese baseball developed in the first four decades of Guomindang rule did not resemble in the least the neat white lines of the baseball diamonds that were home to this movement. In the martial law days of mainlander domination by the Guomindang party and state, baseball was one realm in which Taiwanese people could register their own contributions to Taiwan culture and society. In many ways baseball represented a table of negotiation, where Taiwanese baseball communities exchanged measures of integration for measures of independent expression, measures of "Chinese" identity for measures of pro-Japanese nostalgia, and measures of the autocratic Guomindang state for measures of an independent Taiwanese culture and society.

The Chinese Professional Baseball League: Beginnings, 1990–94

Planning for a Taiwanese professional baseball league began in late 1987, the year that martial law was lifted in Taiwan. The events of this year marked the end of four decades of naked authoritarian rule by the Guomindang and signaled the beginning of a new era in Taiwan. The nation now faced two challenges: defining a unique identity for the Chinese-but-not-really-Chinese island and ensuring Taiwan's inclusion in a global world order. Both of these goals were realized with the creation of the Chinese Professional Baseball League (CPBL), which began play in 1990.

The CPBL consisted of four corporate-owned teams: the Weichuan Dragons, Brother Elephants, President Lions, and Mercuries Tigers. Each team's uniforms clearly demonstrated the effort to present a product that was a pleasurable mix of the global and the Chinese; the teams' names and parent companies were represented on the jerseys and caps in various mixtures of English and Chinese script. The four teams did not represent cities, as teams do in most professional leagues; instead, the teams played weekly round-robin series together, up and down the island's west coast. Each baseball city had fan clubs supporting each of the CPBL's four teams, who provided enthusiastic, flag-waving, drum-beating support but also could at times very easily turn violent. The sight of angry fans—Lions fans in the President Corporation's hometown of Tainan were notorious for this—hurling bottles, cans, eggs, and garbage at opposing players, or even surrounding the opposing team's bus in a mob, was not uncommon in the league's early years.

Another important element of the CPBL was the presence of foreign players (usually called *yangjiang*, or "foreign talents") culled from the rosters of American AA minor league teams. Sixteen American and Latin American players were selected to join the CPBL (with a league limit of four *yangjiang* per team).[8] The presence of these players was meant to add an international flavor to the league and to provide an external stimulus for the improvement of the quality of CPBL play. In a 1993 conversation Jungo Bears pitcher Tony Metoyer described to me how the foreign players also served as "silent coaches" who could share their knowledge of American strategies and training methods with the Taiwanese players. Their many contributions allowed the Taiwanese game to become similar in strategy to the more open or risky style of baseball played in the Americas, and less like the conservative game that suited Taiwan so well in its years of Little League dominance.

Steps were also taken to Sinicize the identities of the foreign players. Each player was given a "Chinese name," which usually sounded something (if only vaguely) like the player's original name and usually bestowed fine and admirable qualities on the foreigner. Freddy Tiburcio, the Elephants' star Dominican outfielder, was called Dibo, or "imperial waves and billows." Luis Iglesias, the Tigers' home run champion from Panama, was called Yingxia, or "chivalrous eagle." These players were photographed for magazine covers dressed in "traditional" Chinese scholars' caps and robes, as Taiwan's baseball public was taught that even in the realm of baseball the Chinese ability to assimilate outsiders was as powerful as ever.

Yet this "assimilation" could occur on the very crassest of terms, as many of the foreign players' "Chinese" names were merely advertisements for products sold by their team's parent corporation. The Mercuries Tigers inflicted names of noodle dishes from their chain restaurants onto pitchers Cesar Mejia and Rafael Valdez. The President Lions, whose parent company specialized in convenience stores and prepackaged foods, did the same with the names A–Q (instant noodles) and Baiwei (Budweiser) for pitchers Jose Cano and Ravelo Manzanillo. Later, the China Times Eagles resourcefully used names from their minor corporate sponsors, dubbing pitcher Steve Stoole "Meile" (Miller Beer), and calling the African Dominican outfielder Jose Gonzalez "Meilehei" (Miller Dark).[9]

The CPBL won several valuable publicity coups in its early years. In 1993 the Los Angeles Dodgers Major League squad visited, only to be beaten in two of three games by Taiwan's CPBL teams. The presence in Taiwan's ballparks of these representatives of the great American baseball traditions only boosted the status of the CPBL in the eyes of Taiwanese and foreign baseball communities.

Besides this conscious effort to connect Taiwanese baseball and culture to international baseball and culture, the CPBL's local composition was also emphasized in marketing the league. The most direct connection was the presence of former Little League heroes who had won such great honors for Taiwan in the 1970s. During their prime years in the 1980s, before the CPBL was founded, these heroes could only play in Japanese or Taiwanese semipro leagues. The CPBL was extremely fortunate to have begun play while this celebrated group could still play well; after a few years it was obvious that the careers of some of these ex–child stars were heading south. But their presence in the CPBL's first years was crucial in making the league a viable enterprise.

Other accoutrements of "traditional Chinese culture" helped cement the league's special Chinese characteristics as well. Fan favorites like Dragons pitcher Huang Pingyang and Lions captain Zeng Zhizhen (known as "The Ninja Catcher") were often featured in magazines that recounted their pursuits of self-consciously Chinese or Taiwanese customs such as drinking fine tea, taking in traditional Taiwanese puppet theater, or collecting teapots or Buddhist paintings. Popular television variety shows even featured noted numerologists and geomancers using these "traditional" Chinese sciences to predict the results of upcoming baseball seasons. Thus, the roots of the CPBL's early success lay in this important effort to combine the local and the global.

Minor League Foreigners and Tensions in "Chinese" Baseball

The CPBL reached its peak popularity, measured by crowd attendance, in its third through fifth seasons (1992–94). In 1993 two new teams joined the league—the Jungo Bears and the China Times Eagles—each loaded with seven young, popular members of Taiwan's 1992 silver medal Olympic baseball team. That same season, the all-sports station TVIS paid NT$90 million (US$3.6 million) to broadcast CPBL games over the next three seasons—hardly American network money but a great improvement over the NT$3,000 (US$120) per-game fee paid previously by Taiwan's major broadcast stations.

But somehow, despite all these signs of vigorous growth, the league's popularity began to wane seriously by 1995, as the game began to lose the local Taiwan flavor it had worked so hard to cultivate. The CPBL mishandled the important balance between the local and the international that was so crucial to sustaining public interest in the league; owners developed a dependence on international networks that made the league simply less appealing.

Perhaps the most visible form of this dependence was the CPBL's reliance on the foreign ballplayers invited to Taiwan to supplement the native rosters. Although most of these foreign players were AA-level minor leaguers who would never reach the American Major Leagues, several of them were able to excel in Taiwan. It became apparent in the league's first year that a team's success could depend heavily on the performance of its foreign "supplements." Teams began putting more emphasis on the foreign element of their rosters, seeing it as the quickest path to improvement—it was certainly easier to wave money at a foreigner with proven skills than to dedicate several years to developing a Taiwanese player from scratch. The situation worsened in 1994 when the board of CPBL owners raised the foreign player maximum to seven per team. In 1995 this ceiling was again raised to ten foreigners per team, and in March 1997 the league owners voted to eliminate all limits whatsoever on roster composition.

Public interest in the league fell consistently as the CPBL became less and less "Chinese" or Taiwanese, and more and more reliant on American and Dominican players. By 1995, 44 percent of the players on CPBL rosters came from outside Taiwan. Many of these *yangjiang* made the situation even worse. Some admitted far too candidly to being baseball mercenaries in Taiwan solely for the relatively high salaries they could demand there. Others alienated local society with their promiscuous and even sometimes brutish behavior; in 1997 *Foreign Pro Baseball Players' Sex Scandals* was published on the topic.

In 1998, commenting on the dominance of foreign pitchers in the CPBL, a *Liberty Times* (Taibei) columnist summoned up ugly images from modern Chinese history in calling the league's pitching mound a "foreign concession" (*waiguo zujie*). Indeed, the predominance of foreign pitchers that season reached ridiculous heights. Of the one hundred CPBL pitchers who took the mound that year, only twenty-two were Taiwanese. The 1998 CPBL champion Weichuan Dragons carried twelve foreign pitchers on its roster (combined record 56 wins, 48 losses, and 1 tie), but only two Taiwanese pitchers (combined record 0-0-0).

In an editorial written in March 1997, a Taiwan sportswriter addressed the problem of the dominance of foreign players in Taiwan baseball differently. He credited the *yangjiang* with aiding the development of pro baseball in Taiwan. However, he reminded fans that the use of these foreigners truly came down to one question: Would these "AAA-level [minor league] foreigners" ever be able to help Taiwan win an Olympic medal in baseball? In terms of national loyalty or the crucial international baseball stage, these foreign players could never truly contribute anything to Taiwan's future.

Fans' own wishes for a more Taiwan-centric CPBL were seen in the votes cast for the annual All-Star Game. In 1997, a season marked by foreign dominance more than any other, fans did not select a single foreigner to the All-Star teams.[10] They preferred marginal (at best) players like Whales outfielder He Xianfan (batting average .218) and pitcher Huang Qingjing (1 win and 9 losses, 5.65 ERA) over the dozens of foreign players who were more deserving by any statistical standard. The presence of the foreign players and managers achieved one of the original goals of the *yangjiang* strategy: the quality of CPBL play improved greatly over the league's first few years. However, it is telling that as the CPBL improved in technical terms, it simultaneously became a subject of such little interest to Taiwanese baseball fans.

The Taiwan Major League

In December 1995 a new chapter in the story of Taiwan baseball began. A group of investors, led by Qiu Fusheng and Chen Shengtian of the Era Communications and Sampo Electronics dynasties, respectively, announced the formation of the Taiwan Major League (TML), which would begin play in 1997. The TML was designed to trump the CPBL, not with better quality baseball but with a media-savvy and authentically "Taiwanese" approach that made the old league's "Chinese" identity look like cheap, outdated gimmicks. This explicitly politicized strategy fit perfectly within the crucial dialectic between globalization and local Taiwanese identity: Pride in Taiwan's unique culture and in the contributions Taiwan can make justifies a place for Taiwan in the international community. Likewise, the pursuit of international (often specifically American or Japanese) trends and symbols can also be understood as solidifying a status for a Taiwan independent of the PRC and its threats of reunification. Mastering this dialectic between the uniquely Taiwanese and the international or universal is necessary for the success of any cultural, social, commercial, or political enterprise in contemporary Taiwan. The TML met these requirements.

Unlike the CPBL, the TML did not allow its productive connections with Japanese and American baseball to overshadow the league's explicitly "Taiwanese" character. Where the CPBL clung to dry stereotypes of "traditional China," the TML's identity was squarely based in Taiwan's unique culture and history. The name of the Naluwan Corporation, which ran the TML, and the names of the four teams—Agan (robots), Fala (thunder gods), Gida (suns), and Luka (braves)—were taken from languages of Taiwan's several aborigine tribes. Team uniforms were designed to reflect "the special characteristics of the aborigine peoples," but also only after "consideration of the colors and design of professional baseball uniforms of other nations."[11]

Another important choice made by the TML was to follow what it called a "territorial philosophy," where each team has a home city or region and its own home field, unlike the CPBL, whose teams never enjoyed a true home team advantage. This "territorial" doctrine dictated that teams take these "home" connections seriously. Before the 1997 season, teams took part in New Year's ceremonies in their home cities and took oaths before city officials to serve as loyal and morally upright representatives of these cities. These hometown loyalties took on more significance with the tragic earthquake that struck central Taiwan in September 1999. The Robots quickly dubbed themselves "the Disaster Area Team" and set up their own Robots van that delivered disinfectants, vitamins, and medicines to the residents of the quake's epicenter.

Participation in the international sport of baseball, as well as impressive connections to powerful baseball networks all over the world, created a cosmopolitan image for the TML. Yet the early success of the TML came from this bold celebration of the local, the authentic, the Taiwanese. Even though the new league offered an inferior quality of baseball than the old CPBL, the TML consistently outdrew its rival at the gates. One random but telling example was a night in September 1998 when 14,385 Jiayi fans attended a TML Braves–Robots game, compared to crowds of 629 and 1,113 that showed up for CPBL games in Taibei and Gaoxiong, respectively.

The TML's official theme song, "Naluwan—Chéng-keng ě Eng-hiǒng"

(Naluwan—True Heroes), was perhaps the finest example of the fascinating mixture of historical and cultural legacies that makes Taiwan society unique and dynamic, and so difficult to fit within most standard models of historical, economic, cultural, social, or political development. The TML anthem, supposedly based on rhythms and patterns of several types of Aboriginal tribal songs, consists of lyrics in Mandarin, Taiwanese, English, Japanese, and Aboriginal languages:

> *Naluwan—True Heroes*
> Take charge—the fervent spirit of the rainbow,
> Our hearts are filled—with great fire shining bright,
> Struggle on—with hopes that never die,
> Start anew—a space for us alone.
> Fight! Fight! Fight, fight! Speed just like the wind,
> K! K! K! Power stronger than all,
> *Homu-ran batta*—truly strong and brave,
> Aaa . . . Naluwan, the true heroes!

Each singing, each playing of this league anthem became a neat and tidy re-creation of the last several centuries of Taiwan history and culture. To be sure, little room for critical analysis of, or retrospection on, this history was allowed in this rousing, commercialized theme song. But the tune was one more way in which the TML sought to portray itself as the true heirs, and "the true heroes," of the proud, complicated history of Taiwan.

"You've Got the F——ing Trouble": The Fall of Taiwanese Pro Baseball, 1997–2001

In the winter of 1997 the future of Taiwan's pro baseball enterprise looked bright. The CPBL was beginning the first year of a rich new television contract with the China Trust conglomerate worth NT$1.5 billion (US$60 million) over three years. The TML stirred up controversy by stealing some of the CPBL's best players and promised to provide healthy competition for the old league.

Unfortunately, 1997 would bring only disgrace, both domestic and international, to the CPBL. In late January 1997, law enforcement uncovered a gambling scandal that revolved around the fixing of CPBL games by ballplayers in return for huge payoffs—often double a player's monthly salary. The nation was shocked by the front-page news that some of the game's greatest and most popular stars had accepted payoffs of NT$300,000 to $500,000 (US$11,000–$18,000) per game that they threw for the local gangs handling the "gambling" on each team. The China Times Eagles threw games most spectacularly; it was revealed that the entire team was bought off regularly for a single team fee of NT$7.5 million (US$270,000) per game.[12]

This scandal, which was later found to be linked to gambling interests in Hong Kong and Macao as well as southern Taiwan, led to the near unraveling of the league as the public learned the sordid details of this enterprise. This was a tricky business; Lions stars Jiang Taiquan and Guo Jinxing lost some NT$200 million (US$7.3 million) of one gambling outfit's money in a 1996 game by accidentally winning after assuring gamblers that the Lions would lose.[13]

No team or player was safe from these gangs and their members' frustrations when their favorite teams won. Loyal Elephants gamblers furious at their team's winning ways kidnapped five Elephant players, pistol-whipping one and shoving a gun down the throat of another. Seven Tigers players (including two Americans and two Puerto Ricans) were abducted at the Gaoxiong Stardust Hotel by gun-packing thugs who used similarly violent ways of "encouraging" the players to throw games. And one day, while picking up his daughter at school, Dragons manager Xu Shengming was stabbed in the lower back by a representative of yet another gambling outfit.

Fewer and fewer fans decided to pay much attention to a league whose games they feared were still being decided by sleazy mob kings. Attendance fell by 55 percent in 1997, a change also due to the easier availability of American and Japanese baseball games via Taiwan's bounding cable TV market. By the 1999 season, fan attendance at most games was below 1,000. One day in October 1999, the two scheduled CPBL games, both crucial to the late-season pennant race, drew just 176 and 116 fans, respectively. During the winter after the 1999 season, the league lost two more teams, as the Mercuries Tigers and three-time defending champion Weichuan Dragons both cited financial pressures in folding their baseball operations.

The fall of the CPBL came at the exact moment when American and Japanese Major League teams were beginning to aggressively scout young Taiwanese baseball talent. In 1999-2000 seven young players who would have starred in Taiwan signed lucrative contracts with American and Japanese teams. The Los Angeles Dodgers, well connected in Taiwan, struck first by signing young outfielder Chen Chin-Feng. Chen was named league MVP in his first U.S. minor league season (California League, Class A) in 1999, and made his Major League debut in September 2002. The Colorado Rockies were next, bagging eighteen-year-old Tsao Chin-hui, toast of the 1999 World Junior Championships, with a $2.2 million contract in 2000. Tsao, who had been scouted by Major League teams since junior high school, was called the "the Hope Diamond of the Rockies' minor league system" and started eight games for the big league club in 2003. The New York Yankees, Seattle Mariners, Seibu Lions, and Chunichi Dragons also invested heavily in young Taiwanese players whose talent the Taiwanese professional game now must live without.

A final humiliation came in March 2001, on the opening night of the TML's fifth season of play. The TML, although not tainted directly by the CPBL's gambling problems, had also seen the popularity of its inferior quality of baseball wane since 1997. By 2001 the two rival leagues, both plagued by several consecutive money-losing seasons, were seriously considering a merger and a further downsizing of the baseball enterprise. The TML shortened the team schedules to just 60 games each (from 84) in 2001 and desperately tried to attract fans with a new marketing gimmick, naming four pop stars as official "spokespeople" for each of the league's teams. Rapper Zhang Zhenyu, spokesman of the Gaoxiong Thunder Gods, was scheduled to kick off the festivities at Chengqing Lake Stadium, along with ROC legislative Yuan speaker Wang Jinping (also TML chairman) and Ronald McDonald. The game itself was to be a milestone in TML history, marking the debut of Taibei Suns manager Li Juming, the former Little League star idolized as Taiwan's "Mr. Baseball." The season got off to an unbecoming start, however, when Zhang enthusiastically performed his song "Trouble," repeatedly screaming in English before the sellout crowd and a national TV audience, "You've got the f——ing trouble! You've got the f——ing trouble!" Zhang's league handlers, not to mention Ronald McDonald, were surely humiliated by this display of bad judgment, but his words were also a very accurate diagnosis of the state of Taiwanese pro baseball at the beginning of the twenty-first century.

Conclusion

On December 31, 2000, Taiwan president Chen Shui-bian made his first New Year's address to the nation, remarks meant to sum up his first seven months in office and to "bridge the new century." Chen had much to discuss, from the political revolution completed by his own victory and his once-illegal party's climb to power, to entry into the World Trade Organization and Taiwan's increasingly tense relations with China. The president summed up his remarks with comments on the unique "Taiwan spirit" forged during the twentieth century, and closed his address with an interesting symbol of the Taiwan experience:

I recently had the opportunity to read some of Taiwan's historical records and was deeply inspired by one picture in particular: a portrait of the Maple Leaf Little League baseball team. In this black-and-white photograph, there was a barefoot aboriginal boy at bat. His face showed full concentration, as he focused all of his energy on his responsibility. Meanwhile, his teammates stood by on the sidelines anxiously watching and giving encouragement. Such a beautiful moment perfectly captures 20th century Taiwan and is a memory that I will never forget.

My dear fellow countrymen, history has passed the bat to us, and it is now our turn to stand at the plate. The 21st century will undoubtedly throw us several good pitches, as well as one or two dusters (*huaiqiu*). Regardless of what is thrown to us, however, we must stand firm and concentrate all of our strength and willpower for our best swing.[14]

It is no accident that Chen chose this image to encapsulate Taiwan's history and identity. (Although he may have understated the case by calling a possible Chinese invasion of Taiwan a mere "duster.")

The history of Taiwanese baseball is an appropriate and crucial window for understanding the complicated histories and cultures of modern Taiwan. Starting with the game's Japanese origins, and then the

5. *China Trust Whales manager Xu Shengming, featured in bookstore advertisement for the official Chinese Professional Baseball League 2004 video game.* (Photo courtesy of Andrew Morris.)

high-profile successes of Taiwanese Little League baseball from the 1960s to the 1980s, baseball was an important avenue by which Taiwanese people navigated the historical relationships with the Japanese, the Chinese Nationalists, and their American allies. Now, in the twenty-first century, as the search for a uniquely Taiwanese identity is given official sanction, baseball is a crucial element of this identity.

Despite the depths to which the professional game's popularity has sunk, recent events still demonstrate the centrality of baseball in Taiwan. Taiwan successfully hosted the 2001 International Baseball Federation amateur championships, a development that speaks to the weight that Taiwan carries in the world baseball community despite efforts by the PRC to shut down this type of international Taiwan presence.

More than a century ago Mark Twain wrote that baseball was the perfect expression of American society, declaring that the game had become "the outward and visible expression of the drive and push and rush and struggle of the raging, tearing, booming nineteenth century!"[15] The same can be said for Taiwan. Baseball has been repositioned at the center of a new Taiwanese nationalism and project of self-definition. In early 2003 President Chen won great face when he was able to achieve a long-awaited merger between Taiwan's two pro leagues, ending the bickering that had robbed baseball of its national unifying power.

The renewed national attachment to baseball is illustrated perfectly by the NT$500 bill issued in December 2000. As the sagely visage of the iron-fisted Generalissimo Chiang Kai-shek is removed from Taiwan's currency for the new millennium, what better indigenous symbol to replace him than an image of the young Little Leaguers who won his regime so much fame in the 1970s? Now, instead of facing the gaze of the Chinese military leader forced on Taiwanese youth for four decades as "Savior of the People," Taiwan consumers handing over NT$500 are inspired by the smiles on the faces of the Puyuma aborigine boys from Taidong County whose victory celebration is portrayed on the bill. These are the healthy and "authentic" faces that Taiwanese people to-day want as representatives of their island nation—and as they have represented for nearly a century, through their national sport of baseball.

Notes

This article has been adapted from an earlier piece, "Baseball, History, the Local and the Global in Taiwan."

1. The Kōshien tournament, founded in 1915, began inviting Taiwan representatives in 1923. From 1923 to 1930 all the Taiwan teams that qualified for Kōshien were Japanese teams.
2. Peng Ming-min, *A Taste of Freedom* (New York: Holt, Rinehart and Winston, 1972), 16–17.
3. Unfortunately, the jubilation over these victories was soon dampened by an unfortunate revelation. The Maple Leaf roster of eleven players included nine ineligible boys who were playing under false names. Months after these victories, the Maple Leaf Elementary School principal, coach, and head administrator were all sentenced to a year's imprisonment by the Taidong County Local Court for these gross violations.

4. Ray Keyes, "Taiwan Team Sprints Upset . . . Tops Santa Clara in L.L. Final," *Sporting News*, September 6, 1969.

5. Laura Li, "Empowering the People: 50 Years of Struggle," trans. Brent Heinrich, *Sinorama* 24, no. 10 (1999): 100–107 (quotation on p. 101).

6. Star Yu Hongkai, from Taidong, had played illegally as a ringer for the 1968 Maple Leaf team and was recruited from across the island for the 1969 Golden Dragons. Guo Yuanzhi, who would go on to star for the Chunichi Dragons in Japan, was also recruited from Taidong.

7. Paul Li, "Baseball Tries to Make a Comeback," *Taipei Journal* 17, no. 45 (2000): 8.

8. Of the nineteen foreigners who played during the CPBL's first season, only two had Major League experience: Tigers infielder Jose Moreno (1980 New York Mets, 1981 San Diego Padres, 1982 California Angels) and Elephants pitcher Jose Roman (1984–86 Cleveland Indians).

9. In 1997 the Sinon Bulls, owned by the huge Sinon Agrochemical Corporation, cleverly named several of its foreign players after the conglomerate's best-selling pesticides.

10. In the CPBL's major statistical categories for 1997, there were the following numbers of foreign players in the top 10: batting average, 8; home runs, 8; runs batted in, 7; and victories, 7.

11. "Qiuyuan quan chong mote'er—zhanpao shanliang xianshen" (Ballplayers moonlighting as models—battle gear unveiled in its glory), *Naluwan zhoubao* 7 (February 1, 1997): 3.

12. Dubbed the "Black Eagles" (Heiying), the team was suspended from the league in late 1997 and formally disbanded in 1998.

13. After being banned from Taiwan professional baseball, Jiang got a second chance five years later in mainland China as coach of the Tianjin Lions of the new China Baseball League, and manager of the PRC national team. The Tianjin team, which evidently has a poor vetting process, also hired fallen Taiwan stars Guo Jiancheng and Zheng Baisheng, also banned in 1997 for throwing CPBL games, as coaches.

14. Chen Shui-bian, "Zongtong fabiao kua shiji tanhua" (The president's century-bridging address) (Taibei: Office of the President of the Republic of China, 2000), available at http://www.president.gov.tw/1_news/index.html; Chen Shui-bian, "Bridging the New Century: President Chen's New Year's Eve Address, Dec. 31, 2000," *Taipei Update* 2, no. 2 (2001): 1–3 (quotation on p. 3).

15. Alan Guttmann, *Games and Empires: Modern Sports an Cultural Imperialism* (New York: Columbia University Press, 1994), 79.

Bibliography

"2005 Far East Heroes." Available at http://www.franksfieldofdreams.com/ 2005feh.htm.

Ching, Leo. "Globalizing the Regional, Regionalizing the Global: Mass Culture and Asianism in the Age of Late Capital." *Public Culture* 12, no. 1 (2000): 233–57.

Connor, Joe. "Teams Investing in Taiwan," June 23, 2004. Available at http:// MLB.com.

Hsiau, A-chin. *Contemporary Taiwanese Cultural Nationalism.* New York: Routledge, 2000.

Morris, Andrew D. "Baseball, History, the Local and the Global in Taiwan." In *The Minor Arts of Daily Life: Popular Culture in Taiwan,* ed. David K. Jordan, Andrew D. Morris, and Marc L. Moskowitz, pp. 175–203. Honolulu: University of Hawai'i Press, 2004.

Roden, Donald. "Baseball and the Quest for National Dignity in Meiji Japan." *American Historical Review* 85, no. 3 (June 1980): 511–34.

Sundeen, Joseph Timothy. "A 'Kid's Game'? Little League Baseball and National Identity in Taiwan." *Journal of Sport & Social Issues* 25, no. 3 (August 2001): 251–65.

Van Auken, Lance, and Robin Van Auken. *Play Ball! The Story of Little League Baseball.* University Park: Pennsylvania State University Press, 2001.

5 | Korea

Straw Sandals and Strong Arms

Hee Seop Choi was on his way to the U.S. Major Leagues and knew he had to work on a few things: hitting a curve ball, making the 3-6-3 double play, and learning a new language. So he started practicing his Spanish. Choi realized if he was going to play for the Chicago Cubs, he had to learn English. But as many as half his teammates would be native Spanish speakers. He had better learn Spanish, too.

By the time Choi became the first Korean to emerge as an everyday player with the Cubs during the 2003 season, he had long rid himself of the translator the team had hired for him. He was speaking enough halting English and fractured Spanish to endear himself to his teammates and make life in a strange land a lot more comfortable. By the time he hit his first home run with the Los Angeles Dodgers, his third big league team, in the spring of 2005, his English was better than that of some Major League announcers.

Playing in the Major Leagues long ago morphed from the exclusive dream of young men and boys across the United States into a burning ambition for ballplayers across the globe. In the morphing, of course, rosters changed. But so did the way players get on the roster. The great baseball writer Ring Lardner once telescoped into a single quote the staggering maw between wanting to be a Major League player and actually becoming one. "Be home real soon, Mom, they're beginning to throw the curve," he wrote in the book-turned-movie *Alibi Ike.*

Killer curve balls still separate the men from the boys a century after Lardner was reaching his prime. But as baseball becomes an increasingly global game in a new millennium, cultural complexities and sensitivities can be as difficult to deal with as anything that happens between the lines.

For decades scores of U.S. Major Leaguers struggled—and all too often failed—to adjust to life in Tokyo, Hiroshima, Osaka, Kobe, and other exotic climes when they were offered lucrative salaries to play in Japan's professional leagues. Probably the most embarrassing cultural bust was former New York Yankees first baseman Joe Pepitone, whose bodacious, self-indulgent ways on and off the field were repugnant to Japanese moral codes. Pepitone lasted just 14 games, batting a miserable .163 with the Yakult Atoms in 1973. He complained that no one spoke English, that McDonald's hamburgers were too expensive, that his long-distance phone bill was too high, that he had to carry his own equipment bags, and that his manager asked him to play when he was hurt. Twice, team management gave Pepitone permission to fly back to the United States during the season, once to finalize a divorce and once to consult his personal physician about an injury. Both times he was supposed to be gone one week. Both times he stayed more than a month. Don Blassingame, a former Major Leaguer who was coaching in Japan at the time, said Pepitone came to him one night and said he was trying to decide what medical condition he could complain about the next day to keep himself out of the lineup.

And there were other Pepitones. One of the most notable was slugger Frank Howard, who twice led the American League in home runs. Howard was thirty-seven and out of shape when he joined the Fukuoka Lions in 1974. He went hitless in his two at bats on opening day, said he was hurt, flew home to the United States for surgery, and never played again. Howard walked away with $80,000 for his two trips to the plate in Japan. But for every Pepitone and every Howard there were others from the United States who worked mightily to fit into an alien culture. Clete Boyer, Wes Parker, Don Buford, Leron Lee, Randy Bass, and scores more excelled in Japan and were embraced by Japanese fans.

Professional baseball was just beginning to become global when U.S. players first started going to Japan in significant numbers in the 1960s, and clearly still was a long way shy of being a truly international game in the 1970s when Pepitone and Howard were playing prima donna in the Orient. But decades later, with the globalization of the game a reality, players on all sides of the Pacific—and the Atlantic, Caribbean, and Mediterranean as well—had learned to accept the need to adjust to strange cultures as readily as wicked curve balls.

Hee Seop Choi wasn't particularly exceptional; that is the point. His struggles to learn English and Spanish, to figure out how to order off a menu written in characters he couldn't understand, and so forth, were typical. The game had changed and so had the ways to get into the game.

Choi comes from a society, which, like many Latin cultures, treasures personal relationships. In Korean culture, people you haven't met simply don't exist. Friends are not easily made, but once made they are never neglected. And colleagues regularly meet outside the workplace to ensure relationships on the job remain smooth. Choi's efforts to learn both English and Spanish were a tribute to his respect for his teammates as much as a practical necessity. And those efforts served him well as he made his way from Korea University in Seoul to Wrigley Field in Chicago.

Missionaries, Military, and Mayhem

Culture is always complex and cultural understanding cuts both ways. While Choi and other Koreans who made it to the Major Leagues embraced U.S. culture, few of their teammates knew much about Korea, or Korean baseball, which has a long, rich history.

The games people play, or don't play, typically mirror their national priorities and customs. Korea is no exception. Baseball became popular in Korea not so much for the game itself but for what the game offered the Korean people. At times it offered a peaceful way to challenge oppressive rulers. Other times it was a convenient tool for politicians to use to sway public opinion. Eventually it became an important part of the nation's economic growth. And, always, it offered an acceptable outlet for the barely bridled emotions of the Korean people.

Korean culture is rooted in Confucianism. Traditionally, within the Confucian framework, emotions are discreetly controlled. Koreans strive to be stoic, but often fail; passionate outbursts are common in the streets of Seoul, on the floor of Parliament, and in the stands at baseball stadiums. Violence is an integral part of Korean society. So, too, is politics. And the two are entwined in the history of Korean baseball.

Missionaries and military personnel from the United States brought baseball to Asia during the late nineteenth and early twentieth centuries. The first games in China, Japan, and the Philippines were played by U.S. sailors and soldiers. In Korea, a missionary named Philip Loring Gillett introduced the game.

Gillett was the son of a prominent surgeon from La Salle, Illinois. Shortly after he was born in 1872, the family moved to Iowa City, where Gillett's father had accepted a position on the faculty at the University of Iowa Medical School. They stayed there until 1885, when the family moved to Colorado Springs just before Gillett's father died.

During his teens and early twenties, Gillett worked as a janitor to put himself through Colorado College, where he played football and baseball and served as chairman of the school's missionary committee. He graduated in 1897, moved back East, and attended Yale Divinity School for a year and a half before enrolling in the International Young Men's Christian Association (YMCA) Training School at Springfield, Massachusetts. Gillett graduated from the training school in 1901 and accepted an appointment as general secretary of the YMCA's International Committee for Korea.

In April 1901, more than two months before graduation, Gillett's superiors already were actively promoting him for the Korean position. A letter in the YMCA archives shows that one of Gillett's supervisors praised him for being "a strong, sturdy Christian man" with a penchant for "winning men to Christ." The letter also singled out Gillett as "a great organizer" who was "exceedingly active in athletic work."

Gillett's passion and penchant for sports figured prominently throughout his missionary career, but it was particularly evident during his first international assignment to Korea, where he introduced baseball and basketball to a culture that, like others in Asia, once considered physical exercise undignified.

Several historical accounts, both in English and Korean, credit Gillett with bringing basketball to Korea in 1903 or 1904—the dates are often contradictory—and organizing the first baseball team at the Hansong

YMCA in Seoul in 1905. The Hansong team was the subject of a 2002 Korean movie, with English subtitles, which fictionalized some aspects of baseball's origins in Korea but paid homage to the game. Titled simply YMCA *Baseball Team*, the movie does an impressive job explaining the complex, important role baseball played in helping foster self-esteem and national pride among Koreans at a time when the country was increasingly under the domination of Japanese occupiers.

The YMCA team held several scrimmages and played informal games in 1905. However, historians widely consider the first formal organized baseball game in Korea to have taken place on February 11, 1906, between the YMCA team and a squad from the German Language Institute of Seoul. By all accounts the game was a colorful affair, though the final score seems to have been lost or forgotten. The game was played in an area known as Hullyonwon, then a training ground for military recruits near the current site of Seoul Stadium. Some of the players wore high leather boots and pristine white uniforms. Others took the field wearing straw sandals and traditional Korean clothing.

At the time of the first game, the YMCA already was famous for being "the center of the [Korean] basketball world" and for hosting "football afternoons," which brought young players together for feisty soccer matches.[1] Basketball and soccer caught the fancy of Koreans quicker than baseball did. But a series of compelling factors—social, political, cultural, and martial—affected baseball's acceptance and development in Korea.

Most significant among these was the presence of baseball-loving Japanese soldiers and administrators as an army of occupation in the Korean Peninsula from 1905 to 1945. Baseball may have been brought to Korea by a U.S. missionary, but it would be the passions and policies of Japanese soldiers, administrators, and educators that enabled the game to survive and prosper to the point where it would become an integral ingredient of local culture.

Learning to Sweat

Japan exerted strong influence over Korea for centuries, particularly during the last two decades of the nineteenth century. That dominion was consolidated in September 1905 with the signing of the Treaty of

Portsmouth, which formally ended the Russo-Japanese War and recognized Japan's undisputed supremacy in Korea. Three months later the Korean emperor signed another treaty making Korea a Japanese protectorate.

A decade earlier, in July 1895, when Korea ostensibly was being protected by Japan during the Sino-Japanese War, a series of sweeping social and educational reforms had been announced in Korea. Among them was the introduction of a new approach to physical exercise—similar to the cultural reforms that took root in Japan during the Meiji Restoration and in China during the "self-strengthening movement," both of which opened doors for Western ideas and indirectly led to the introduction of baseball in those countries. The underpinnings for reform in Korea were straightforward and merely repetitions of the rationale used to promote similar attitudinal adjustments in Japan and China.

By late 1905, when Gillett introduced baseball to Korea, the new attitudes about physical education had begun to take hold, especially under the influence of Christian missionaries and Japan's military occupation forces. Colonial authorities used the school system and athletics to indoctrinate Korean youth with Japanese ways and at the same time undermine traditional Korean values. They eliminated such things as the study of Korean history and Korean language and actively promoted baseball. A Korean journalist summed up the Japanese influence neatly. Baseball, he wrote, started to be "deeply rooted" in Korea the moment the Japanese took control.[2]

It is not surprising, then, that it was a group of Korean students home on holiday from Tokyo in the summer of 1909 who provided what the Korean Baseball Organization later called "the turning point for Korean baseball." A newspaper article decades later recalled the moment:

On July 21, 1909, twenty-five Korean students studying in Tokyo, led by Yun Ik-hyon, formed a baseball club and scored a large-margin victory over a selection of foreign missionaries in Korea. . . . The Korean students were excited over the victory and had a series of baseball matches while touring provincial areas. As a result, the students played a great role in the popularization of baseball across the nation.[3]

While baseball clearly was beginning to enjoy a strong measure of popularity by 1909, most accounts agree the game came into its own in 1910—the year Japan formally annexed Korea. In February that year, Hansong High School and Hwangsong Christian School played a game Korean historians still refer to as "the foundation of Korean baseball." The game was played in the dead of a typically bitter Korean winter with two umpires—one from the United States and one from Japan. A crowd of some two hundred fans watched, officially signaling baseball's transformation from a fringe pastime to a mainstream sport. "That baseball game is now regarded as important in the history of Korean baseball," a Korean reporter wrote. "Korean baseball was consolidated with increasing attention from the people in Korea."[4]

In his annual report for 1909–10, Gillett listed what he called "facts of encouragement" about the past year's work. He wrote briefly about the improved physical facilities of the Seoul YMCA, then launched into a glowing account of the association's athletic involvement. "The base ball team, pioneer team for Korea, reached its top notch of enthusiasm when they succeeded in both tying and defeating teams composed of Americans picked from among the missionaries and resident business men. The scores were 20–20 and 10–8. The significant thing about these athletics features is that the young men of the country are thereby being led to adopt a new ideal of energetic manhood."[5]

By 1912 teams from the Seoul YMCA were playing more than 60 games a year and the association's top squad rarely lost. The popularity of the game, and athletics in general, was mind-boggling even to the missionaries who started it all. "It seems almost incredible to those of us who have seen the Korean young men five or more years ago trying to play ball or enter into athletics," wrote one of Gillett's colleagues. "The remark of a Korean gentleman seeing a foreigner covered with perspiration from a game of tennis, 'Why don't you have your coolie do that work' will not be heard from this generation. Like the Korean top-knot and American horse car it is a thing of the past."[6]

A Japanese Game

Missionaries tended, reasonably enough, to see the popularity of sports as a validation of their efforts. As one official of the Seoul YMCA wrote, "The enthusiasm and zeal to learn more about Western customs is seen on the base-ball diamond, in basket ball, in football."[7] But Korean attitudes about baseball seem to have been shaped by forces closer to home—culturally and geographically. Even as early as 1910, many Koreans perceived baseball to be a Japanese game or, if not strictly a Japanese game, then certainly a game the Japanese had embraced and mastered to a degree worth emulating.

As such, baseball offered an intriguing outlet for young Koreans opposed to Japanese military rule. The sport became a way for them to both appease and challenge their occupiers. Just as it did in other countries at other times, sport provided a vent for political, as well as physical, frustrations. It brought Koreans and Japanese together in "nonpolitical commonality," offering an opportunity for the downtrodden to peaceably challenge their political masters.

Korean and Japanese teams began routinely playing one another—at venues in both countries. Another group of Korean students on summer vacation from school in Tokyo defeated a Japanese squad in Korea, then returned to Japan in November 1912 to play 6 games against Waseda University, a powerhouse of collegiate baseball then and since. The *Korea Times* hailed the Waseda series as "the first time in Korean sports history that a Korean sports team had overseas matches."[8]

In his annual report of 1912–13, written in September 1913, Gillett refers to a YMCA team that traveled to Tokyo to play a series of games against Japanese university squads. "This has been a great year for athletics in the Seoul Association. Our baseball team beat every Korean team in the country and went to Tokyo to play the championship teams there. They were badly walloped by the university teams but when playing boys of their own age (middle schools) they captured one game, tied another and lost one."[9]

While the YMCA teams enjoyed great success, even winning the Seoul interscholastic championship in 1914, Japanese teams generally dominated baseball throughout Korea in the early years of the twentieth century. In 1915 a tournament held on the grounds of Yongsan Station featured seven teams—six Japanese and one Korean. The Korean team, Osong, advanced to the finals only to be beaten. But the Korean crowds appreciated the efforts and, in the words of one observer, were "only briefly deflated."

Missionaries, especially those involved with the YMCA, remained active in promoting baseball. In 1917 the sports club of the Chongno Central YMCA sponsored what proved to be a memorable baseball tournament featuring six high school teams. Competition was especially keen and tempers rose steadily until the final day of the Yonghap Baseball Tournament, when police had to be called to break up a riot that broke out over a dispute about the batting order. The *Korea Times* called it "the first violent game in Korean baseball," but it hardly was the last. In sports, as in politics and almost every other endeavor, the Korean penchant for resorting to fists over words is legendary. The phrase "fighting spirit" is invoked with monotonous regularity in Japanese baseball. In Korea the phrase has been taken literally with similar regularity since that turbulent tournament in 1917.

Violence and Change

The first decade under Japanese annexation helped foster an appreciation of athletics, especially baseball, among Koreans. But it also bred anger and discontent. By 1919 opposition to Japan's colonial rule was widespread enough to spawn a series of demonstrations for Korean national independence that began March 1 in Seoul and spread quickly throughout the country. An estimated seven thousand people were killed by Japanese police and soldiers before the uprising was suppressed nearly a year later. Sixteen thousand people were wounded, forty-six thousand were arrested, and forty-seven churches and two schools were destroyed by fire. Eventually known as the March First Movement, the yearlong uprising convinced the Japanese occupiers to modify their policies. As one scholar noted, "The March First Movement caused the Japanese government to review its colonial behavior, introduce limited reforms and pursue the so-called 'cultural' or 'conciliation' policy on the basis of 'Nisen Yuwa' (harmony of Japan and Korea)."[10]

Baseball was a convenient tool to foster cultural conciliation. One of the first social organizations established to promote greater harmony in 1920 was the Chosun Amateur Athletic Association, which declared its intent to ensure "baseball games were more actively staged." The organization pulled together ten teams—five company teams and five from middle schools—to participate in the first Chosun National Baseball Championship in 1920.

The Yanks Are Coming

Korean baseball got an important boost in 1922 when the Herb Hunter All-Americans, a team of U.S. Major Leaguers, stopped briefly in Seoul on a winter tour of Asia that included a series of games in Japan and brief exhibitions in Shanghai and Manila. In Seoul the Koreans assembled an All-Star team of their own to play the Major Leaguers. Not surprisingly, they were overmatched, losing 21–3. But as the *Korea Times* later rationalized, "The score was not so important as learning the American players' superb baseball skills for the Korean team."[11]

Baseball was so popular by then that construction was begun on a major stadium in Seoul. The facility opened in 1925, a year before the University of Seoul was established, and regularly hosted high school and intercollegiate games. But it was three years before a Korean player had the clout to hit the first home run out of the park. The memorable moment came during a 1928 match between Yonhi (Yonsei) University and Kyongsong (Seoul National) University. The player who hit the home run was outfielder Lee Yong-min, who went on to become a national hero and was named to one of the Japanese teams that played against Babe Ruth, Lou Gehrig, and the U.S. Major League All-Stars on their historic tour of Japan in 1934—the last tour of the Orient before World War II.

Despite the new stadium and interest among high school and college players, baseball in Korea essentially faded for a decade from the mid-1930s through the mid-1940s. The outbreak of the Sino-Japanese War left little time for leisure. Some baseball still was played, of course, but the game essentially disappeared until the war ended in 1945.

Once peace came, however, the game was resurrected quickly. As the *Korea Times* reported, "With the liberation of Korea from . . . Japanese rule in 1945, baseball also awoke from its . . . hibernation to become more active than before." One of the first sports organizations founded after the war was the Taehan Baseball Association, which promised to be "vigorous in promoting baseball interest in the post-Liberation era as never before."[12]

Baseball's swift postwar resurgence was fueled by the presence of U.S. troops stationed in southern Korea. The soldiers who waged war from

1950 to 1953 were, more often than not, die-hard fans of the game, which was enjoying probably its golden era at the time. They spread the gospel of baseball so well that by 1954, a year after the fighting stopped, South Korea was accepted into the International Baseball Association.

A series of successes in international competition, beginning in the early 1960s and carrying through the 1970s, transformed baseball from a pastime into a passion in Korea. The South Koreans defeated Japan to win the fifth Asian Amateur Baseball Championship in 1963, then hosted and won the Asian tournament again in 1971 and 1975. A third-place finish at the World Baseball Championships in Italy in 1978 reinforced the growing belief that Korea had the talent to compete with anyone. But when South Korea upset Cuba and the United States to finish as co-champions with Japan at the World Baseball Championships in Tokyo in 1980, then followed that by upsetting the United States to win the gold medal at the World Youth Baseball tournament at Newark, Ohio, in 1981, the game officially became a national mania.

Political Hardball

The steady rise in baseball's popularity in the early 1980s came at a time when political and social conditions in Korea were unraveling. Anti-government riots broke out in Pusan in October 1979 and had to be suppressed by the military. A month later President Park Chung Hee, who had come to power in a 1961 coup, was assassinated. The strong military crackdown that followed led to a bloody uprising in Kwangju in May 1980 and the subsequent closure of all universities and colleges across South Korea.

In August 1980 Chun Doo Hwan was elected president and two months later a new constitution was approved, ushering in the Fifth Republic of Korea. The political situation had stabilized enough by January 1981 for martial law to be lifted, and the government actively began trying to put a kinder, gentler face on its authoritarian image. Baseball became an important part of those efforts. As it had been during the Japanese occupation, baseball became a convenient and important instrument of cultural conciliation.

From its birth in December 1981, there never was any doubt that one of the primary objectives of the Korea Baseball Organization (KBO) was to provide an outlet for restless and increasingly rebellious elements of society, particularly young males. As the authors of one study on sports and politics in Korea wrote in 1993, "the start of pro baseball in the country did much towards diverting the public's interest from politics to sports."[13]

The government's role in orchestrating that diversion and the economic significance of baseball on the national economy became obvious at the first public meeting of the league's top officials. Each of the six charter teams was owned by a major conglomerate that was closely tied to the government. The first commissioner of the KBO, elected unanimously and waiting in the wings with a prepared text when the results were announced, was Suh Jyong-chul, a former defense minister and president of the Korea Anti-Communist League. In addition to his impeccable political connections, Suh brought solid baseball credentials to the job. He learned the game in Japan as a youngster, playing first base and batting cleanup for Tachi Commercial High School in Miyazaki Ken, where he studied. Later in life, while serving as chief of staff of the Korean Army in 1961—the year of the military coup that brought Park Chung Hee to power—Suh managed the Korean Army baseball team.

At the inaugural meeting of the KBO in December 1981, Suh and representatives of the six company-owned teams laid down elaborate ground rules that ensured professional baseball would mirror the autocratic ways of doing business—and running the government—in Korea. Play would begin in March 1982 and for five years no professional team could scout another's players. The six teams would share income equally. A salary cap was in effect, players were rated and paid according to their ratings, and contract fees for managers and coaches were carefully categorized.

In the first few months of 1982, the government made clear that the introduction of professional Korean baseball was merely part of a comprehensive campaign to ease political tensions and win the hearts and minds of the younger generation. The first gesture came in January 1982, when President Chun lifted a midnight curfew that had been in effect in Seoul since 1945. Not long afterward, students in middle schools and high schools were freed unexpectedly from having to wear the uncomfortable military uniforms that had been imposed on successive generations of youngsters since the Japanese colonial era.

In March, just two weeks before the start of Korea's first professional baseball season, the government announced it was taking the "magnanimous gesture" of granting amnesty to 2,863 political prisoners. As part of the pardons, a government spokesman said the life sentence against leading dissident Kim Dae-jung would be reduced to twenty years. Kim originally had been sentenced to death for sedition after a show trial that lasted just six minutes. Eventually, even the new twenty-year prison term was eased and Kim was released from prison two days before Christmas 1982. He was flown to the United States, where he spent most of the next fifteen years in exile. Kim came to be known as "Asia's Nelson Mandela" because of the similarity of his suffering to that of South Africa's leading anti-apartheid activist. Like Mandela, Kim Dae-jung was elected president of his country after years of political persecution and went on to win the Nobel Peace Prize. Kim's election in December 1997 was the first time a Korean opposition candidate won, and he received the Nobel Peace Prize in 2000 for his work in calming one of the last danger zones of the twentieth-century cold war by promoting closer ties with Stalinist North Korea.

Support the National Economy and Train Like Spartans

The same week in March 1982 that the government announced its wholesale amnesty and the reduction of Kim Dae-jung's sentence, Korean newspapers began running a series of profiles on each of the teams in the new professional baseball league. Like a number of other articles published in the run-up to opening day (and for weeks after), the team profiles were notable mainly for the heavy-handed way in which they promoted baseball and social values, linking both with the success of the country and nation building.

"Samsung Organizes Team to Expedite National Unity," read the headline on a profile of the new Samsung Lions, who represented the east coast region of Kyongsang-pukto and featured a team made up mostly of players from that area. The headline on the article was taken directly from a quote by team president, Lee Kunhee, vice chairman of the Samsung Business Group. "[The] major objective of the Samsung Lions to participate in the professional baseball is to expedite national unity and building national strength through sports and to encourage actively the social environment," Lee said. "[The] purpose of the founding the Samsung Lions team is to support [the] national economy and its development while providing social welfare of the nation through Samsung spirit and to enhance the business development of Samsung Business Group of companies."[14]

A similar profile of the Haitai Tigers emphasized the "harsh Spartan training" the team had undergone in its first spring. "Manager Kim [Dong-yeb] set up the rules of five points that the players must adhere to in camp. They must have clean uniforms, drink no wine, avoid smoking, be thoroughly health oriented, and not play cards." Part of the manager's "Spartan" training session was a daily drill called "American knocking," in which players were forced to field a series of line drives and grounders hit from a distance of just five to ten meters.

The manager of the Sammisa Superstars also stressed personal behavior in his preseason rundown. "Always act as a good baseball player. Get dressed properly and be punctual," Park Hyon-shik told a reporter when asked what he demanded of his players. Unlike most of the other managers, Park set his sights low, saying his goal for the season was "staying out of the cellar position among the six clubs." And he was less of a disciplinarian. The Superstars were the only team that spring to tolerate even moderate drinking among its players—a somewhat surprising exception since manager Park proclaimed himself a teetotaler.

Like his counterpart on the Samsung Lions, the manager of the Lotte Giants felt compelled to emphasize the role baseball could play in promoting national unity—coupled, of course, with proper behavior. "We want to become a team loved by the fans across the country by showing high quality and fair playing," he said. On the eve of the first game Prime Minister Yoo Chang-soon reiterated the theme that had been hammered home by government ministers, baseball managers, and the media all spring when he declared that "the inauguration of professional baseball teams will create a momentum to enhance national concord and harmony."[15]

Yahoo for Yagoo

The long-awaited birth of Korean professional baseball in 1982 was everything it was meant to be. The commissioners of the only other two professional baseball leagues at the time—Bowie Kuhn of the United States and Takeso Shimoda of Japan—were in the stands. President Chun Doo Hwan, his ample belly bulging under a vest and tie, threw out the first pitch. And thirty thousand fans were jammed into bunting-draped Seoul Stadium.

Pregame ceremonies lasted for two and a half hours with hundreds of high school cheerleaders, dance troupes, and rural bands parading around before players from all six teams in the new league were called onto the field to swear an "athlete's oath" of good behavior and fair play. The game itself was broadcast live in Japan and Korea and couldn't have been scripted better. The MBC Blue Dragons, owned by a broadcasting conglomerate, came back from 5–0 down to defeat the Samsung Lions 11–7 on a grand slam home run in the bottom of the tenth inning.

After the game most newspapers and media were filled with predictable praise and euphoria about the "historic moment in Korean sports." But it was interesting to note the focus of one newspaper columnist who looked at the game from a different perspective and saw in the sport things he clearly felt were most noble in Korean society in general. "The umpires were firm and authoritative," wrote columnist Kim Young-won. "Their showy gestures added to the excitement and fun. But it was their firm attitude that pleased the fans most."[16]

As exciting as that first game had been, the attention of most baseball fans in Korea quickly shifted to their true passion—the annual high school tournament. In Korea, as in Japan, the country almost comes to a stop when the spring high school championship begins. *Time* magazine summed up the fever with one sentence in a 1982 article: "Playoffs among [Korea's] 52 high school teams are so popular that they are televised during hours of low electrical demand so that games will not cause brownouts." But *Time* saw hope for the future of professional *yagoo*—the Korean word for baseball: "Some fans are dreaming even now that in ten years South Korea will be ready to challenge the U.S. in a real *yagoo* World Series."

That never happened, of course, at least not on a professional level. The KBO has prospered, but not in proportion to the talent levels of Korean players, the best of whom often play in the Japanese professional leagues. In his superb 1977 work, *The Chrysanthemum and the Bat*, Robert Whiting writes about the roles foreign players from the United States and Korea played in Japanese baseball. "The American is not the only 'outsider' in Japanese baseball, he's just the most visible," Whiting notes. "Koreans also fall into the same category. But while the American is merely resented, the Korean is often looked down upon." Whiting claims many Koreans born and raised in Japan played baseball because the game offered a way up and through Japan's strict social hierarchy. Even so, the escape route was open only to Koreans who suppressed their heritage by assuming Japanese names and trying to pass for natives. Most did it so well that even their Japanese fans were duped. A favorite activity in Japanese ballparks to this day is "Korean spotting"—trying to figure out which players, if any, are second-generation Koreans.

Whiting quotes another knowledgeable writer who calculated that there were so many Korean players in Japan, "if you removed them all there wouldn't be any more Japanese baseball."[17] To underscore Whiting's point, few realize that Masaichi Kaneda, considered the greatest pitcher in Japanese baseball history and nicknamed the "God of Pitching," was a Japan-born Korean. Scores of other stars in Japan's two professional leagues were born in Korea and emigrated to play baseball.

Much has changed in the three decades since Whiting broke cultural and historical ground with *The Chrysanthemum and the Bat*. Korean stars now have a native outlet for their talents, which many are eager to pursue. But the level of play in Korean professional baseball is still universally regarded as inferior to that of Japan and the United States. But it is improving rapidly. By 2005 most Major League scouts considered the level of talent in Korea roughly on par with AA or AAA ball in the United States. And, increasingly, the best of the best can play with the big boys anywhere.

In 1993 all of Korea celebrated when the Los Angeles Dodgers paid $1.2 million to sign Park Chan Ho, an economics major and star pitcher at Han Yang University. Park went to the States, Westernized his name to Chan Ho Park, and radically changed his pitching motion, which for years featured an excruciatingly long pause at the top of his windup. Japanese pitchers often use the same pause and compare it to *ma*, the dramatic pauses so essential to Kabuki dialogue. In his book, *You Gotta Have Wa*, Whiting quotes a fan of the famous Japanese relief pitcher Yutaka Enatsu, who claimed to know the secret of his hero's success: "He was good because he knew how to use the *ma*. He waited for just the right moment—a lapse of concentration by the batter—to deliver the pitch."[18] But umpires and fellow professional players in the United States took one look at Park's *ma* and cried foul over something they had never seen before. Park took it all in stride, quietly altered a lifelong habit, and was a pitching star in the Major Leagues within two years.

Park, like his one-time Dodger teammate Hideo Nomo of Japan, was a national hero back home. And like Nomo, all of Park's starts in the Major Leagues were broadcast live to millions of sleep-deprived fans half a world away from where he was pitching. That is, until 1998, when Korea and the rest of Asia were hit hard by an economic downturn. "To save $3 million in foreign exchange, [Korean] viewers polled by broadcasters voted not to buy the live television rights to Los Angeles Dodgers baseball games," *Asiaweek* magazine reported before the start of the 1998 season. "By doing so, they pass up watching the wildly popular Park Chan Ho." In fact, the poll was just that. It didn't change policy. Park's appearances still were shown live in Korea when a cable channel picked up the rights for about $1 million, and the telecasts were cited by some as yet another reason for the decline in attendance at professional games.

Red Sox Instead of Straw Sandals

While Park was the first Korean in the Major Leagues, others followed. Choi was the first position player, but half a dozen Korean pitchers found spots on U.S. professional teams. In 1997 the Boston Red Sox made headlines by signing two Korean hurlers, Lee Sang-Hoon and Kim Sun-Woo, both of whom eventually made it to the majors.

Lee, who already had pitched several seasons professionally in Korea, got off to a bad start in the United States. His contract with the Red Sox was voided on a technicality and several Major League scouts rushed to

Cerritos, California, in February 1998 to watch him pitch in a workout session in hopes of signing him. Lee showed up overweight and apparently out of shape. One scout said Lee was "incapable of pitching off a mound" and complained his bosses were angry at him for wasting the expense of getting to Cerritos. Lee, for his part, claimed there had been some confusion about the session. He said he was unaware he would be asked to work out in front of the scouts. Lee pitched that season for the Chunichi Dragons in Japan and redeemed himself enough to make it to the majors with the Red Sox in 2000. He appeared in nine games, giving up four runs in 11⅔ innings, before returning to Korea where, in 2003, he signed what then was the richest contract in Korean baseball history to close games for the LG Twins.

Kim Sun-Woo had been the youngest member of Korea's 1996 Olympic team. As part of their deal, the Red Sox agreed to help Kim complete his degree requirements at Korea University and invited his college teammates to spring training at Fort Meyers, Florida, in 1998. Kim eventually made it to the majors as well, breaking in with the Red Sox in 2001 and going 3-0 for Boston in 2002 before being traded to Montreal.

The Red Sox seemed to have a penchant for Korean pitchers. Besides Lee and Kim Sun-Woo, the Sox traded for Byung-hyun Kim, who, like Chan Ho Park, became a national hero in Korea. "B.K.," as he was known by his teammates, broke into the majors with the Arizona Diamondbacks in 1999 as a twenty-year-old. He earned a save in his Major League debut against the New York Mets, then struggled with control the rest of the season, despite striking out better than one hitter per inning. Kim emerged during the 2000 season as one of the most feared relievers in the game only to earn a place in baseball lore by suffering through a nightmare World Series in 2001. In game four against the New York Yankees, Kim gave up a game-tying two-run homer to Tino Martinez with two outs in the bottom of the ninth inning, and then a game-winning home run to Derek Jeter with two outs in the bottom of the tenth inning. The next night Kim gave up a two-run game-winning home run to Scott Brosius with two outs in the bottom of the ninth inning.

As Brosius circled the bases after that third unbelievable home run, Kim dropped to his haunches on the mound and suffered a thousand deaths in front of a hundred million viewers. But he came back. A week later he was a world champion when the Diamondbacks rallied to win game 7 of the series. And just seven months later, pitching again in Yankee Stadium for the first time since his ignominy, Kim got the final six outs to preserve a 9–5 regular season interleague win against New York. With his teammates rushing to congratulate him, Kim stood on the mound and hurled the baseball he had just thrown as hard as he could into the outfield. The ball cleared the left-field wall and landed in the netting, just about the spot where Brosius hit his home run. "It was just for fun," Kim said through an interpreter. "It would have been a loss of face if it didn't get over the fence."

Imports

The globalization of Korean baseball officially became a two-way street in 1998 when the KBO reluctantly followed the lead of Japan's professional leagues and voted to allow foreign players on its rosters. That year each team was permitted to "import" two foreigners. The number later was increased to three. Many clubs, however, still limited their signings to one or two foreigners.

Asia was in the midst of a devastating economic slump in 1998 and the eight teams in the KBO signed only ten "imports" that first season. Most were from the United States and Latin America, and the clear standout was Florida native Tyrone Woods, a power-hitting first baseman who signed with the Dooson Bears. Woods was a dominant player with the Seoul club for five seasons before moving to Japan.

The move to bring in foreign players was an attempt to improve the caliber of professional baseball in Korea. But it provoked more than a little nationalistic resentment among fans and a number of players groused about lost jobs. In an effort to ease those concerns, the KBO expanded rosters to provide two more spots for Koreans. Even so, an informal poll of several players by a Korea-based journalist revealed significant objections to the inclusion of foreign players.

In 1996, two years before the league voted to allow foreign players, Thomas St. John, a Korea-based journalist, interviewed a number of KBO players and said they were "equally divided" on the idea of allowing imports. Interestingly, the split was along generational lines, with older

Korean players noting that "imports" could help improve the quality of play, while younger players complained that "imports" were taking jobs from locals. On the eve of the 1998 season, with the economy in dire straits, the generation gap had slammed shut. St. John was unable to find a single Korean player who supported the use of foreign talent. "I definitely do not want them to come," said a player who asked to be identified only by his family name, Lee. "They will be my teammates and I will treat them the same as others. [But] now is just not the right time. A foreign player's salary used to be equal to that of about three [Korean] players. Now it equals about eight."[19]

Within a couple of years the Asian economy rebounded and Korean players were drawing dramatic salary increases. Foreigners often still made considerably more money, but at the start of the 2000 season a record thirty-two Korean players were earning 100 million won or more. The 100-million mark was a psychological barrier, much like becoming a millionaire in the United States, though 100 million won was worth about us$89,000. By 2003 the 100-million-won mark was shattered six times over when closer Lee Sang-hoon, the one-time Red Sox reliever, signed the richest contract in the history of the KBO. His 600-million deal with the LG Twins was worth $500,000.

Polluting Purity Again

Just as has happened in the United States, soaring player salaries in Korea spawned some fan alienation. Korean fans, like their counterparts in Japan, have always been somewhat ambivalent about professional baseball. The baseball-loving Japanese took nearly six decades to organize the professional game—and even then they needed the emotional catalyst of a triumphant tour by U.S. Major Leaguers to make the move acceptable. Before the 1934 tour by Babe Ruth, Lou Gehrig, and their fellow All-Stars, few Japanese believed professional baseball could succeed in their country. "The sport was undeniably popular," Whiting writes, "but tradition-bound Japanese were expected to remain loyal to favorite college teams, leaving pros with no one to cheer them on. Furthermore, monetary considerations would, it was argued, so dilute the purity of the sport that right-thinking people would turn away in disgust."[20]

That same question of "purity" of sport was far less an issue in Asian cultures by the time the KBO took the field in 1982. Still, there were concerns that the advent of professionalism would diminish amateur baseball, which was beginning to bring so much international honor and prestige to Korea in the early 1980s. Mindful of these concerns, KBO organizers met with officials of the Korea Amateur Baseball Association and drew up a set of strict rules to prevent the professionals from draining the young talent that fed both the Korean national squad and various university teams. The regulations stipulated that high school or college students must graduate before turning pro. High school graduates who were playing on company teams had to spend at least three years with the team before turning pro. College graduates had to spend two years with their company teams. And members of the Korean national team had to seek permission from the commissioner of the KBO to turn pro.

In its lead editorial the day the first professional baseball game was played in Korea, the *Korea Herald* welcomed the "dawning of pro sports" but worried the new day might bring with it unwanted complications—particularly to the amateur game. "Some caution may be expressed at the outset about the possible excesses in recruiting ballplayers and holding games. Granted, a professional sport implies commercialism. However, it should adhere to a code of conduct based on integrity and dignified sportsmanship. . . . Augmenting the physical strength and prowess of the people is an important part of our nation building."[21]

A quarter century later, professional baseball is alive and well in Korea, but the amateur game still dominates. South Korea has remained a world-class power at all levels of amateur baseball. The South Koreans followed their 1981 title at the Youth Baseball Championships with another gold medal—again upsetting the United States—in 1994. They won back-to-back Little League World Series Championships in 1984–85. And the annual high school tournament continues to attract a staggering nationwide following every spring.

Korea fielded a series of highly competitive Olympic teams for years, then finally won a medal at the Sydney Games in 2000 when professionals were allowed to compete. The KBO shut down for several weeks that season so its best players could go to Australia. They came home national heroes after Korean southpaw Koo Dae-Sung outlasted Japanese ace Daisuke Matsuzaka in a magnificent pitchers' duel that enthralled an overflow crowd of more than fourteen thousand and gave Korea a bronze medal—the first Olympic medal in Korean history. After being carried off the field by his players, Korean manager Kim Euong-Yong was near tears. "The win against Japan is more meaningful than a bronze medal," he said. "Since I was young, Korean players are taught we have to always beat Japan. We got a medal and beat Japan, so I'm very glad."[22]

Quiet Riots

The Olympic victory was the most emotional in Korean baseball history until Spring 2006, when a team of KBO and major league professionals won the first 6 games of the inaugural World Baseball Classic. The tournament featured the best players from the top 16 baseball-playing nations competing for their home countries for the first time. Team Korea defeated Japan twice in the opening rounds of the tournament and came within 1 win of making the finals against Cuba at San Diego's PETCO Park. The amazing run created a frenzy among fans back home and the huge Korean community in Southern California. But Korean baseball fans hardly need rousing international performances to stir their passions. Even seemingly trivial midseason games in the KBO are emotional affairs. Just one example came during a July game in 1996 when the LG Twins were being trounced 6–0 by the lowly Ssangbangwool Raiders at Chamsil Stadium in Seoul. The Twins certainly were playing poorly enough, but the umpires weren't helping much either. Late in the game 3 Twins fans finally became so irate at one call that they started angrily shouting and demanding a meeting with the offending umpire. When a policeman stepped in to try calm matters, he was beaten. Next a door was smashed. Suddenly, more than 150 Twins fans joined in the mayhem. Ah, just another night of fun at the ole ballpark in Korea.

In truth, this particular fracas was a little unusual. Two hundred riot police had to be called in and it took them fifty minutes to restore order. But only 3 people were arrested. And hardly anyone in Korea gave the incident a second thought. Korea is one of the few places in the world where a riot can be quiet—perhaps not literally quiet—but of so little consequence that it is quickly forgotten the next day.

Violence is an integral, and accepted, part of Korean culture—not just on the baseball field but in all walks of life. A phrase heard often in Japanese baseball is "fighting spirit." The Japanese even give out a fighting spirit award during the annual Japan Series. Koreans invoke "fighting spirit" as well. But in Korea the phrase takes on a whole new meaning. In Japan the emphasis is on "spirit." A player is revered for his hustle and heart. In Korea the emphasis clearly is on "fighting."

In *The Chrysanthemum and the Bat* Whiting discusses the role of violence among the Japanese, who played such a prominent role in preserving and promoting Korean baseball. "Violence just isn't supposed to happen in Japan," Whiting writes. He points out that violence does occur in Japan—both on the playing fields and elsewhere. But he rightly notes that violence is the extraordinary exception to acceptable behavior. "When this happens," he writes, "Japanese players will lash out with an intensity seldom seen in American ballparks."[23]

Violence in Korea, on the other hand, is a socially accepted way of expressing everything from political frustration to sporting failure. Student riots and union demonstrations are regular, accepted, and often choreographed exercises. During the early 1990s, Korean students regularly doused themselves with gasoline and leapt from buildings to protest government repression. A Korean demonstrator once bit off the tip of his finger in front of a group of Western journalists and used his own blood to scribble the name of opposition leader Kim Dae-jung on a wall to vent his rage at the government.

Emotional venting—particularly violent emotional venting—is part of Korean culture. That is one reason beer sales are banned in Korean ballparks—even at games of the OB Bears, whose animal nickname is a clever allusion to the team's sponsor, the Oriental Brewery, makers of OB Beer. But the absence of alcohol does little to diminish the fervor of the fans. Riots and near riots are relatively routine. That is not to say Korean baseball is Asia's answer to ice hockey, where occasionally a game interrupts the fight. Long stretches pass during the Korean season without chaos. Still, violence—often physical violence, but at the very least violent emotion—is an accepted part of the game in Korea. It is accepted on the field and in the stands.

Baseball in Korea is the product of a pair of sometimes parallel yet distinctly different influences: U.S. missionaries and Japanese imperialists. The missionaries weren't always religious, though Philip Gillett, the "Father of Korean baseball," certainly was. A new generation of "baseball missionaries"—U.S. soldiers in Korea after World War II—rekindled the game at a time when it easily could have died. On the other hand, not every Japanese imperialist came in conquest. The owners of the Yomiuri Giants, Hanshin Tigers, and other Japanese teams that provided opportunities for Korean professional players for decades after World War II performed as important a role in the salvation and safekeeping of baseball in Korea as their colonial forefathers who decreed the game be used to indoctrinate Korean youth into Japanese ways.

No one who sets foot in a Korean ballpark can doubt the Japanese influence. A missionary from Illinois may have introduced the game to Korea, but the Japanese nurtured baseball and kept it alive for decades. Almost everything in the Korean game—strategy, scoreboards, managing styles, cheerleaders—more closely resembles baseball the way it is played in Japan than the way it is played in the United States.

What distinguishes Korean baseball, however, is not the indisputable Japanese influence on the game or its long ties to the U.S. military and U.S. missionaries. It isn't even necessarily the relative propensity for violence among fans and athletes alike. The most distinguishing element of Korean baseball is the level of political involvement.

Baseball always has had strong political ties. It has been used as a tool of diplomacy by the United States, Japan, China, and almost every country where the game has held sway. The Japanese certainly turned to baseball as an instrument of cultural conciliation during their colonial rule of Korea. And the Japanese government hardly hesitated to impose political and ideological constraints on the game in their own country during World War II.

But the unabashed way the Korean government went about establishing professional baseball in the 1980s as a diversion and channel for political and social unrest is probably unparalleled. Baseball and politics have always gone hand in glove in Korea—with a little passion thrown in just to spice things up. Remember that the next time a Korean reliever turns and hurls a ball from the pitcher's mound over the left-field fence or a first baseman from Seoul orders in Spanish from the menu at a Mexican restaurant. It's all part of the globalization of the game.

Notes

1. Guttmann, *Korea*, 689.
2. Lee, "U.S. Missionary."
3. Lee, "U.S. Missionary."
4. Lee, "U.S. Missionary."
5. Report of P. L. Gillett, general secretary, Seoul, 1909–10, YMCA Archives, 370.
6. Report of Lloyd H. Snyder, September 30, 1912, YMCA Archives, 624.
7. Report of Lloyd H. Snyder, undated (ca. 1910), YMCA Archives.
8. Lee, "U.S. Missionary."
9. Report of P. L. Gillett, 1912–13, YMCA Archives, 791–92.
10. Wells, *New God, New Nation*, 103.
11. Lee, "U.S. Missionary."
12. Guttmann, *Korea*.
13. Larson, and Park, *Global Television*, 159.
14. "Samsung Organizes Team to Expedite National Unity," *Korea Times*, March 27, 1982, s4.
15. "Chun Fetes Birth of Pro Ball," *Korea Herald*, March 28, 1982, 1.
16. "Pro Baseball Era," benchmark column in *Korea Herald*, March 30, 1982, 4.
17. Whiting, *Chrysanthemum and the Bat*, 203.
18. Whiting, *You Gotta Have Wa*, 50.
19. Thomas St. John, "Ten Foreign Players in Korea to Face Hardship this Season," *International Baseball Rundown* 7, no. 3 (1998): 9.
20. Whiting, *Chrysanthemum and the Bat*, 3.
21. "Dawning of Pro Sports," *Korea Herald*, March 27, 1982, 4.
22. Quoted at a postgame news conference in Syndey at an event the author managed as the senior media manager for the Olympic baseball competition. Also quoted by Agence France Press reporter Jim Slater in a dispatch from Syndey headlined, "Koreans Beat Japan to Capture Baseball Bronze," September 27, 2000, available on LexisNexis.
23. Whiting, *Chrysanthemum and the Bat*, 53.

Bibliography

Dixon, W. Gray. *The Land of the Morning*. Edinburgh: J. Gemmell, 1882.

Guttmann, Allen. *From Ritual to Record: The Nature of Modern Sports*. New York: Columbia University Press, 1978.

———. *Games and Empires: Modern Sports and Cultural Imperialism.* New York: Columbia University Press, 1994.

———. *Korea: Its Land, People and Culture of All Ages.* Seoul: Hakwon-sa Ltd., 1960.

———. *A Whole New Ball Game: An Interpretation of American Sports.* Durham: University of North Carolina Press, 1988.

Korean Baseball Organization. *A Guide to Korean Pro Baseball.* Seoul: Korean Baseball Organization, 1996.

Korean Overseas Information Service. *A Handbook of Korea.* 9th ed. Seoul: Ministry of Culture and Information, 1993.

Larson, James F., and Heung-Soo Park. *Global Television and the Politics of the Seoul Olympics.* Boulder CO: Westview, 1993.

Lee Su-wan. "U.S. Missionary Taught Koreans Baseball Skills." *Korea Times,* March 27, 1982, p. s2.

Lone, Stewart, and Gavan McCormack. *Korea since 1850.* Melbourne: Longman Cheshire, 1993.

———. "Political Hardball?" *Sports Illustrated,* April 14, 1986, p. 22.

Wells, Kenneth M. *New God, New Nation: Protestants and Self-reconstruction Nationalism in Korea, 1896–1937.* Honolulu: University of Hawai'i Press, 1990.

Whiting, Robert. *The Chrysanthemum and the Bat.* Tokyo: Permanent Press, 1977.

———. "East Meets West in the Japanese Game of *Bèsubóru.*" *Smithsonian* 17, no. 6 (September 1986): 108–20.

———. *You Gotta Have Wa: When Two Cultures Collide on the Baseball Diamond.* New York: Vintage, 1989.

2 | The Americas

6 | Dominican Republic

Forging an International Industry

Professional baseball in the United States is being Latinized. Consider the following: Arturo Moreno became the first Latino owner of a Major League franchise when he bought the Anaheim Angels in 2003. The previous season Omar Minaya became the first Latino general manager of a Major League franchise, while Tony Pena and Luis Pujols became the first Latinos to manage against each other in a Major League game. Moreno is Mexican American; the rest are Dominican. Major League teams all over the country are paying increased attention to their Latino constituencies by providing broadcasts in Spanish, presenting Hispanic promotions (e.g., Spanish Night, Outstanding Hispanic Student Award), or simply by offering more Spanish content (e.g., music, food) at the game. Hispanic Americans have responded with increased attendance and greater consumption of merchandise. Baseball enthusiasts are quick to point out that the most visible dimension of Latinization is taking the form of increased numbers of Latin American players among the ranks of professional ballplayers. The 2005 season opened with 242 (of 829) foreign players on Major League rosters, of which 204 were Latin American. Latin Americans made up 84 percent of foreign players and 25 percent of all Major Leaguers, a figure that has grown dramatically in the past two decades. Much of this Latinization has revolved around baseball in the Dominican Republic. This chapter will examine the rise of Dominican baseball to national and international prominence.

For North Americans the increased presence of Dominican

ballplayers in MLB and their ability to elevate every level of excellence has come as a mild surprise. Dominicans have been Most Valuable Players (George Bell, 1987; Sammy Sosa, 1998; Miguel Tejada, 2002; Vladímir Guerrero, 2004; Albert Pujols, 2005); Cy Young winners (Pedro Martinez 1997, 1999, 2000; Bertolo Colón, 2005); Rookies of the Year (Alfredo Griffin 1979, Raul Mondesi, 1995; Carlos Beltran, 1999; Rafael Furcal, 2000; Albert Pujols, 2001; Angel Berroa, 2003); and batting champions (Matty Alou, 1966; Rico Carty, 1970; Julio Franco, 1991; Manny Ramirez, 2002). The game had been thought of as quintessentially American for so long that anything other than a token presence by foreigners was met with raised eyebrows. For the Dominican Republic and other Latin American countries around the circum-Caribbean (Cuba, Puerto Rico, and Venezuela), however, baseball has been the central sporting institution for over a century.

Dominican baseball ascension within MLB mirrors the sport's cultural importance on the island as well. Baby boys often have tiny baseball mitts placed in their cribs while still in the hospital in the hopes that they might one day honor their families as a professional player. This symbolic gesture also veils the family's hope for release from their economic straitjacket and feeds national pride attached to the sport. The relationship between privation and baseball is a powerful one, and most journalists and scholars writing about Dominican baseball have noted it. Baseball's importance, however, is also bound up with culture and history. The remainder of this chapter examines the most salient features associated with the Dominican ability to develop the sport.

Origins and Early Years of Dominican Baseball

Cubans brought the game of baseball to the Dominican Republic around 1890. Fleeing from the civil war that was raging in their country and the distinct likelihood that slavery in Cuba would end, members of the slaveholding, sugarcane-growing class emigrated to the Dominican Republic. They encountered a moribund sugarcane industry, which they quickly took over and mechanized. Other compatriots followed, among them brothers Ignacio and Ubalde Aloma, who were employed in Santo Domingo as ironworkers. Although they are credited with organizing

6. *Scoreboard in La Romana's stadium shows a little of the face of Dominican baseball. Soldiers and kids leisurely hang out at a game.* (Photo by Alan Klein.)

the first Dominican teams, the game was no doubt played among Cuban expatriates earlier.[1] The sport was also brought into the interior of the country by another Cuban, Dr. Samuel Mendoza y Ponce de Leon, at about the same time. Baseball grew quickly, first among the elite, later trickling down to the masses—a trajectory that seems to reflect the diffusion of sport in most countries.[2] The sons of some of these elite families formed the first professionally oriented team in the country in 1907. Licey (named after a river) formed the cornerstone of Dominican professional baseball, and the team still exists today. Professional teams appeared in short order in two other major Dominican cities: Santiago in the north, and San Pedro de Macoris in the east. The fourth and final team, Escogido, was formed in 1921. Escogido resided in the capital of Santo Domingo along with Licey, and they soon became rivals. The nature of the game in those years was a cacophony of tournaments played within and between the teams in these cities, but the rivalry between the two teams in the capital was the most heated and came to be known by local scribes as "the eternal rivalry."[3] On May 14, 1921, the blue pinstripes of Licey squared off against the red of Escogido in what would be known as the "queen's championship"; Licey's owner, predicting a win, arranged to have a beauty queen offer a toast to his squad at the game. This, he thought, would unnerve the Escogido team.

A young woman, considered the most beautiful in the republic, the Señorita Esperanza Pereyra, won the title of "queen" in her native town of La Vega and was invited to the game. Don Geo Pou, president of the Blues (Licey), personally went to La Vega and drove the beauty queen to the capital in his car. The queen was to assist in the game, but couldn't make her entrance earlier. The managers of Licey were afraid of losing and only when they had a three-run lead in the eighth inning did the sovereign arrive to make the championship toast.[4]

The game was all but won when a substitute outfielder for Licey, Loco Lamberto, misplayed a ball with the bases loaded. Three runs scored, and Licey lost 6–5. Lamberto was made a goat for all time, and the batter, Mateo de la Rosa, became known as "the batter that made the queen cry." The beauty queen, believing her image soiled in fashionable Santo Domingo, sobbed uncontrollably before thousands of Licey fans. She had no idea that she would become the stuff of legend.

Baseball powerhouses from Cuba and Venezuela began playing in the Dominican Republic during the early 1920s. They raised the caliber of the sport by fostering heightened competitive standards for local players. When the Venezuelan team, Concordia, toured in September 1933, they brought with them some of the most highly regarded players of the day (e.g., Tetelo Vargas and Luis Aparicio, whose son went on to play in the majors, and Negro League legend Josh Gibson). The Dominicans, eager to test them, threw their pitching ace Abejita Ruiz, who was said to have the best curve ball of his time. Ruiz beat the highly touted foreigners, setting off a wild celebration in the capital.[5] Pitchers all over the island began working on their curve balls as word of Ruiz's exploits made the rounds.

Competition among the four premier teams intensified during the mid-1930s, particularly after the capital (renamed Ciudad Trujillo, after the dictator) team lost to San Pedro de Macoris in 1936. San Pedro's owner elevated the stakes by loading the team with Cuban players. Regional politics then entered the sport. Trujillo's megalomania extended to winning in baseball, so when the capital lost in 1936, sportsmen in the city decided they had had enough. Trujillo's operatives (Trujillo himself cared little for the game) approached the top Negro Leaguers, particularly Pittsburgh Crawfords superstars Satchel Paige and Josh Gibson. In 1937 Cuban superstar Martin Dehígo and Dominican Tetelo Vargas played, as well as almost a dozen Negro Leaguers. Ciudad Trujillo won because of its acquisitions (and some timely arrests), but the extravagance came at a price. The owners went bankrupt, and Dominican baseball slid into an abyss. For the next thirteen years baseball reverted to amateur club baseball, but no one who watched the game played in the 1930s or 1940s would argue that the caliber of play had not been diminished, and there were fewer outside superstars.

While the sport was being played in urban centers such as Santiago, San Pedro de Macoris, and the capital, it was quietly flourishing in the refinery towns throughout the eastern part of the island. The *ingenios* (refineries) surrounding San Pedro served as the seat of some of the most intense competition on the island and had a major role in the development of many players coming out of the San Pedro area.

For years the managers of the refineries would field teams and vie with one another for local bragging rights. To maximize their chances, refinery managers (the father of Yankee legend Billy Martin was one) rewarded cane workers by giving them time away from cane cutting. By itself, this was sufficient inducement for workers to develop their baseball skills, since cane cutting was arduous and debased labor. With gladiatorial incentives competition to get on a team intensified, and this spilled over into the games themselves. Contests between refineries were raucous affairs, known locally as "wild ball."[6] "These games were bigger than the World Series," recalls Austin Jacobo, an organizer of those games. "When you go to any of these refineries, baseball was the only thing you gonna see. There was no movies. They don't want [to drink] coffee in the house. Everybody was on the field. So when you lose a game, everybody was crying or fighting. If you go to Angelina and they win, they fight you. If they lose, they fight you. It was because they were so excited, you know? And if the umpire calls a bad play, you can bet you're gonna fight."[7]

Postsegregation Latin Baseball

The aftermath of the 1937 season was most felt in the absence of foreigners playing in the country and the relative decline of structured competition. Locally, baseball remained highly competitive, even if underfunded. This scaled-back state of affairs continued until 1951, when a group of wealthy Dominican sportsmen decided to reclaim the luster that had graced Dominican baseball thirteen years earlier. They secured backing from the government, established a symmetrical schedule of play, and once again began attracting foreigners. This brief five-year period was to remind the international baseball community of the wealth of talent in Dominican baseball.

The year 1955 marks the beginning of MLB's relationship with Dominican baseball. This initially took the form of arranging to have Dominicans play their baseball in the winter so as not to compete with American summer baseball. Complying with MLB's structural demands opened the door for various teams to enter the country in search of talent. Of course what underwrote the entire effort was the signing of Jackie Robinson in 1946 and the resulting breakdown of American baseball's racial barrier. With color no longer an impediment, teams like the New York Giants and Pittsburgh Pirates began to send scouts into the Dominican Republic, Cuba, and Venezuela.

Ozzie Virgil is usually credited with being the first Dominican to play MLB when he joined the New York Giants in 1956, but his family emigrated to New York City when Virgil was a boy. It was Felipe Alou who was the first Dominican from the island to play MLB when, in 1958, he came up to play for the Giants. Few teams looked at the Dominican Republic as a serious source of talent in the 1950s, in part because Cuba enjoyed the better reputation for developing talent. With Castro's successful revolution and the subsequent embargo instituted against Cuba after 1969, the flow of talent shifted suddenly to the Dominican Republic. The success of the three Alou brothers (Felipe, Mateo, and Jesus), Juan Marichal, and Manny Mota with the Giants fueled more interest, and other teams began to forge "working relations" with Dominican teams. The Americans would send prospects to play in the Dominican Republic, and in turn Dominican teams would find and help cultivate

Dominican talent for their American partners. More important, North American teams began to think of the Dominican Republic as a source of good and inexpensive talent.

The scouts that came to the island essentially treated their work along "hit-and-run" lines. Scouts like Alejandro Pompez (Giants) and Carlos Pascual (Washington Senators) were among the first on the island. Operating loosely, they generally stayed only long enough to have some locals arrange a tryout in the capital and to sign prospects. Unscrupulous behavior occurred regularly enough that the Dominican government attempted to intervene; but like most things in the country the attempts were haphazard. Notwithstanding the irregularities, the numbers of Dominicans coming to MLB continued to climb. Two Dominicans entered the Major Leagues during the 1950s; 22 in the 1960s; 38 in the 1970s; 65 in the 1980s; and 133 in the 1990s. The rosters on opening day 2005 had 91 Dominicans (figures would grow during the regular season), with almost 1,500 playing in the minor leagues.

The Academy System

Beginning in the mid-1980s, two cutting-edge Major League teams (Toronto Blue Jays and Los Angeles Dodgers) built the first baseball academies in the Dominican Republic. Epy Guerrero (Blue Jays) and Ralph Avila (Dodgers) both realized the value of scouting talent from the island rather than from a distance. They knew that because they lived in the country they could build the kind of presence that would allow their teams to more extensively sign players. In short, they localized Major League presence by building academies to develop players, and they did so independently of the amateur and professional teams on the island. Guerrero built his complex in 1986, just north of Santo Domingo. Avila prevailed upon Dodger owner Peter O'Malley to purchase a swath of land thirty minutes outside of Santo Domingo and build a facility that would allow the Dodgers to house and develop Dominican talent. With a Dominican academy the team would be less dependent on the hit-and-run tactics of finding, signing, and developing players. Additionally, an academy would provide signed players who were not yet ready for rookie ball in the United States a place to train.

Getting visas for qualified players is tightly controlled so that there are always more candidates than visas. The U.S. Department of Labor grants visas to foreign workers, and MLB receives a limited supply of these visas. Each team has between thirty-four and forty-two visas depending on how actively they sign foreign players. In the late 1980s not all teams used their visas, which meant that there were more for others. Still, even for the most active teams there were more players than there were visas. A Dominican (or Venezuelan) facility that could develop all of a team's players who weren't ready to be sent to the North American minor leagues would be of great value. The Dodgers facility, Campo las Palmas, was far and away the best academy on the island. It contained two state-of-the-art playing fields, spacious dorms, eating and recreational accommodations, and sufficient land to grow much of the food needed for the players. They employed fifty people to keep it running. An impressive number of players came out of that facility, going on to carve out careers in baseball (e.g., Pedro Guerrero, Jose Offerman, Jose Viscaino, Ramon Martinez, Raul Mondesi, and Pedro Martinez).

While Campo las Palmas was comfortably able to house forty players and half a dozen coaches, other academies were considerably more modest. In some of these academies players slept in relatively cramped *penciones* (apartments, or small hotels), were provided per diems for food, and played on rented fields. However, Dominican poverty was so widespread that virtually any accommodation was deemed adequate. The small-market Kansas City Royals, for instance, were able to produce a dozen Major Leaguers with their modest facilities. As the 1990s began thirteen Major League clubs had concocted some version of an academy.

More and more teams began to realize that signing Dominican players was becoming critical to success in the United States. Dominicans became increasingly proficient at the game, and the number of Dominicans in the American Major League climbed. The excellence could now be measured in milestones and titles won (George Bell led the American League in home runs in 1987; Joaquin Andujar was a 20-game winner for the Cardinals in 1986). More important, it was cost-effective to sign Latino players. For what a top college draft choice would cost in the United States (approximately $500,000), one could sign 100 Dominican prospects and be reasonably assured that half a dozen would become Major Leaguers.

Academies, however, had a negative impact on Dominican baseball: they weakened the amateur leagues. Until the rise of the academies Dominican amateur leagues were the primary vehicle of talent development, fostering the skills and playing experience of boys until they were old enough to sign with a Dominican professional club or Major League organization. The academies short-circuited this current, acting as magnets for young hopefuls who were migrating to them in ever-increasing numbers. The tryouts held there might result in a contract or a thirty-day trial period at the academy with a possible contract at the end. The Dominican professional teams that had relied on the amateur leagues as a feeder system saw prospects going to academies instead. Hence, North American baseball was structurally becoming more dominant in the Dominican Republic as it increasingly dictated the terms of their relations with Dominican baseball, and was strategically placed to intercept the flow of talent. If we think of the development of Dominican baseball players as a commodity chain that began in the Dominican Republic and ended in North America, then through its academies MLB was seemingly in control of both ends of the chain.

Contemporary Dominican Baseball

Contemporary Dominican baseball is characterized by the following: (1) an intensified presence of MLB; (2) increased support by the Dominican government in efforts to "grow" more players for export; (3) the continuation of Dominican professional baseball; and (4) the beginnings of a two-way flow of resources and control of the sport. Dominican baseball is becoming an American-dominated industry, and all Major League teams have embraced the idea of having a greater presence in the Dominican Republic. Teams with no academies made certain that they secured them; those with a modest presence improved them. Even the Japanese team, the Hiroshima Carp, built an academy. The Dominican government has encouraged MLB by subsidizing the building of baseball facilities throughout the country and providing coaching at all amateur levels. Some of the governmental involvement is in the form of elevating baseball to the level of national ideology. Travel around the capital and you confront enormous banners of Pedro Martinez or Vladimir Guerrero admonishing youth to stay in school, or highly publicized governmental functions at the Presidential Palace honoring individuals who have played key roles in baseball. When Miguel Tejada won the American League's Most Valuable Player award in 2002, he was honored by Dominican president Hipolito Mejia at the palace.

Dominican Winter League and Dominican Summer League

Governmental assistance to baseball has a long history. The Dominican Winter League has received government subsidies since it was first established in its modern guise in 1951. At that time the Dominican government advanced as much as $300,000 a year to teams so that they might bid for better players. Since it began in 1951, the Dominican Winter League has been anchored by the four primary clubs (Licey, Escogido, Aguilas, and Estrellas Orientales) that have formed the backbone of Dominican baseball since the beginning of the twentieth century. To this mix other clubs have come into existence and expired. Until the era of free agency when player salaries escalated and included multiyear contracts, the Dominican Winter League had a full slate of Dominican Major Leaguers. Matty Alou (NL batting champion in 1966) recalls, "In those days it was better baseball because all the big leaguers used to play here. We didn't make as much money as they do now, so we had to play here. I played for Escogido every year for 23 years. When I was sick, I played. When I won the batting title [playing for the San Francisco Giants], I played; didn't miss one year." There was a sense of responsibility to the Dominican public for their early support as well: "The fans expected us, and we owed them that much for believing in us when we were nobodies."[8]

Since the late 1980s, however, many fewer Dominican Major League stars are committed to playing winter ball at home. One can still find a blend of Major Leaguers and solid AAA players on teams, which makes for an exciting brand of baseball. During the 2002 season games I attended between Licey and Escogido, rosters included several journeymen big leaguers (i.e., Enrique Wilson, Abraham Nunez, Ruben Mateo), as well as a number of excellent Dominican and American AAA prospects.

It is the fans that lend the vibrancy to the game, however. That has remained unchanged over the century that organized play has occurred. Dominican fans are deeply loyal to their teams and bring a level of raucousness not normally seen in North America: a *brujo* (witch or wizard) casting spells upon the visiting team; merengue being danced throughout the stadium; informally organized wagering in sections of the park; or more intangible things like the familiarity with one another (the ease of conversation, running up tabs with vendors, the joking, teasing, and even taunting that goes on among those in attendance).

The Winter League's season (November to early February) culminates in the spectacular Caribbean Series, which pits the champions of the Dominican Winter League against winter league champions of Mexico, Venezuela, and Puerto Rico. Host countries are rotated, and wherever it is played there is a carnival atmosphere. With national bragging rights at stake, the Caribbean Series often attracts stars from the various countries. Dominicans are often favored in this series, and the presence of their fans can incite crowd hostilities.

The Dominican Summer League is much younger and does not garner anywhere near the interest of Dominican fans that the Winter League does. Growing out of the academy system, it is essentially a rookie league affiliated with MLB, a recognized extension of the National Association of Professional Baseball Leagues. As Major League clubs began investing in their academies they saw organized league play as a natural extension of their operations. The competition between clubs has generated an excellent rookie league, one that enables the coaching staff to evaluate their players more effectively, in time moving them "up" to North America. Venezuela also had a summer league, but with political tensions in the country on the rise, many clubs have folded their Venezuelan rookies into the Dominican Summer League. While this represents a growth in the professionalism of baseball in the country, it also marks an increased presence of MLB in the country. The league is subsidized and maintained by Major League clubs and MLB in general.

The *Buscón*

With the amateur leagues withering as a consequence of Major League academies, where would the twelve- to sixteen-year-old talent that feeds the academies and Dominican Summer League be honed? This void was quickly filled by the *buscón* (from *buscar*, to find), an individual who locates, develops, and then links his prospect with a team. For this he receives a percentage of the signing bonus. Between my first study (1987–90) and my return in 2002, the *buscón* was the most significant development. Estimates have their numbers between 1,500 and 2,000.

The *buscón* seeks out young players (typically in the twelve- to seventeen-year-old range) or, if he is well established, players seek him out to be groomed into prospects that might interest Major League clubs. *Buscónes* work with these youngsters, provide them a level of nutrition to further their physical development, secure the competition that can enhance their skills, and oversee their mental preparation. When and if the time comes, the *buscón* uses his ties with various organizations to arrange a tryout and hopefully get him signed. For this he demands a percentage of the signing bonus. Because it is completely unregulated, the determination of how much the *buscón* receives is negotiated from case to case. He might get 20 percent or even as much as 50 percent. What is difficult to assess is how much *buscónes* invest in their players. They could put in years of upkeep (food, housing, training expenses) for which they would seek compensation. They also figure in the losses they take on players in whom they have invested but never sign. In a sense the *buscón* becomes a de facto baseball academy, amateur league, and agent.

The *buscón* runs the gamut from small operator to large enterprise; from modest to well-appointed. "They look like little academies," noted Royals academy director Luis Silverio. "They have fifty, sixty, seventy, even a hundred kids working out. The kids will pay maybe twenty pesos a month for that bird dog [*buscón*] to work him out. Sometimes these guys go around and play games in different parts of the country." Louie Eljaua, Red Sox international scouting director, characterizes the *buscón* as a small-scale operation: "Unless they're funded by someone, or like Soto, or an agent with a camp, you'll see guys with little programs. They'll have four or five players, beat-up baseballs; they're playing on run-down fields. Small time really."

Some *buscónes* have baseball backgrounds; others do not. Ex–Major Leaguer Ramon Martinez pitched for twelve years in two organizations.

When he retired he returned to his hometown of Manoguayobo and opened his own academy. Martinez's fifty prospects play in a high-end facility with a new dorm, ample playing fields, and full-time coaching. Samuel Herrera, by contrast, never played baseball. He came to the ranks of *buscón* after having taught college calculus. His half a dozen players live in comparatively modest quarters and play with used equipment. But even Herrera has had players signed in his five years as a *buscón*. As he phrased it, "I've won the lottery seven times."

If those more closely affiliated with North American interests are put off by the unregulated nature of the *buscónes* and the periodic theft of signing bonuses, there are others who perceive their role as valuable. Silverio concludes, "This may sound nuts, but they go places our scouts don't go. There are some dangerous areas here, places where you can't throw a tryout. These *buscónes* cover all these areas. I was in La Romana two weeks ago at 9:30 in the morning. Tuesday. There were seventy guys working out there. There are hundreds of these guys [*buscónes*] out there in every remote area. They definitely have become an important part of getting talent."

Red Sox academy director Jesus Alou concurs: "I think they're benefiting baseball, even if some of them are crooked. They're getting kids interested in playing. There are so many baseball programs going on in the Dominican Republic that are run by *buscónes*. They might not know how to teach the kids the best way to play ball, but they've got them in a camp! They've got them interested in baseball, and that keeps them away from bad things." Ben Cherington, Red Sox farm director, agrees, noting that parents he has dealt with want their kids to be taken by a *buscón* because they are assured their sons will have better food and medical care than they would receive at home.

The *buscón* fashioned a place for himself out of all proportion to what anyone in MLB might have originally figured. *Buscónes* are an influential Dominican presence in a North America–dominated enterprise. Because some *buscónes* have been implicated in wrongdoings and questionable dealings, Major League teams and the Commissioner's Office have preferred to keep them at arm's length. Typical of the many comments I heard is the following from a scouting director: "Trust me, some of these guys you don't want over for dinner. They're a whole other element." These views are fueled by the *buscónes'* quasi-legitimate status and ethnocentrism regarding Dominicans.

Journalists in particular are a major source of this ethnocentrism.[9] While there are hundreds of *buscónes* in the country, few writers examine any more than the most publicized and self-promoting of them. Enrique Soto is, perhaps, the most controversial and successful *buscón* in the Dominican Republic and, not coincidentally, the most written about. While he has been responsible for finding some of the most successful Major Leaguers (Miguel Tejada was one of his finds), he also victimized Danny Aybar, one of his charges. Soto absconded with almost half of Aybar's signing bonus. This blatantly criminal act brought out several investigative reporters—most notably Steve Fainaru of the *Washington Post*—who seized upon Soto as the embodiment of *buscónes* everywhere. His characterization of the Soto-Aybar relationship was almost Dickensian, replete with references to Soto "plying" the young man with nutrients to fatten him up for sale. Soto's efforts at making Aybar more literate extended only to teaching him how to write his name, "then [Soto] drove him into the capital, Santo Domingo, where Aybar printed his signature on a contract to receive $1.4 million from the Los Angeles Dodgers. . . . And then, to secure his investment Enrique Soto stole Willie Aybar's money."[10] Other accounts of *buscónes* mention the occasional scoundrel, but none characterizes them all as thieves or "street-level entrepreneurs," or reduce the country to a baseball "breeding ground for exploitation and corruption" as did Fainaru.[11]

Buscónes represent a strategic layer of contemporary Dominican baseball, and understanding them as an institution nestled between MLB and Dominican baseball illuminates not only the ethnocentrism of others but also the nuanced nature of Dominican life and economics. Soto should not be judged solely by his reprehensible actions with regard to Aybar. If that were the case, he'd be out of business and in a Dominican prison. Instead he continues to enjoy remarkable success because he helps many more than he might ever harm. Former Red Sox director of international scouting, Louie Eljaua, grudgingly conceded that Soto's players appear at tryouts and games in immaculate uniforms bearing the name of his academy. He provides them with the best equipment and nutrition. Most important, he can deliver. He has had more players signed than anyone else. For those familiar with the culture and mind-set of developing nations, this carries an inordinate amount of social weight. Soto's actions may be criminal, but he continues to gather hope-fuls around him because he knows how to build hope, pride, and talent; in the Dominican Republic this trumps conventional morality. Escaping poverty is more important than obeying the letter of the law. Journalists like Fainaru fail to comprehend the nature of economic development in the Dominican Republic when depicting Soto as simply a criminal. He's much more. Depicting all *buscónes* as being like Soto compounds the error.

The MLB Commissioner's Office opened a branch in Santo Domin-go in 2000 in an effort to oversee all baseball developments. That they would locate the first foreign office in the Dominican Republic validates the country's preeminent status in the world of baseball. MLB's decision to oversee baseball in the Dominican Republic began to build in the 1990s in direct relation to the ever-intensifying search for new talent, the uneven way in which young rookies were treated, and the manipu-lation of birth documents by teams and individuals alike. Rafael Perez, the commissioner's Dominican point man, is responsible for bringing all academies under a uniform policy in which they are required to com-ply with standards set by MLB. This has met with success. Less successful have been the efforts of Perez and associates to regulate the visa pro-cess that includes validating the birthdates of Dominican players. He points out that the vast majority (approximately 98 percent) of fraudu-lent documents are those of players who are older than they claimed to scouts, agents, and teams. There are a very few signings involving play-ers younger than 16 ½, the MLB minimum signing age. Since the terror-ist attack of September 11, 2001, the U.S. State Department has tight-ened up the visa process, and all birth certificates are now thoroughly screened. MLB has done its share by insisting on a more thorough vali-dation process, one that uncovers numerous cases of fraud each month. Less successful have been MLB's efforts to organize and regulate *bus-cónes*. But MLB has recently joined the Dominican Republic's Commis-sioner of Baseball to push forward legislation to organize them into an association to better control their activities. Unfortunately, there is little incentive for *buscónes* to join an association of *buscónes* that seeks to regulate them—which would reduce their share of signing bonuses.

Two-way Flow of Influence

The view of Dominican baseball presented thus far is one in which North American interests dominate. Though this is true in general, there is evidence that reciprocal relations are emerging.

We have discussed the *buscón* as a Dominican presence inserting himself into player development. That *buscónes* are not appreciated in most American baseball circles underscores the argument that they are perceived as Dominican intrusions. In the context of anthropological discussions of the "informal economy," *buscónes* occupy a somewhat counterhegemonic position: they are local entrepreneurs, difficult to control, and indispensable to the commodity chain. *Buscónes'* position is aptly summed up by the outspoken and flamboyant Enrique Soto, who noted that "if teams invest, they're organized. If *buscónes* invest, they're thieves."[12]

Dominicans who forged successful baseball careers in the United States are increasingly investing their riches in the construction of baseball facilities that will serve as academies for Major League teams. At least half a dozen of these Dominican-owned facilities have been built and leased. The ability of Dominicans to function in the capacity of owners of state-of-the-art facilities is, from a political and economic standpoint, significant.

The reciprocal flow of influence is also more subtle. It extends to Dominicans who originally emigrated to the United States and then returned home to enhance their chances of being signed, as in the case of Osvaldo Creque Jr. He repatriated to San Pedro de Macoris and skipped his senior year at John F. Kennedy High School in the Bronx as part of a calculated effort to attract the attention of *buscónes* or Major League scouts. There is an irony here, as journalist Justin Brown points out, when you have "kids dropping out of American high schools so they can play amateur baseball in a country where most local players are trying to leave."[13]

Another undocumented development that signifies the degree to which Dominican baseball has penetrated both nations is the replication of Dominican baseball schools in the United States. Over a thousand miles from the unkempt baseball factories of the Dominican Republic, in cities with large Dominican populations, baseball schools like those in their homeland have cropped up. These are usually makeshift batting cages fabricated in someone's basement, to which baseball wannabes flock. They may range in age from nine to nineteen, but they share a desire to imbibe baseball secrets that will give them a leg up on the competition. We are seeing Dominicans as agents in an enterprise that is increasingly transnational.

Conclusion

Dominican baseball is unlike baseball anywhere else in the world. Dominicans have played the game for over a century, and in the course of the search for upward mobility they have fashioned a level of competition that has bred excellence. The sugar refineries, the semipro teams of the 1930s and 1940s, and the academies all fostered a high level of play forged through competition. Poverty and competition combined to create a Dominican pipeline to the pros.

Structurally, MLB has inserted itself into the Dominican game for over fifty years through rogue scouts, the academies, the Dominican Summer League, and the establishment of the MLB Commissioner's Office. While the flow of influence has been heavily one-sided, it does not go unanswered—Dominicans also promote their own interests.[14] For this reciprocal flow to become truly meaningful, however, the overall economic forecast must improve for the Dominican Republic. Major League Baseball International, the business wing of the Commissioner's Office, has worked hard to develop, or "grow the game," in the Dominican Republic, but the third world economic base of the country hinders that movement. Were the Dominican Republic as economically advanced as Japan, for instance, the two-way flow of influence would have reached equilibrium long ago. Japanese ability to buy MLB franchises, to promote corporate sponsorships, and to sign television contracts with MLB for more than $300 million all speak to this.

Because it is the only shared space in which Dominicans dominate, baseball is consciously a source of intrinsic and extrinsic pride, an area in which Dominicans can point to someone connected by only a few degrees of separation to someone who has derived stature and wealth through the game. What is also increasingly apparent is that while the game is going global, it is not synonymous with American control of the playing or administration of the game. At this juncture it is Dominican labor that represents the most globalized piece of the game, but there are signs that Dominicans are increasingly able and willing to invest capital and provide governmental support to bolster their presence. There is no doubt that MLB will in the coming years find foreign partners at all institutional levels, and one of them will be Dominican.

Notes

All quotations not formally cited come from interviews conducted by the author throughout 2002 in the Dominican Republic.

1. Two of the earliest teams were El Cerveceria and El Cauto in 1891.
2. Beezley, *Judas at the Hockey Club.*
3. Klein, *Sugarball,* 18.
4. From an interview with Cordova, in Klein, *Sugarball,* 33.
5. From an interview with Cordova, in Klein, *Sugarball,* 33.
6. Klein, *Sugarball,* 24–26.
7. Quoted in Klein, *Sugarball,* 24–26.
8. Quoted in Klein, *Sugarball,* 30.
9. Fainaru, "Business of Building Ballplayers"; Forero, "Cultivating the Field of Dreams"; Strauss, "Caribbean Baseball Agents Ruling the Roost."
10. Fainaru, "Business of Building Ballplayers."
11. Forero, "Cultivating the Field of Dreams"; Salisbury, "Search for Dominican Talent"; Souhan, "Baseball's Frontier."
12. Quoted in Fainaru, "Business of Building Ballplayers."
13. Brown, "Diamonds in the Rough."
14. Klein, *Sugarball.*

References

Beezley, William. *Judas at the Hockey Club and Other Episodes of Porfirian Mexico.* Lincoln: University of Nebraska Press, 1987.
Brown, Justin. "Diamonds in the Rough." *Christian Science Monitor,* March 25, 2002.
Fainaru, Steve. "Business of Building Ballplayers: In Dominican Republic Scouts

Find the Talent and Take the Money." *Washington Post*, June 17, 2001.

Forero, Juan. "Cultivating the Field of Dreams." *Newark Star Ledger*, July 5, 1998.

Klein, Alan. *Growing the Game: Globalization and Major League Baseball*. New Haven: Yale University Press, 2006.

———. *Sugarball: The American Game, the Dominican Dream*. New Haven: Yale University Press, 1991.

Ruck, Rob. *The Tropic of Baseball*. Westport CT: Meckler, 1991.

Salisbury, Jim. "Search for Dominican Talent No Longer a Hit or Miss Affair." *Philadelphia Inquirer*, July 23, 2002.

Souhan, Jim. "Baseball's Frontier: Latin American Academies Spawn Major League Talent." *St. Paul Star Tribune*, June 17, 2003.

Strauss, Joe. "Caribbean Baseball Agents Ruling the Roost." *St. Louis Post Dispatch*, December 25, 2005.

7 | Cuba

Behind the Curtain

Between innings at the Estadio Latinoamericano in Havana, as ushers sold sweet coffee to those in the box seats behind home plate, we fell into a candid conversation with a high-ranking Cuban baseball official. Such moments don't happen very often on the island.

It's as though a huge, black curtain separates Cuba from the rest of the world. That's how life here was once described to me. Sometimes Cubans can hear what's going on beyond that curtain. But rarely does it move enough in the trade winds for them to catch a real glimpse of what's going on beyond their shores.

As a consequence, what passes for communication between our country and theirs is usually carefully phrased sentences, often spoken only after a look over the shoulder to see who may be listening. Cold war bromides prevail even though the world has changed so much since the revolution in 1959, the Cuban missile crisis, and the Bay of Pigs, and the two nations still remain only ninety miles apart as the crow flies. But every now and then the curtain does move. Both sides catch a glimpse of each other and so often the link between these two disparate worlds—capitalism and what's left of socialism—is baseball.

"What would happen if the United States lifted the embargo tomorrow?" we ask, watching how the baseball official licks his lips and gazes at those around him. "Maybe a freighter, a big one from Rawlings or Wilson docked in the harbor and they began to unload all kinds of equipment. Baseballs, gloves, bats—everything that's so needed down here?"

The baseball official looks out toward the game, seemingly ignoring my traveling partner, Milton Jamail, and me. He has that faraway look in his eyes that I have seen so often in this beautiful yet cursed land. At first I think he will shrug off such hypothetical questions. After all, what's to be gained? We've heard those excuses before. He'll be like so many others and swiftly move the conversation to something safe like how deftly the third baseman has just fielded that hard-hit grounder. How the first baseman has stretched to make the out. Commenting on such excellent play and leaving out the most obvious conclusion: that either player would have a chance at playing Major League ball if the world was somehow different. If it wasn't so entrenched in the past.

"What would happen?" the baseball official repeats. Yes, we answer. What would happen if such a ship rolled past the Old World castle that marks the entrance to Havana harbor and tied up at the ancient piers? "What would happen?" the baseball official said, his voice now low and serious. "Only that the world as we know it would change forever."

Such is the power of baseball in Cuba. It can break through the hypothetical and make people think, even dream. That's the way it's been for more than a century on this island. In the United States the national pastime will always be the game of red, white, and blue bunting and Mom's apple pie. Yet the sport is just as important in Cuba and throughout much of the Caribbean, but for completely different reasons. When Spain controlled the island, sneaking off to play baseball was a radical, sometimes dangerous, hobby. In playing baseball, many Cubans turned their back on the old colonial ways and showed their preference for a new, independent nation.

More than a half century after Fidel Castro's revolution, the debate still rages about him and baseball. Is he a national hero or the devil incarnate? It depends on which side of the Straits of Florida you have that conversation. But any student of history concedes that Castro's decision to play baseball and form a ragtag barnstorming company from his improbable army called Los Barbudos (the Bearded Ones) was a stroke of genius. For Castro knew how important baseball was and will always be for Cuba. Los Barbudos played a series of exhibitions in the months after Castro took control of the island in 1959. The new president sometimes took the mound to show off his loopy curve ball for cheering baseball aficionados. That Castro has outlasted nine U.S. administrations and counting is a credit to his understanding of his country's soul more than any success in national health or education.

Was Castro a legitimate baseball prospect? It depends on who you talk to or what you choose to believe. According to Tad Szulc's acclaimed biography, *Fidel: A Critical Portrait*, Castro was an impressive athlete before enrolling in Havana University's law school in 1945. While attending Belen College, a preparatory school, he was the institution's top athlete, starring in track, table tennis, basketball, and baseball.

In doing the research for his book, Szulc had full access to Castro and his closest associates. Szulc says that Castro was so determined to be Belen's best pitcher that he often practiced "until eight o'clock in the evening at the school's sports grounds. Long after the catcher got tired and left, Castro would go on throwing the ball against the wall."[1]

Whether such effort attracted the attention of Major League scouts has never been confirmed. While researching my novel, *Castro's Curveball*, I spoke with several scouts and players from the old Cuban winter ball league. Some dismissed such speculation about Castro's prowess, while several insisted that Castro was good and had even pitched batting practice for them. Legend has it that the Washington Senators and New York Giants were interested in signing Castro in the waning years of World War II. At that point Castro wasn't overly politically active and hadn't fully aligned himself with the growing revolutionary factions in Cuba.

Roberto González Echevarría, a former semipro catcher and now a Yale University professor, says in *The Pride of Havana* that the story of Castro being a top prospect "is a fabrication by an American journalist whose name is now lost, and is never told in Cuba because everyone would know it would be false."[2] González Echevarría turned up only one trace of Castro's pitching career. In a 1946 game between the law and business schools at the university, an "F. Castro" was found in the box score. He was a pitcher and on the losing end of a 5–4 decision.

Searches by the Baseball Hall of Fame in Cooperstown, New York, only turn up a *Sport* magazine article that appeared in 1964. In it Don Hoak, who spent eleven years in the Major Leagues and several winters playing in Cuba, details a strange evening at the ballpark in Havana. The year was 1951, and it wasn't unusual then for students to come out of the stands and interrupt a game to protest the government or the hold that such U.S. corporations as United Fruit had on their country. Once again baseball was seen as one of the paths to an independent nation.

Hoak relates that one night a tall, skinny student wearing a white shirt, black pants, and suede shoes took the mound with Hoak next up at the plate. Hoak maintained that the interloper was Castro. "Left-handers as a breed are eccentric, but Castro, a right-hander, looked kookier than any southpaw I have known," Hoak later told *Sport*. Hoak fouled off two Castro pitches before the field was cleared of demonstrators.

So the question still remains: Was Castro a legitimate prospect? Probably not. But right when you're ready to dismiss such notions, somebody steps out of the past. A few years ago in Havana, we were talking with several fans and one of them, an old man, claimed to have played baseball with Castro as a boy on the eastern end of the island, where they both grew up. The usual questions about hometown and schooling were asked in trying to catch the old-timer in a lie. But he fielded all the queries flawlessly. Finally, Milton Jamail asked, "What did Castro throw?"

"So-so fastball, sneaky slider at the knees," was the reply. "But his best pitch was a curve ball. Castro had a great curve." Oddly appropriate for all that happened over the last half century, don't you think? Whether or not Castro was ever a prospect, Cubans still play the game of baseball anywhere they can. In alleyways, city parks, and in the wide country fields, kids exhibit an enthusiasm reminiscent of stickball in the United States during the 1950s. The equipment may be as primitive. That's why I recommend that anyone who goes to Cuba take along a few new baseballs and hand them out to the children on the street. You'll know you've changed somebody's world forever by the stunned looks you receive.

In 1959 Castro's rebel armies took control of Cuba. During the succeeding years he would steer the nation toward communism and link it with the Soviet Union. Few of his countrymen realized what Castro had in store for the island as rebel army tanks and soldiers streamed into the capital. But at least one ballplayer was wary of the new regime and what the future held for his homeland.

Orestes "Minnie" Minoso sat in his trademark Cadillac as the military parade tied up traffic in Havana soon after the Batista regime fell. Passing rebel soldiers recognized him and called for Minoso to join them. The ballplayer left his car and was about climb aboard one of the military flatbed trucks when something stopped him in his tracks. Something didn't feel right about the whole situation. Minoso claims that from that moment on he never trusted the Castro government. Despite the cheering crowds and what seemed to be answered prayers, he hung back. In fact, not long after that he began to make plans to leave the island and resettle permanently in the United States. It would prove to be a costly process, as he owned several high-rise apartment buildings and a fleet of taxis. By pulling out of Cuba, he knew he would lose a lot of money.

"Call it a gut feeling," Minoso explained years later, "but I was always suspicious of [Castro]. I kept quiet at first, but kept an eye and ear open as to where his government was heading. When I became convinced beyond doubt that he would take all freedom away from the Cuban people, I made up my mind to leave."[3]

Of course, Minoso wasn't the only one to make that decision. The exodus began in earnest as Castro methodically destroyed the old social order and moved Cuba rapidly toward a Marxist-Leninist way of life. Soon after taking power, despite touring the island playing ball and pitching before the cheering crowds, Castro abolished the professional teams that had existed for decades on the island. Cubans would play amateur baseball, with the country's new president routinely questioning national team coaches about game strategy and roster moves.

The Cuban revolution and the subsequent events had a profound impact on the U.S. baseball community. Almost everywhere the ripples spread. The Minnesota Twins, for example, had already released Tony Oliva when the Bay of Pigs debacle took place. All flights back to Cuba were canceled, so the Twins decided to keep him. Three years later, Oliva became the first rookie in Major League history to win a batting championship.

George Genovese was managing with the Giants' minor league affiliate in El Paso. On his roster was Jose Cardenal, who was from Mantanzas, Cuba. Cardenal was listed as an infielder, but Genovese soon realized that he didn't have a future at any of those positions. "Jose hadn't shown much in spring training and he was about to get released," Genovese says. "So, I decided to take him along with me to El Paso and make an outfielder out of him. If he couldn't make it, I'd release him then so he could stay in this country. I knew if he went back to Cuba, he would never get out."

The move to right field paid off. Cardenal homered in his first game for El Paso and went on to hit 36 home runs that season. He played 18 seasons in the Major Leagues, including appearances in the 1978 League Championship Series and the 1980 World Series. He became a confidant to the Cuban players who would follow—Rafael Palmeiro, Jose Canseco, and Orlando "El Duque" Hernandez.

On a corner of the main park in Havana, the famed Esquina Caliente, or "Hot Corner," they know all about these players and much more about the game. They gather here daily, almost always men, under the royal palm trees to discuss nothing but baseball. A perpetual Hot Stove League. Those at Esquina Caliente know the statistics, maybe even the game, better than most American fans. But because of government crackdowns, the barriers that have existed for a half century between these two nations, they can hear the gospel of the game but they are rarely afforded a glimpse of the game's Major League stars.

On one trip to Havana's Central Park to talk baseball, I brought along several copies of *USA Today Baseball Weekly*, a publication I helped found in the early 1990s. Other than baseballs, nothing is more coveted on this island than news from the outside world. The cover story for this particular issue was about players who were nearing the end of their careers—Cal Ripken, Dennis Eckersley, Mark McGwire. How would they be remembered? How did they stack up against the all-time greats?

The issues disappeared in a heartbeat. Little can make one more popular in Havana than to come bearing baseball gifts. But a few minutes later a middle-aged man with a stogie in hand returned to me and pointed to the cover photo of a grim-faced McGwire with a bat in his hands. "This is what McGwire looks like?" he asked, and I could only nod my head. The man saw the quizzical look on my face. "I just

7. (top) *Esquina Caliente (Hot Corner) in Havana, where fans come to discuss baseball seven days a week.* (Photo by Tim Wendel.)

8. (bottom) *Pitching in the park.* (Photo by Tim Wendel.)

thought he would be different," he replied, and once again I was reminded of one of the major contradictions about Cuba. They may hear, but they are rarely permitted to see.

That is difficult for those of us in the rest of the world to truly comprehend. Every day we are bombarded by images of the rich, powerful, and famous. We may not care about the latest Hollywood or even sports celebrity, but like it or not we'll sooner or later know enough about Brad Pitt or Jennifer Lopez or certainly Mark McGwire to pick them out of a crowd. In Cuba such intimacy, generated by satellite TV or the magazines found in your doctor's waiting room, doesn't exist. So, you have such strange situations as Radio Rebelde, what at one time was Castro's clandestine station during the revolution, now specializing at night in baseball broadcasts and sports talk radio. That's curious enough, but in the station's dilapidated studios you'll find Edel Casas, who can name the Cy Young winner or MVP in either league in any year. The man may be a walking baseball encyclopedia, but if Mark McGwire walked into his studio one night, even Casas wouldn't recognize him.

The disconnect between image and accomplishment occurs time and time again. In Cuba they love baseball and know it as well as we do. But when the Baltimore Orioles played an exhibition game in Havana in 1999, what Cuban fans were hungry for was to gaze upon a team of Major Leaguers. Burn those memories into the brain forever.

This was driven home to me on my first visit to Cuba in 1992. I had gone to cover a series of exhibition games between the United States and Cuban Olympic teams on the eastern end of the island, not far from where Castro supposedly embraced the game as a boy. The American team was loaded with future Major Leaguers—Nomar Garciaparra, Phil Nevin, Jeffrey Hammonds, Charles Johnson. But they were no match for a veteran Cuban squad that included Victor Mesa and Omar Linares—two of the best ballplayers who would never play in the majors.

Early on in the first game an old man sat down in the aisle next to me. "Tell me about the Minnesota Twins," he said. Now this was during the off-season after the glorious team of Kirby Puckett, Jack Morris, and Kent Hrbek had defeated the Atlanta Braves in one of the best World Series ever played. Even though we were years away from MLB's attempt to eliminate the Twins and the Montreal Expos, already the economic constraints were enveloping the newly crowned champions. I told the old man it would be difficult for them to repeat. They couldn't re-sign every star they had. Plus, the team was getting older. Many had had career years. It would be difficult for them to duplicate such prowess at the plate and return to the Fall Classic.

"I know all that," the Cuban told me.

"ok," I replied. "What do you want to know?"

"I need to know, what do they look like?"

What do they look like?

Since then I've written two books about baseball in Cuba and the Caribbean. Some of it, in the beginning, was simply following up on the assignments that were given to me. But the fascination with this star-crossed land of bright sunshine and gallows humor began when the old man asked me that strange question: What do they look like?

In my tourist Spanish, I went around the diamond describing the 1991 world champion Minnesota Twins. It wasn't easy and at times I was at a loss for words, tongue-tied as I too often am with Spanish. Somebody like Puckett or Hrbek is difficult to describe in English let alone in a second language. As I spoke, I gazed out toward center field, where Hammonds was playing a few yards in front of a sign that read "Socialismo o Muerte"—Socialism or Death. When I was finished I turned back to the old man. His eyes had begun to well with tears. He stood up and clasped me on the shoulder and said, "Thank you. Now I know."

One last story about Cuba and the disconnect that exists between there and here, between baseball's past and its present. When presidents and dictators become too entrenched in daily life, things are rarely as they seem or as they should be. Still, the desire for something better can be as captivating as it ever was.

In 1999 the Baltimore Orioles and the Cuban national team played a two-game exhibition series; the first game was in Havana and the second a few weeks later in Baltimore. The first game was an extra-inning affair with the Major Leaguers barely winning. In the follow-up the Cubans trounced the Orioles, just as they had the young U.S. Olympians seven years before. Even though protesters came onto the field, eerily reminiscent of Castro's budding revolutionary years, and Linares finally got his due, posing for photographs with Ripken, for me the most memorable moment belonged to Andy Morales. His home run delivered Team Cuba's final runs in the 12–6 victory. As the infielder rounded the bases he almost began to dance. He raised his arms in the air and nearly stumbled as he rounded second base.

After the game several Orioles grumbled that Morales had shown them up. You're not supposed to exhibit too much emotion in baseball, at least not at the professional level. Back home in Cuba, Morales was feted by Castro himself. So why did he try to defect a year after that exhibition game? Why, when he was sent back to Cuba, did he try again sixteen months later and this time make it to south Florida?

Some would say he simply wanted a better life. He had seen firsthand the luxurious existence of a Major Leaguer, and the riches that can be earned for hitting a ball with a bat and sending it soaring into the night sky. But perhaps this one time it wasn't all about the money. In the United States, actually in much of the world, you can compete against the best. Have a knack for stocks and bonds? Go to Wall Street. Ready to lead a nation? Come to Washington. But if you play ball in Cuba, all you hear about is the Major Leagues. You know the names—McGwire, Sosa, Griffey, A-Rod. You may not recognize them, but their statistics are memorized and repeated word for word. Handed down from fan to fan. That's what the U.S. Olympians, the Baltimore Orioles, and many in MLB have never understood about any exhibition series between the United States and Cuba.

The real Cuba lies in the shadows and the alleyways—anywhere baseball is played. The essence of this land rides the night air like a piece of music that grabs your attention, only to dissolve when you stop and try to determine where the tune is coming from. In Havana they often say that maybe tonight the world will sink into the earth. The waiting for something better might come to an end. Their prayers may be answered.

Because of such feelings, baseball isn't just a game in Cuba. Maybe it never was. With all that's happened over the last half century, baseball has never been more important in Cuba. Many, like Andy Morales, play to prove that they belong. They will chase that dream as far and as long as they can. For in Cuba, baseball is perhaps the only thing that will allow them to change their world as they know it. Change it forever.

Notes

1. Szulc, *Fidel*, 120.
2. González Echevarría, *Pride of Havana*, 8.
3. Quoted in Wendel, *New Face of Baseball*, 19.

Bibliography

Augenbraun, Harold, and Ilan Stavans. *Growing Up Latino*. Boston: Houghton Mifflin, 1993.

Dickson, Paul. *The New Dickson Baseball Dictionary*. New York: Harcourt Brace, 1999.

Fainaru, Steve, and Ray Sanchez. *The Duke of Havana: Baseball, Cuba, and the Search for the American Dream*. New York: Villard, 2001.

González Echevarría, Roberto. *The Pride of Havana: A History of Cuban Baseball*. New York: Oxford University Press, 1999.

Jamail, Milton H. *Full Count: Inside Cuban Baseball*. Carbondale: Southern Illinois University Press, 2000.

Price, S. L. *Pitching around Fidel*. New York: Ecco, 2000.

Regalado, Samuel O. *Viva Baseball!* Urbana: University of Illinois Press, 1998.

Rucker, Mark, and Peter C. Bjarkman. *Smoke: The Romance and Lore of Cuban Baseball*. Kingston: Total Sports Illustrated, 1999.

Szulc, Ted. *Fidel: A Critical Portrait*. New York: William Morrow, 1986.

Wendel, Tim. *Castro's Curveball: A Novel*. New York: Ballantine, 1999.

———. *The New Face of Baseball: The One-Hundred-Year Rise and Triumph of Latinos in America's Favorite Sport*. New York: Rayo–Harper Collins, 2003.

8 | Cuba

Community, Fans, and Ballplayers

Cuba, as one friend put it, "is the most boring place in the world when there's no baseball." In the summer there's nothing to talk about, but during the season, he opined, everyone comes alive with baseball. Baseball provides a vibrancy that fuels the workers in the factories, energizes the old men, and feeds the dreams of young boys. Taking my cue from him, this essay explores the world of Cuban baseball by examining the fans' social connections, historical and current, real and imagined, to baseball.

Since 1995 I have been studying the cultural aspects of Cuban baseball. In the late 1990s I spent two full seasons in Havana attending every game played at the Estadio Latinoamericano. During games I chronicled fans' actions and words to understand the relationship among fans, national identity, and the government. I also interviewed fans, athletes, coaches, journalists, and officials. Here, I will use one particular game during the 1998 pennant chase in the Serie Nacional, the premier Cuban league, to look at Cuban fans' place in baseball. As will be seen, some aspects of being a fan are no different than those in the United States, but others are specific to Cuba. First, I will provide some historical background, which will be followed by a discussion of the contemporary dynamic between players and fans.

Historical Rivalries

Baseball arrived in Cuba sometime in the late 1860s or early 1870s. University students returning from the United States are credited with bringing the first equipment and organizing the first clubs. These young men were among Havana's wealthy, and their nineteenth-century games were major social events. Clubs hosted a Sunday afternoon game and then provided a dinner and dance for the visitors, players, and elite members of Havana society. Because players mingled with their spectators after their afternoon's exertions, a heightened degree of familiarity existed between ballplayers and these socially elite fans. Some of these privileged supporters were even allowed into the clubhouse while athletes changed into their uniforms prior to a game. Some even assisted players in getting dressed. Described in what may be the first written history of baseball, Wenceslao Gálvez y Delmonte, a historian and shortstop, chronicled his preparation for a game against Habana in 1889.

One by one we, the Almendares players, arrive at Aurelio's Gymnastic Club. . . . The most enthusiastic or most presumptuous [fans] come in to see us get dressed, witnessing it all, somewhat indecorous at certain points. And in their delirium for the team they might praise the beauty mark on so-and-so's right thigh. They help us with our toilette, tying the string on our undershirts and the brand new blue silken scarf, which was purchased at the Chinese boutique.

"How about dedicating a hit to me today? I have already seen the *habanistas* [Habana's players] at the gym on Consulado Street. Don't strike out. Have you had much wine?" They continue in their impertinent and foolish manner until it is time to leave.[1]

While Gálvez y Delmonte's social equals were permitted to enter the clubhouse during athletes' preparations, supporters of lesser social standing had to wait outside for the players to emerge for their journey across town to the rival club's ground. These early games, more than athletic contests, were premier social *events*. They were galas that attracted the attention of a broad spectrum of society and were places to see and be seen. Even traveling by carriage from one social club to another for a baseball game attracted attention along their passage through Havana's streets. Gálvez y Delmonte describes one such journey from the gymnasium where his team changed to the home team's field for an afternoon game.

No sooner do we appear outside the gym door than the curious began to stop in their tracks and stand in front of us, and those who recognize us point us out to their friends as if we were some sort of monument.

"There's Carlito Macía," pointing his finger at my teammate.

"Look, that's Alfredo Arango."

"So fat? I thought he was much thinner."

"Well, I'll prove it to you. Psst, psst, hey aren't you Alfredo Arango? . . . Yeah, man, that's him. He just doesn't want to answer."[2]

Their arrival, as Gálvez y Delmonte describes it, stopped pedestrians in their tracks. Some climbed trees and flagpoles to catch a glimpse of the players on their way to the field. Baseball games were also civic events, as they attracted thousands that celebrated Cubanness at a time when declarations of Cuban identity were challenges to the Spanish colonial regime. In short, baseball was revolutionary a hundred years before Castro's revolution. Promoted in nationalist terms by the wealthy most interested in Cuban independence, baseball represented all that was supposedly civilized and modern about Cubans. While the rhetoric justifying the game was couched in nationalistic jingoisms, the physical sites of the game were primarily limited to the capital in much the same way as early American professional baseball was limited to the Eastern seaboard. The emergent rivalry between Habana and Almendares reflected a local enmity that lasted more than sixty years, much like the Yankees-Dodgers rivalry before the latter moved to the West Coast.

During the so-called Golden Era of Cuban baseball (1930s–1950s), this rivalry formed the core of Cuban baseball fans' passion. Played out almost weekly during the winter months, these two teams along with the others in the professional league were all located in the various boroughs of Havana. Habana and Almendares dominated the Cuban professional league, which never consisted of more than six teams. The other teams often seemed to provide a foil in setting up a dramatic season-ending, climatic confrontation between Habana and Almendares. Identified by their respective colors, red and blue, their enmity was based on local passions. Elderly fans recalled these intense games as ones that divided families. One fan explained that in his youth he was a "Blue" while his brother was a "Red." This sibling rivalry drove their mother crazy since it meant that he often shunned whatever his brother did, refusing to eat the same foods at mealtimes as his brother, wear the same clothes, listen to the same music, or like the same girls. Whatever position his brother took, he took the opposite. The brothers' rivalry reflected the passion that fueled Cuban fans.

Cuban baseball was not limited solely to this one isolated professional league. Major League teams had toured Cuba playing exhibition games since the early 1900s. In the 1940s the Havana Cubans played in the Florida International League, followed by the Sugar Kings in the International League in the 1950s. Powerhouse amateur teams, such as Hershey and Telefónico, run by American-owned corporations, also attracted significant amounts of attention. Regional amateur leagues existed throughout the island, but none of those leagues or the professional league qualified as a true "national" league that involved teams from all regions of the country.

The Cuban Revolution altered the entire structure of Cuban baseball. The nationalization of many foreign-owned private holdings accelerated the dismantling of the existing baseball structures. The Sugar Kings were moved to New Jersey and longstanding amateur clubs like Hershey disappeared as their holdings were taken over by the government. The rivalry of Habana and Almendares also dissolved as the government reorganized baseball to harness the country's immense and untapped athletic talent. The Castro regime set about constructing stadiums in provincial capitals that did not have large stadiums as part of a program to make sport available to the entire populace. And the private clubs, where the original baseball teams had formed and which possessed some of the country's best facilities, were opened to the public.

New leagues and tournaments were created that emphasized the connections between the various regions of the country in a way that had not existed previously. This was most apparent in the Serie Nacional. Beginning with four teams in 1961, the Serie Nacional united the island in one competition. Played every winter since, the Serie Nacional expanded to sixteen teams divided into Western and Eastern conferences, Occidente and Oriente. Each conference has two four-team sections. Before the Cuban Revolution there was no single league that encompassed the entire country, and there were none of the regional rivalries that exist today.

The structure that emerged from the revolutionary reorganization proved vibrant; instead of rivalries just within the capital city, regional rivalries emerged based on geographic differences, the most passionate being between the capital and the two outermost provinces. The rivalry between Havana's Industriales and Pinar del Rio (the latter from the province on the western edge of the island) gradually replaced the Habana and Almendares rivalry. Since both Industriales and Pinar del Rio compete within the Occidente conference, they have met more often than any other two teams in the Serie Nacional, mirroring the Yankees–Red Sox rivalry in MLB. And they often play for the right to represent the Occidente in the Campeonato de la Serie Nacional. The other major rivalry is between Industriales and Santiago de Cuba, the team from the cultural capital of the eastern tip of the island. This rivalry has intensified as the teams from Santiago have won more championships in the past ten years than any other club.

The Cuban Revolution not only reorganized baseball but ended up reaffirming the importance of an athlete's ties to his local community. The Revolution abolished the economic disparity within Cuban baseball in which the richest teams, like Habana or Almendares, could afford to hire the best players away from amateur teams. Players now train and develop their skills in their hometown or province throughout their entire career. Players are now truly representatives of their community—the Serie Nacional requires all players to live in the geographic area of the team for which they play, as do all other leagues whatever the level of competition. Thus, all players for Industriales must have been born in and must live in the capital. All players for Pinar del Rio must come from the Pinar del Rio, and so on. Each of the fourteen provinces has one team and the capital has two, Industriales and Metropolitanos. Hence, Cuban ballplayers remain a part of the social and athletic community in which they grew up. Throughout the interviews I conducted, the players often talked about the importance of representing their neighborhood, their town, their province, and their country.[3]

Another consequence of the residency requirement is that players are likely to spend their entire career with one club. Players cannot be traded—that would make them commodities from the Cuban viewpoint and that only happens in capitalist societies. However, a player

9. Advertisement for a Havana sporting goods distributor. (Photo courtesy of the National Baseball Hall of Fame.)

can switch teams if he moves to another province, but Cubans are rarely allowed to change residence. Cuban officials are not blind to talent, however. If a young prospect's advancement is blocked because there are older talented players within the province at his position, he may be transferred to another province where he will get to play.

Fans as Part of the Game

Ballplayers' connections to local communities are historical legacies of the game in Cuba. Cuban ballplayers became celebrities in part by remaining attached to part of their local communities. Castro's rise to power did not create these connections. Ironically, the turn toward socialism sundered the baseball connections between the United States and Cuba and also limited the disparities between wealth and poverty, thereby preserving these connections. Cuban athletes are not the media-hyped celebrities placed on pedestals and removed from human interaction, so commonly seen in the United States. Cuban athletes openly express responsibility to their sport and to neighborhood communities. There is a distinct sense of civic duty instead of individual entitlement in their actions and words. Almost every player I interviewed credited his development as a ballplayer partly to the encouragement of neighbors. The athletes' physical immediacy and proximity in everyday life to local people reinforce these connections. A morning conversation with a Cuban friend made this all too apparent.

A few days before a game between Industriales and Cienfuegos, my friend Carlos and I sit in the driveway of his bakery talking about Industriales.[4] I mention the play of one of the outfielders and Carlos interrupts with a suggestion: "Let's go talk to him. His apartment is just a couple blocks away." He ignores my protests that surely this star of the team does not want to be bothered at home by some strange foreigner. Carlos stands up and shouts into the bakery, "Flaco! We're going to talk to Murrieta. We'll be back later."

Carlos leads me down a tree-lined street to an apartment building and up to the third floor. I argue again that Murrieta will not want to be bothered. Carlos laughs, "What else will he be doing at one in the afternoon but lounging about? Besides, he doesn't have a game today so there's nothing for him to prepare for. He'll be there." The interior stairwell to the third floor is unlit and dark, a stark reminder of everyday difficulties residents in Havana face. Carlos reaches through an iron grating and pounds on a worn, wooden door. Shuffling can be heard and then the door opens. Standing before us in a pair of shorts, flip-flops, and a threadbare t-shirt is one of the premier players in all of Cuba, Ivan Murrieta. Carlos explains who I am and why we are paying him a visit. Murrieta smiles graciously and unlocks the iron gate that serves as a screen door, quite common in Cuba; air can circulate while providing some security. He invites us in, offers us coffee, and we proceed to sit and talk about life on the road in the Serie Nacional and other baseball topics.

Two hours later Carlos and I are back at the bakery with a lunch appointment with Murrieta for the next day to continue our conversation. I tell Carlos that I cannot believe we just went and knocked on the door of Industriales' star player in the middle of the day. "Why not?" Carlos argued. "He's a guy like the rest of us. He makes his living playing baseball but he still puts his trousers on one leg at a time."

Carlos's point was driven home over the next few days as we visited Murrieta several more times. Soon I began to notice Murrieta on the streets, heading into shops, and graciously mixing with neighbors. Shopkeepers and pedestrians know who he is but no one gawks or follows him, not even young boys who aspire to be ballplayers. The locals do not appear to believe that associating with Murrieta enhances their own status. One boy who plays on Murrieta's street simply shrugs, "Admiring him won't make me a better player."

Certainly, Cuban ballplayers are privileged. They travel throughout Cuba, and some travel overseas. They have opportunities that their neighbors will never have. Yet this difference in social position is not so great that they are removed from the everyday concerns of community life. They, like their neighbors, need to be creative in obtaining the basic necessities in a dire economic environment. Their mutual struggle helps connect sports heroes with their neighbors as people rather than as icons.

Interactions between fans and players are not limited to everyday encounters on Havana's streets. Players' families, friends, and neighbors arrive at Estadio Latinoamericano before games and spend time chatting with the ballplayers as they prepare for games. Such encounters between athletes and fans feed the passion of the crowds and fuel the rivalries. This became especially clear to me after a tense game in the Serie Nacional of the 1997–98 baseball season.

The late afternoon sun beat upon the wooden seats of the Estadio

Latinoamericano, slowly sapping their brilliant color. The diamond gleamed in the sunlight, a contrast of rich, red clay and damp, green grass. It is an hour before the scheduled start of a game between Industriales and Cienfuegos, a team from eastern Cuba. There are 5 games left in the season, and for the first time in over a decade, it appears that Industriales may not make the playoffs. Pinar del Rio has already clinched the section championship and a playoff spot. Only the four teams with the best records in each conference make the playoffs, and Isla de la Juventud has a 2-game lead over Industriales with five to play. Two of those five are head-to-head clashes between Isla de la Juventud and Industriales. To qualify, Industriales must beat Isla in both games but they also cannot afford to lose any of their other remaining games.

An hour before game time, a few players have left the shade of the dugout to loosen up. It's hard to believe that muscles could be tight in the humid heat. Three players seated on the outfield grass stretch as an older man in slacks and *guayabera* (a tropical dress shirt) stops and talks to them. They laugh and banter before he pats one of the players on the shoulder and then disappears into the dugout. Other players step out of the dugout and talk through the backstop with other early arriving fans in an easy, friendly manner. They joke and laugh until thirty minutes before game time.

The old man who had disappeared into Industriales' dugout reemerges and clambers over the third base rail into the stands. He ascends the cement steps to where I sit, and we catch up on the latest news. Eddie is part of the spectacle of Cuban baseball. He leads fans in cheers and he starts chants in support of their beloved Industriales. I ask him what he was doing on the field. "The players need to know how much everyone will shout their support, so they better push their bodies and skills to their limits. I explained to them how important victory today is to all of us. There'll be 30,000 here tonight. All shouting at them and that energy will provide the difference." He adds that he was on the field to "help" some of the players relax and assure them that they have the fans' support. It might sound trite, but the crowd's support does seem to play a role in the outcome of the game.

In the seventh inning of this critical game, Industriales leads Cienfuegos 2–1. The crowd has been quiet the past two innings as Industriales failed to get a base runner. But now Industriales has men on first and second with one out. The left-handed batter has a full count. With the pitch, the runner on second breaks for third. The batter checks his swing, and the catcher fires the ball to third base. The third base umpire calls the runner out. The players for Cienfuegos assumes it is the third out and run off the field. The batter begins to return to the dugout, thinking he has struck out.

As Industriales' players on the base paths return to the dugout, their manager and the on-deck batter shout at the home plate umpire, "What is the call at home?" The umpire calls the pitch a ball. It is ball four; the batter has walked. It also means the runner thrown out trying to steal third base is not out but is forced to third base by the base on balls. So what initially appeared to be the end of the inning is now bases loaded with one out.

All three Industriales runners quickly return to their bases, but Cienfuegos remains seated in the dugout as their manager races out to argue with the umpires. He screams at the home plate umpire, gesturing toward the third base umpire. The two umpires confer and then the third base umpire signals out again. Satisfied, the Cienfuegos manager jogs off the field.

The decision appears to make no sense since it looks like the umpires have declared four outs for the inning. Whatever the interpretation, it seems the umpires do not know what had happened. Only later it became clear that the Cienfuegos manager had appealed to the third base umpire as to whether the Industriales batter had checked his swing in time or not. The umpire said he had not. The home plate umpire had not made an initial call on the pitch because he was waiting to see if there would be an appeal on the swing. With the appeal, the inning is now over.

Now it is Industriales' turn for bewilderment and anger. The entire team leaps out of the dugout and runs onto the field to argue. Fans erupt, swarming out of their seats and onto Industriales' dugout roof, which is normally off-limits. They crowd five rows deep, screaming at the umpires. Hundreds more push to get onto the already packed roof. Eddie races down the stairs to get close to the field. The fans are furious and confused as the ruling makes no sense. A fan grabs me by the front of my shirt and shouts in my face, "How can he [the third base umpire] make that call for strike three? You can't watch two plays at once." Another fan howls through the backstop, "That son of a bitch umpire used to play for Industriales fifteen years ago. Now, every call he makes goes against Industriales!"

The fans' anger continues unabated; a voice over the PA system announces that fans must calm down and return to their seats or Industriales will forfeit the game. The announcement has the opposite of its intended effect: the fans scream even louder from the dugout roof. Industriales' coaches and players, who are already on the field, turn to face the screaming horde just above their heads and plead with them. They cajole the fans to calm down, playing on their loyalty and desire to see Industriales win and pointing to the scoreboard, which shows Industriales ahead 2–1 after seven innings. A forfeit will cost Industriales any chance of catching Isla de la Juventud in the race for the final playoff spot. Their entreaties begin to have an effect, and the fans grudgingly return to their seats.

The game resumes with Cienfuegos at bat in the eighth inning. The fans chant in support of Industriales' pitcher, who is throwing a magnificent game. By the ninth inning, the crowd ratchets up the noise with each strike that he throws. He retires the side in order and Industriales' fans howl with glee. His teammates burst out of the dugout to congratulate him on the mound. Then, in response to the fans' chanting and rhythmic clapping, players and coaches turn to face the stands, tip their caps, and applaud the crowd. Their acknowledgment of the crowd's support encourages the fans to cheer even louder. Later, some fans gather at Industriales' entrance to the stadium to further applaud their heroes as they leave the stadium. The players and coaches begin to head for their homes, some in cars but many on foot. Murrieta emerges and several of us walk with him toward our homes.

The fans that associate with players are not looking to bask in their reflected glory. They see themselves as an integral part of the spectacle that is Cuban baseball. Likewise, the players acknowledge that the fans contribute to the passion play in which they compete. The relationship between the club and its supporters is based on social relationships fostered and nurtured in the neighborhoods where the players grew up and lived. Many of the most ardent supporters have known the athletes since they were little boys. In short the relationship is much more personal and human instead of one of worshipers adoring a deified figure on a pedestal. The status that Cuban baseball players enjoy is not based merely on their athletic prowess but on their presence within their communities. This has been a constant throughout Cuban baseball's long history, and was enshrined in the revolutionary era of Cuban baseball. Socialism—with low but equal wage scales imposed across the country—and the reinforcement of local pride in one's own community has kept Cuban sports heroes on a human scale. To represent one's community, whether town, province, region, or country, on the diamond is an honor and privilege, not a right, in Cuba. The handful of American tourists I encountered in Estadio Latinoamericano during my two seasons in Havana expressed nostalgia for the good old days of American baseball before free agency when Major Leaguers were approachable. Such sentiments have contributed to the interest in U.S. minor league baseball in the United States. Fans can interact with the players on a more personal basis, and a few even host players in their homes for a season. Of course, in time, the same forces that severed professional athletes from their communities in the United States could happen in Cuba. How it will all play out remains to be seen, just like each inning in baseball, wherever it is played.

Notes

1. Wenceslao Gálvez y Delmonte, *El Base Ball en Cuba* (La Habana: Imprenta Mercantil de los Herederos de Santiago S. Speneer, 1889), 98–99.
2. Gálvez y Delmonte, *El Base-Ball en Cuba*, 97.
3. The only exception to this residency regulation is the team that represents Isla de la Juventud, which has a very small population. Promising prospects are often transferred to Isla's team because one of Cuba's elite sports academies is located there.
4. All names of contemporary Cubans have been changed to protect players and coaches who talked with me from any potential reprisals that could arise because they did not have official permission from the National Commission of Baseball. While I am not aware of any players suffering such re-

criminations, this research was conducted at a time when several prominent players defected, making Cuban officials nervous about any foreigner poking around the Estadio Latinoamericano.

Recommended Reading

Baird, Katherine. "Cuban Baseball: Ideology, Politics, and Market Forces." *Journal of Sport and Social Issues* 29, no. 2 (2005): 164–83.

Brock, Lisa, and Bijan Bayne. "Not Just Black: African-Americans, Cubans and Baseball." In *Between Race and Empire: African-Americans and Cubans before the Cuban Revolution*, ed. L. Brock and D. Castañeda Fuertes, 168-204. Philadelphia: Temple University Press, 1998.

Burgos, Adrian, Jr. "Entering Cuba's Other Playing Field: Cuban Baseball and the Choice between Race and Nation, 1887–1912." *Journal of Sport and Social Issues* 29, no. 1 (2005): 9–40.

Carter, Thomas F. "Baseball Arguments: Aficionismo and Masculinity at the Core of Cubanidad." *International Journal of the History of Sport* 18, no. 3 (2001): 117–38.

———. "The Manifesto of a Baseball-Playing Country: Cuba, Baseball and Poetry in the Late Nineteenth Century." *International Journal of the History of Sport* 23, no. 2 (2005): 246–65.

Fainaru, Steve, and Ray Sanchez. *The Duke of Havana: Baseball, Cuba, and the Search for the American Dream*. New York: Villard, 2001.

González Echevarría, Roberto. *The Pride of Havana: A History of Cuban Baseball*. New York: Oxford University Press, 1999.

Jamail, Milton H. *Full Count: Inside Cuban Baseball*. Carbondale: Southern Illinois University Press, 2000.

Rucker, Mark, and Peter C. Bjarkman. *Smoke: The Romance and Lore of Cuban Baseball*. Kingston: Total Sports Illustrated, 1999.

9 | Puerto Rico

A Major League Steppingstone

Our two families moved to Puerto Rico in the years after World War II, when our fathers accepted positions in international banking and government: Frank's father the banker and Tom's an economist for Operation Bootstrap—the ambitious government program that paved the way for Puerto Rico's postwar industrialization. Frank was born in San Juan and Tom was two years old when his family embarked on a four-day voyage from Baltimore to San Juan. The ship carried lumber to help rebuild the island, which was devastated by a recent hurricane.

Growing up we were both avid followers of the Puerto Rico Winter League (PRWL), a professional league with a three-month season that began after the U.S. World Series and ended before spring training. We both attended games at Sixto Escobar and Hiram Bithorn Stadiums, home fields for the capital area's San Juan Senadorers (Senators) and Santurce Cangrejeros (Crabbers), respectively. Radio broadcasts in Spanish and newspaper coverage provided our daily dose of box scores, league standings, and player statistics.

We idolized the Crabbers and many of its native players, some of whom made names for themselves in the Major Leagues, including future Hall of Famers Roberto Clemente and Orlando Cepeda. Rubén Gómez, who pitched for the New York Giants, was the father of a grammar school classmate of Tom's, whom he remembers joining them in pickup games after school, pitching for both sides.

Our fathers took us to our first games. In 1954 Frank watched

Willie Mays get his first hit for Santurce. Throughout the game, fans taunted the opposition with whistles, cowbells, and conga drums. They waved white handkerchiefs, chanting "Ese es tu papá!" (He's your father!) as Rubén Gómez shut down the opposing batters.

Tom remembers the open betting and money changing hands through a chain of fans between the losing bettor and the winner. Fans used hand signals—e.g., five fingers up for five dollars that, say, Tony Pérez would get a hit. That was a lot of cash then, as the average worker on the island made about $1.50 an hour. The stakes were higher during a March 1965 spring training game at Bithorn Stadium between the New York Yankees and the Washington Senators. Fans a few seats away from Tom bet $10 on whether Roger Maris would swing at the next pitch; $25 whether Mickey Mantle would walk, strike out, or hit a home run; and $15 on how far Frank Howard would hit the ball in pregame batting practice.

As adults our passion for the game transformed itself into research projects on Puerto Rican baseball, which resulted in articles and several books. Interviews were conducted with many of our childhood heroes, a few quotes from which appear in this essay. First, though, a brief history of how baseball came to Puerto Rico and evolved, then how the PRWL compares to professional baseball in the United States, and finally, the status of professional baseball on the island today.

The Early Years

It is generally acknowledged that the Cubans introduced baseball to Puerto Rico shortly before the end of the Spanish-American War in 1898. A newspaper box score appearing in June 14, 1896, documented the first reported game as Borínquen, the Carib Indian name for the island, played Almendares, a team of Cuban expatriates. The newspaper deemed the game "dangerous for human beings and a silly form of entertainment."

After the Spanish-American War, military and civilian personnel from the United States arrived on the island. Soon playing venues expanded, leagues formed around the island, and teams were established in the larger public high schools and universities. American military personnel were given time off from their duties to play pickup and club games. Differences in playing styles between the local players and their American counterparts began to be noted. For example, the natives were more demonstrative and vocal, using infield chatter and offering encouragement to their pitchers and hitters.

Initially the game was played mostly by the educated middle class, but it later trickled down such that dockworkers, sugarcane hands, and farmers—of all skin tones—were also playing. By 1918 barnstorming teams from the Major Leagues and the Negro Leagues visited the island, as did Cuban All-Star teams led by legendary players Cristobal Torriente, Adolfo Luque, and Martín Dihigo, the latter being the only player in the world elected to the baseball Hall of Fame in three countries: the United States, Cuba, and Mexico.

The visiting teams exposed more Puerto Ricans to baseball and motivated Puerto Rican baseball aficionados and corporate sponsors to form Puerto Rican All-Star teams of their own, who would play in the Dominican Republic and Venezuela. Some of the new Puerto Rican clubs took their names from North American companies (e.g., Wrigley) and North American products (e.g., Buick and Sherwin-Williams), illustrating the close economic ties between Puerto Rico and the United States. Two Puerto Rican barnstormers who relocated to the Dominican Republic and Venezuela each earned the title of father of Dominican and Venezuelan baseball.

The first Puerto Rican baseball stadium with a scoreboard was San Juan's Escambrón Stadium, completed in 1932, with a seating capacity of 13,000 and clubhouses with shower facilities. It was soon renamed after the boxer Sixto Escobar, who won the world bantamweight title in 1934. The Cincinnati Reds held their 1936 spring training there and played against local Puerto Rican stars. Their presence added to the locals' knowledge of the game and appreciation of good baseball. Unlike in the United States, where the color ban was still in effect, Puerto Rico offered a convivial environment for fans and players of different racial and ethnic backgrounds. Black and white players mixed freely and often established lasting friendships.

The Middle Years

Baseball's popularity grew with the founding of the Semi-Professional

League in 1938, and two years later the professional PRWL was established. The latter featured mostly Puerto Rican players with a few Cuban and Negro Leaguers. The early stars were Hiram Bithorn, who became Puerto Rico's first big leaguer (1942 Chicago Cubs); Pedro Cepeda, a shortstop and father of the Hall of Famer Orlando Cepeda; Pancho Coímbre, outfielder with the Negro League New York Cubans in the 1940s; and Luis Rodríguez Olmo, who played for the 1943 Brooklyn Dodgers. Whereas Bithorn and Olmo's fair complexions made it possible for them to play in the pre–Jackie Robinson Major Leagues, the dark skin of Cepeda and Coímbre excluded them.

Puerto Rican fans still recall their own version of the Bobby Thompson "shot heard round the world"—the "Pepelucaso." In the seventh and deciding game of the 1950–51 island championship between perennial winner Caguas and Santurce, a record 16,700 fans packed into Sixto Escobar Stadium. The stakes were high as the winner not only would be the island champion but would earn the right to represent Puerto Rico at the Caribbean World Series in Venezuela. With the score tied at two in the bottom of the ninth and with two outs, light-hitting José "Pepe Lucas" St. Clair came to bat for Santurce. As contact was made, there was no doubt that the ball would clear the left-field fence. Pandemonium broke out in all corners of the ballpark. Caravans of fans in honking cars reveled throughout the capital city until the early morning hours. Santurce had waited twelve years for its first championship.

Playing in the United States

Puerto Ricans playing pro baseball in the United States confronted the ugly face of racism, particularly in the American South where "Whites Only" signs were evident and players of color could not stay in the same hotels as their white teammates. Víctor "Vic" Pellot Power related an incident at a restaurant where the waitress said to him, "We don't serve Negroes," to which Vic replied, "I don't eat Negroes, I eat rice and beans." In 1953 Vic was playing well in the Yankee farm system but had not gotten a call-up to the big club. "I had now been with the Yankee organization three years and [was] the American Association [AAA] batting champ. They did not bring me up. There were problems at Yankee Stadium where black people from Harlem together with Puerto Ricans picketed the stadium. This bothered the Yankees. Frequently the press would ask me why the Yankees didn't bring me up. I told them that the Yankees weren't ready for a colored person on their team."

Similarly, Saturnino Escalera was with a Cincinnati Reds farm team heading north when they stopped in Atlanta for their last spring training game. He was told blacks weren't allowed to play in Atlanta and to stay in his hotel room. When the NAACP asked him for a comment, he said, "I am not black, I am Puerto Rican."

Nicknames

In Puerto Rico players often acquire colorful nicknames that may reveal the local culture and the intimate relationship island fans enjoy with the players. Josh Gibson's moniker was "Trucutú," based on an island cartoon hero. Bob "El Múcaro" (the owl) Thurman was nicknamed for his hitting prowess during night games. Willard Brown was nicknamed "Ese Hombre" (that man) for becoming the dominant player in the post–World War II period. Some native players used a childhood nickname in their baseball career, such as Luis Rodríguez "El Jíbaro" (country boy) Olmo; Orlando Cepeda was called "Peruchín," the diminutive for "Perucho," his dad's nickname; and Juan "Igor" González was known as Igor since age ten for his interest in "Mighty Igor," a pro wrestler. Second baseman Jim Gilliam earned the sobriquet "Black Sea" since nothing eluded him, Rubén Gómez—"El Divino Loco"—had permission to ride to away games in his sportscar, instead of the team bus, and drove wildly. Nicknames of American players could be transformed in Puerto Rico. Willie Mays was the "Say Juey" (not "Say Hey") kid, since *juey* is a land crab, and Mays played for the Santurce Crabbers.

Puerto Rican team names also tell stories. For example, the Guayama Brujos (witches) referred to local residents who practiced a local form of voodoo; Aguadilla's Tiburones (sharks) referred to the prevalence of sharks off this west coast town; the Caguas Criollos' name refers to the local landed gentry; Ponce Leones (lions) came about when their team owner was photographed with a whip in his hand, appearing to be a lion tamer; Bayamón's constant traffic jams helped team officials and fans choose Vaqueros (cowboys), named after the city's "cowboy drivers"; the Carolina Gigantes derive their name from a legendary seven-foot-eight-inch native once dubbed El Gigante de Carolina; and the Manatí Atenienses (Athenians) were named after that municipality's rich cultural heritage.

Imported Players

PRWL teams have long been allowed to use "imports"—players not from Puerto Rico or the neighboring U.S. Virgin Islands. PRWL rules permitted three imports per team during the early years (1938–42) and up to ten per team from the mid-1950s to the mid-1980s when Major League clubs had working agreements with Puerto Rican teams. Each of Puerto Rico's six teams is now permitted six imports on their active roster. During the first two decades, imports mostly came from the Negro Leagues. Satchel Paige (1948) and Bob Thurman (1955) made their Major League debuts after stellar winter performances in Puerto Rico. Some later imports came from elsewhere in the Caribbean and Latin America, such as Dennis Martínez (Nicaragua), Chili Davis (Jamaica), Tony Pérez (Cuba), Manny Sanguillén (Panama), and Manny Mota (Dominican Republic). An import used to be allowed to replace a Puerto Rican big leaguer if the latter opted not to play winter ball, or got hurt.

The quality of the imports and their ability to produce for their respective clubs often determined whether a team had a winning or losing season. Reggie Jackson had already played three full MLB seasons when he arrived in Puerto Rico in 1970 to play on a team managed by Frank Robinson, who later became the first African American Major League manager. Cal Ripken Jr. was a twenty-year-old prospect when he first played in the PRWL. Ray Miller—Baltimore's pitching coach at the time—was his Puerto Rican manager, and Cal wanted to impress him and the Orioles' management.

We had a lot of big league players in Puerto Rico. A lot of the pitching was AAA, so the level was between AAA and the big leagues. So coming out of AA [1980] and AAA[1981] I had to compete at a higher level and learned quite a few things playing in the sixty-game season. . . . [I]t allowed me to reach the big leagues before I was twenty-one, and part of my goal in baseball was to reach the big leagues early and be able to play a long, long time. I don't think I'd have reached it without Puerto Rico.

Many scouts and managers believed that if a prospect could succeed in Puerto Rico, he could play in the majors. Hank Aaron went to Puerto Rico as a nineteen-year-old second baseman in October 1953. When Aaron did not hit well, there was pressure from the media and the fans to replace him with a better import. Mickey Owen, player-manager for Aaron's team, recalled,

I knew where I could get a better second baseman than Aaron. . . . [O]ne day I hit him a few fly balls and he went to them easy, and he threw good. I said, you're not an infielder, you're an outfielder. I never told Aaron how to do anything except once. I told him to hit one to right field, and he hit a bullet there.

Aaron saw Major League pitching almost every day, and after moving to the outfield he began hitting again. Aaron, who tied for the home run title and helped his club win the pennant, later said that Puerto Rico had been an important steppingstone and a confidence builder in his getting to the Major Leagues.

Tony Gwynn played two winters in Puerto Rico (1982–84) to make himself a better player:

In a sense, it's just like playing Major League baseball. . . . [T]here were so many guys down there that had so much experience, it enabled you to learn about what it was going to take to be successful at this level. . . . [A]nytime somebody asks me about winter ball, and they say they're going to Puerto Rico, I say "GO." You're going to learn a lot about the game. . . . [I]f you go down there and do your due diligence . . . there's no question that you'll come back a much better player.

Salaries, Money, and Gifts

The top PRWL imports made about $1,500 a month from the mid-1950s to mid-1960s, which after inflation is even more than today's top monthly PRWL salaries of about $4,500. Jim Northrup, for example, recalled making $1,500 per month in 1964–65, more than his $1,330 monthly salary as a rookie with the 1965 Detroit Tigers. It was common for imports to make more money than native players, at least through the 1980s when Rickey Henderson made $7,000 per month plus a Rolex watch from team management for setting the all-time PRWL single-season stolen base record.

The players could also pick up a little extra cash from fans who gave money to players for game-winning hits and fine pitching during La Epoca Romántica (the Romantic Period) of 1938–49. After Roy Campanella's grand slam in the 1940–41 final series contest, for example, excited fans put dollar bills into Campy's hand as his teammates carried him on their shoulders. Ponce's mayor ran onto the field to shake the hand of a player after he hit a game-winning homer against the New York Yankees in a 1947 spring training game, and the player enriched himself by $70 from fans passing the plate. Wilmer Fields received $125 from fans who passed money through the wire mesh at Escobar Stadium after Fields homered off Satchel Paige in 1948. When Arecibo's Claude Raymond won a tiebreaker game in 1962 to clinch a playoff spot, one fan thrust a $100 bill into his hand.

In the 1950s cash was given to the players by archrival San Juan or Santurce fans, depending on the outcome of the City Championship. Don Liddle, who pitched for the 1952–53 San Juan Senators, recalled the evening when he received cash from a fan under unusual circumstances. After besting Santurce and their ace, Rubén Gómez, Liddle received a police escort back to his apartment. As Liddle was leaving Escobar Stadium someone jerked his pants and the policeman hit the fellow with his billy club. When Liddle got to his apartment, there was $300 stuffed into the back pocket of his uniform.

Conditioning and Training

Puerto Rican ballplayers were generally smaller and less muscular than their American counterparts, though this began to change in the 1970s when better diets, improved health care, and successful social and educational programs such as Head Start were introduced. No longer do the Puerto Rican players just play infield and outfield positions. In the 2003 Major League postseason, four of the starting eight catchers were from Puerto Rico—Ivan "Pudge" Rodriguez (Marlins), Jorge Posada (Yankees), Javy Lopez (Braves)," and Benito Santiago (Giants). Of the four, only "Pudge" is under six feet tall, and his two hundred ten pounds is all muscle.

Today youngsters benefit from the expertise and experience of native professional players, coaches, and scouts who provide clinics around the island in their free time. In a 1999 interview with Frank, Jorge L. De

Posada talked about his approach to training his son, who now is the New York Yankees catcher.

I kept him [Jorge] out of little leagues until he was eleven years old because early on kids get hit with hard balls and then don't want to play anymore. Up until then, all he hit and played with was a plastic bat and rubber balls. We took it real easy until he gained confidence. When he started to play organized ball as a youngster, I never let him use an aluminum bat. Today, the "pop" he gets when he hits, and the way the ball jumps off his bat, comes from developing strong hands with the wooden bat. Later on, I also got him into cycling and bought him a rowing machine for conditioning and strong leg development.

Fans

Puerto Rican baseball fans are said to be very knowledgeable about the game, which they follow year-round. In the town *plazas, colmados* (mini grocery stores), workplaces, and homes, fans discuss the finer points of the game. They are passionate about the game as well, as the behavior of fans during one rain delay illustrates. John Strohmayer, who had pitched into the fourth inning of a 1970–71 game when a downpour halted play, recalled,

It had rained all week, so fans did not look forward to another postponement. Within 20 minutes the entire infield was covered with two inches of water . . . so everyone went into the clubhouse and started getting undressed. I put my arm in a bucket of ice. Somebody came into the clubhouse ten minutes later saying it had stopped raining. No way, anytime it rained like that in the States, the game was finished. Fans from the neighboring houses went home and got their wheelbarrows. A big pile of loam was under the stands and put to use. Work was completed forty minutes later and play resumed. That epitomizes the word "fan." I felt a lot of satisfaction when I was able to perform well—so much appreciation on the part of the fans, more so than any other place I played.

Ballparks

PRWL ballparks are similar in size and amenities to AAA ballparks in the United States (although we have not yet seen the new Roberto Clemente Walker Stadium in Carolina, nor Manatí's new Pedrín Zorrilla Stadium, named after the man who signed Roberto Clemente to his first professional contract).

Four of the six stadiums have artificial surfaces. This is an adaptation to the tropical climate that produces torrential downpours, which pose serious drainage problems on natural grass fields that in turn require the rescheduling of games, a threat to revenues. When the city of Ponce won the bid to host the 1993 Central American and Caribbean Games, it installed the first artificial surface at Paquito Montaner Stadium.

Puerto Rico's baseball stadiums now present a more corporate and less intimate appearance than they used to. Bithorn Stadium's huge amount of foul territory, for example, makes the fans feel more removed from the players. And its location in a business district on a busy highway, across from the island's first major mall, has meant congestion and parking problems. The prevalence of company signs and sponsors on today's outfield fences reinforces the corporate environment. In contrast, the old Sixto Escobar Stadium was a stone's throw from the Atlantic Ocean and was caressed by ocean breezes. With the trade winds blowing out toward left field, screwball-throwing Rubén Gómez mostly pitched right-handed batters low and away, whereas at Bithorn Stadium, when the wind came in from the outfield, Gómez threw up in the strike zone, conducive to hitting fly balls. Pine trees formed a backdrop in the outfield at Sixto Escobar, unlike the high-rise condominiums and office buildings fans now see behind the fences at Bithorn.

The clubhouse atmosphere in Puerto Rico tends to be more informal than in the U.S. Major Leagues, making it easier for journalists to converse with and interview players and managers. After a game Puerto Rican players typically go home to eat and sleep, whereas the imported foreign players stop at fast food restaurants for a snack or meal prior to returning to their apartments.

Concession stands at today's ballparks feature a standard fare of American fast foods—Pizza Hut, Taco Bell, Kentucky Fried Chicken—in addition to local products such as *platanutres* (plantain chips), *bacalaítos* (fried codfish), and rum and fruit drinks. One can still get oranges and *piraguas* (snow cones) outside the ballpark.

Recent Developments

Today Puerto Rico is less of a Major League steppingstone because U.S. Major League clubs have the option to send their top prospects to other winter leagues in the Dominican Republic, Venezuela, and Australia. And for younger prospects there is the Arizona Fall League. A greater number of native players now have the chance to play in the PRWL.

One encouraging development in Puerto Rican baseball has been the establishment of a baseball academy—a high school whose goals include the development of disciplined players and students. The brainchild of former Texas Rangers pitcher Edwin Correa, the academy produced twelve prospects in the 2004 Major League draft, the most players ever selected from one high school. With the assistance of two $200,000 grants from MLB, the academy has a strong academic component that has been missing in the academies established by Major League clubs in the Dominican Republic and Venezuela. The attainment of a solid high school education should help the Latino prospects better integrate into American professional baseball and perhaps accelerate their climb through the minor league system.

The establishment of a Major League team in San Juan has been the dream of many Puerto Rican fans and some investors. MLB helped Puerto Rico experiment with the idea when in 2003 and 2004 it scheduled the Montreal Expos to play 43 regular season games in Bithorn Stadium. The Expos were greeted with great fanfare and high expectations. Thirteen million dollars was spent to upgrade the forty-two-year-old stadium, including a new artificial surface, an expanded home clubhouse, a new scoreboard and video board, and six thousand additional seats. While average attendance at the games for both years exceeded that of Montreal's home attendance, it was far less than many had hoped for. Overall attendance was hurt by higher than usual ticket prices (ten-dollar bleacher seats to eighty-five-dollar box seats behind home plate) and a lack of big-name Latino players on some visiting team rosters. An annoying financial quirk for the Expos players was a 20 percent tax levied by the Puerto Rican legislature on all income earned while playing in Puerto Rico. Expos players were now paying income taxes in three separate countries.

Maintaining a dedicated fan base continues to be a challenge for

PRWL officials and ball club owners. They need to provide a commodity that is competitive with other local venues. Ballparks must offer reasonably priced seats, safe and accessible parking, and ancillary entertainment such as mascots, and *pleneros* (popular musical groups) in the aisles. Giveaways, free transportation from low-income housing projects, clinics for youngsters, and more televised games are all being pursued to increase the fan base and get more spectators in the seats. To capitalize on the rivalry between the Dominican Republic and Puerto Rico, a midseason interleague All-Star game has also been established.

We cherish our PRWL memories—the San Juan–Santurce City Championship, the open betting, the constant chants, discussing strategy with fans, and perhaps most of all, how our PRWL launched the big league careers of so many fine American and native ballplayers.

Bibliography

Brau, Salvador. *Historia de Puerto Rico.* Rio Piedras, Puerto Rico: Editorial Edil, 1978.

Costas, Rafael. *Enciclopedia Béisbol Ponce Leones.* Santo Domingo, Dominican Republic: Editoral Corripio, 1989.

Crescioni Benítez, José A. *El Béisbol Professional Boricua.* San Juan, Puerto Rico: First Book, 1997.

Otto, Franklin. "Playing Baseball in America: Puerto Rican Memories." *Nine* 4, no. 2 (Spring 1996): 362–76.

Van Hyning, Thomas E. *Puerto Rico's Winter League: A History of Major League Baseball's Launching Pad.* Jefferson NC: McFarland, 1995.

———. *The Santurce Crabbers: Sixty Seasons of Puerto Rican Winter League Baseball.* Jefferson NC: McFarland, 1999.

Verducci, Tom. "Puerto Rico's New Patron Saint—Like Clemente before Him, Ranger Slugger Juan González Is a Hero and an Exemplar to His Countrymen." *Sports Illustrated,* 1993.

10 | Nicaragua

In Search of Diamonds

Baseball rules the Nicaraguan airwaves, but soccer balls now ricochet in Managua's poorest barrios. I began to notice the shift in preference only a few hours after returning to Nicaragua for the first time in fifteen years. Before that, descending the plane staircase onto the steamy tarmac at Managua International Airport, the first things that struck me were the flashy advertisements on luggage carts for cell phone plans, luxury cars, and rum. As if the airport's change of name from Sandino International wasn't reminder enough that the leftist Sandinistas were no longer in charge. Nicaraguans, worn out by war with the unrelenting U.S.-funded Contras, a U.S. trade blockade, skyrocketing inflation, and political censorship, voted the revolutionary leaders out of power in 1991, ushering in a return to capitalism. Foreign investment poured into the city and the landscape of Managua was soon speckled with Radio Shacks, Pizza Huts, and Mobils on the Run.

Riding into the city behind a silent cabdriver who tailgated with only inches to spare, I was shocked by the sheer number of children and families in tattered clothes along Carreterra Norte selling cell phone covers, car mats, and other paraphernalia, and by the increased road traffic in a city that scarcely had cars in 1988.

The driver was taking me to Barrio Jonathan Gonzalez, where fifteen years earlier I had hung out with the barrio baseball team and become friends with Efrain Rosales, pitcher and manager of the squad. I had met Efrain on my first afternoon in Nicaragua, while exploring Managua on foot. I spotted him down a dirt road monitoring two boys who were playing catch with a ball of black duct tape. Although I had been researching baseball culture for twelve months in Asia and Latin America, I still felt a thrill the first time I saw someone playing baseball in a new setting. Ballparks and neighborhood sandlots were like welcome mats laid out by the local community, enabling me to connect with people more easily. After I greeted Efrain and told him about my research, he joyfully showed me his notebook, which contained a roster for his recently formed squad. Over the next two and a half months I often watched the barrio team play, attended ball games with Efrain at National Stadium, and even accompanied him to his hometown on remote Ometepe Island in Lake Nicaragua. Fifteen years later I was returning to Nicaragua to look at how baseball had changed, and I was excited about rekindling an old friendship and reconnecting with a country I'd experienced as a twenty-two-year-old, fresh out of college.

As the cab approached the barrio, I recognized nothing. The road was lined with new strip malls, gas stations, and a soon-to-open warehouse supermarket. But the barrio itself seemed more disheveled and forlorn than ever. Although I'd read how Nicaragua had slipped below Haiti to become the poorest country in the Western Hemisphere—reeling from Hurricane Mitch, famine in the countryside, and rampant political corruption—I had naively hoped that the absence of war would have improved things. But for all its harsh conditions fifteen years earlier, the barrio then had been graced with *malinche* trees that bloomed pink petals and provided shade. Farmland and open fields once bordered it, and many residents owned chickens and pigs. Now the *malinche* trees and livestock were gone, and the neighborhood was hemmed in by development—a forgotten ghetto. In poll numbers cited that week in *La Prensa* and *Nuevo Diario*, I would discover the extent of the poverty: 46 percent of Nicaraguans were underemployed or unemployed, 46 percent lived in a state of poverty, surviving on less than a dollar per day, 40 percent resided in homes without plumbing, and 30 percent were without electricity.

Unable to find the street address I had given him, the driver doubled back on a parallel dirt street and passed to the right of two metal bars in the road. They served as goal posts for some young men who were playing soccer in the road. This struck me as odd, because over nearly three months in 1988 I had never seen soccer being played in the barrio or elsewhere in the country. Instead the streets had teemed with stickball games, played with a doll's head, rolled-up masking tape, socks, or small plastic jugs for balls.

Discouraged by the driver's inability to find the street, I exited the cab at the barrio entrance and approached a young woman seated at the edge of the road. I described Efrain and his mother, Carmen. Rain started falling hard as her daughter led me through a narrow alley, turned right, and stopped in front of a well-kept corrugated hut with a fenced-in yard. The girl stood at the locked gate and called out, "Don Efrain!" After she'd made a few shouts that failed to get a response, I asked, "Are you sure this is Efrain Rosales?"

"I don't know his last name, but his first name is Efrain."

The girl's mother appeared around the corner and asked her daughter to go look for Efrain in the neighborhood. As she ran off in the rain, it suddenly let up, like someone turning off a tap. I asked the woman if she was sure it was Efrain Rosales and repeated that his mother was Carmen Rosales. She chimed in, "From Ometepe Island." She said it with such confidence that I felt joyful anticipation and relief. Then, from the distance, I saw the girl walking back with a man. I approached him slowly, still not convinced it was him. "Efrain Rosales?" I said. He nodded, looking me over unsurely. "Do you remember me? I'm Dan Gordon." With that, recognition dawned on Efrain's face. He shook my hand enthusiastically and embraced me, then invited me into his hut.

The only frills in Efrain's cramped abode were a toaster, an aging tiny black and white Sony television, and a small transistor radio, all sitting together on a workbench, and a set of kitchen knives on the wall. I'd come bearing baseball-related presents—a Red Sox yearbook, a box of baseball cards, a ball signed by Luis Tiant—figuring we would pick up where we had left off in our discussions on Nicaraguan baseball, which we'd talked about continually on my previous visit. Efrain received the gifts politely, set them down, then said that Nicaraguan baseball had fallen in popularity in recent years and that he had lost interest. Efrain had remained captain of the neighborhood team for six years, but in

1994 the team had folded when the barrio's rustic baseball diamond was paved over to make a highway. Ironically city officials christened the road Pista Dennis Martinez, after the first Nicaraguan to reach the Major Leagues and the winningest Latin American pitcher of all time. After that Efrain no longer played or followed baseball. "I followed our national team for a while and they always lost," he said. "So I said, 'Enough with that!' It didn't make me happy, so I left it."

King of Sports

Efrain's disavowal of a sport he had once loved—one that had preoccupied and sustained him through poverty and civil war—reflects a growing trend in Nicaragua. Although Nicaragua's national pastime is as popular as ever in some regions and young ballplayers from those areas are emigrating in record numbers to Major League organizations, in Managua and many other parts of the country baseball seems to have lost its meaning. Attendance has reached all-time lows and increasing numbers of young people are turning to soccer, basketball, and other sports.

Old-timers and many of those within the game, however, still view baseball as *el deporte rey* (king of sports). "Baseball here is as big as apple pie back in the States," says Anibal Vega, a veteran outfielder on the Nicaraguan national team, who was raised in California. "People here are more passionate with their baseball and they take it more seriously."

Vega plays winter ball for the Granada Tiburones and San Fernando of Masaya, two of the traditional teams in the national league. Four others are the Indios of Boer, Team Leon, Esteli, and Team Chinandega, and competition among them has evolved into highly charged rivalries.[1]

As I revisited Nicaraguan ballparks, Vega's descriptions of blissfully serene and respectful fans that on occasion turn sarcastic and rowdy resonated with me. San Fernando fans dressed in ornate Nicaraguan folkloric costumes lead the crowd at Masaya's Roberto Clemente Stadium in indigenous dancing to marimba music. When the Indios of Boer visit, fans often hurl oranges in unison at the opposing team's players—unpeeled when they wish to make a statement. The pelting grew so frequent in 1993 that league officials shut down the stadium for two weeks as punishment. In more recent years stone-throwing incidents have occurred outside the stadium, where large groups of youths from one team target fans of the other.

"Fans here love you, but they hate you," says Vega, who in 1992 helped lead San Fernando to their first national championship in fifty years. "They'll throw stuff on the fields—bottles, mango seeds, big mangos, all kinds of stuff. Sometimes you have to stop the game."

Efrain and I had experienced a more serene atmosphere at a national team exhibition game we attended in Managua in 1988. Enticing aromas filled the air from the moment we arrived at Dennis Martinez Stadium (then called Rigoberto Lopez Perez in honor of the assassin of Anastasio Somoza Garcia). On the ramp leading to the ticket gate, fans leisurely stopped to buy fried pork rinds, which were served with coleslaw and yucca on a banana leaf. In the stands, which held 30,000 fans and were often filled in those days, vendors sold mangos, coconuts, newspapers, cigarettes, chewing gum, chocolate coins, chocolate chip cookies, fried plantains, and small plastic bags of Victoria Beer (consumed by puncturing a small corner with one's teeth and sucking). The only events that seemed to get a rise out of the docile crowd were the occasional updates over the sound system of Dennis Martinez's outing that evening with the Montreal Expos and the zany dancing of the home team's batboy, Keith Taylor. Efrain told me that the batboy pretended to hex other teams. He would blow powder at them and carry around in an attaché case a wooden coffin containing an effigy that represented the team.

Because travel between the two coasts is expensive for Nicaragua's professional teams, the Atlantic Coast region rarely fields teams in the professional league. The Atlantic Series, an annual tournament between second-division teams from jungle-enclosed fishing villages along the coast, has been an outlet for baseball-loving Costeños since 1952. Rather than canceling seasons during the bloody civil war of the 1980s, teams armed themselves with rifles and white flags when they traveled through the war zone to away games.

"The Atlantic Series has a beautiful history," says Roger Taylor Mora, a former coach in Bluefields. "It's part of our culture on the Atlantic Coast." As part of an evolving fusion of the cultural pastimes of their ancestors—Miskito Indians, former slaves from the Caribbean, African Americans who resettled in the region, and European and Asian tradesmen—reggae and old-fashioned country music are played loudly and nonstop during the games; fans have been known to hold processions with coffins, toads, and candles to cast mock hexes on the local team's opponents; and players and fans good-naturedly rib one another in a mixture of English, Creole, Miskito, and Spanish.

Evolution of a Game

In 1888 an American named Albert Adlesberg introduced Atlantic Coast cricket players to baseball. At the time, the Mosquito Coast was a British protectorate with a strong cricket tradition. Adlesberg, a lumber trader who routinely visited Bluefields, assumed correctly that locals would adapt well to a sport that called on similar throwing and batting abilities. Initially the locals played barehanded using balls made from the sap of rubber trees and tree limbs as bats. Then Adlesberg returned from a trip to New Orleans with balls, bats, and gloves. By 1889 the first two clubs, White Rose and Southern, were formed, representing the northern and southern barrios of Bluefields. A league developed and baseball immediately upstaged cricket as the region's favorite pastime.

Three years after baseball took root along the Caribbean coast, a few dozen Nicaraguan youths from the Pacific Coast cities of Granada and Managua, who were studying in universities in the United States, brought home baseball equipment and formed clubs. Few details are known of Pacific Coast baseball during this era. The local newspapers did not regularly carry sports pages until the 1920s and the teams did not have scorekeepers. One of the earliest recorded traces of baseball was a prolonged, fierce campaign in the Managuan newspaper *El Duende* in 1893 to ban baseball. Newspaper editor Juan de Dios Matus argued that the game was too common in the streets and posed a threat to pedestrians. Soon after city officials in Managua and Granada prohibited street baseball. But when Jose Santos Zelaya took over the country in a coup in 1893, one of his first moves to win over the public was to lift the ban.

Around the turn of the century, baseball teams sprung up throughout the Pacific Coast region. The vast majority derived their names from geographical locations or countries at war during the era: Boer, Japon, Russia, America, Manchester, Waterloo, Chile, Argentina, Paris, New

York, and Chicago. In response to the high demand for baseball equipment, a Managua harness maker unstitched a glove one of the ballplayers had imported from the United States, studied its design, and began producing waterproof gloves made from the rubberized seats in horse carriages.

The U.S. occupation of Nicaragua from 1912 to 1933 accelerated the spread of baseball. Twenty-seven hundred U.S. Marines landed in the country to protect U.S. fruit, mining, and transportation interests from a popular uprising and preserve the ruling Conservative government. Taking advantage of the curiosity and enthusiasm of Nicaraguan youth when the troops played baseball among themselves, military leaders set up children's leagues and tournaments in Managua's barrios. The first recorded international game in 1914, between Boer, the most famous team in the history of Nicaraguan baseball, and a group of ballplayers from the U.S. military ship *Denver*, resulted in a 6–5 victory for the home team. In *The American Review of Reviews* in 1916, Clifford D. Ham (collector general of customs in Nicaragua) described the efforts of the Marines to popularize the sport as a "step towards order, peace and stability."[2]

While the success of the U.S. campaign is debatable, baseball fever continued to grip the nation. Among the Pacific Coast stars of the era were pitcher Julian Amador (nicknamed the "White Ape"), who won 24 consecutive games for the famous club San Fernando of Masaya. Far and away the biggest stars from the Atlantic Coast region were the brothers Jorge and Stanley Cayasso. Their barnstorming tour of the Pacific Coast in the early 1930s was part of what Nicaraguan baseball historians identify as the catalyst for modern baseball in Nicaragua. As I sat with ninety-four-year-old Jorge Cayasso, both of us in rocking chairs in his tidy cement home, behind a boxing gym his family had set up, he described the arrival in the West of his team, Navy, from the Atlantic Coast to play the first ever series of games between the Caribbean Coast and Pacific Coast players. "We are a poor people," noted Jorge, with the widest of grins. "No resources. But I'm going to tell you something. I played catcher, pitcher, third baseman, and whatever position. I just wanted to play."

Navy had set out for the Pacific Coast intending just to see the world.

As a gimmick, they named themselves after a branch of the military and sported sailor caps. Many of the Navy ballplayers were also jazz musicians—including Jorge, who played banjo and guitar. They played ball during the day against the Pacific Coast teams and jazz at night on the bandstand at the municipal marks. Their music caused a sensation, and Pacific Coast residents took to dancing in the park. Few had experienced their fluid and happy style of music or heard the strumming of a banjo. The Pacific Coast people saw the player-musicians of Navy as exotic. When they walked in the streets with their sailor uniforms and black skin, people followed them. On the playing field, they became known for their elegance, athleticism, and speed. When the country formed its first national team for the 1935 Central American Games in El Salvador, many of the former Navy players were selected. Although Nicaragua finished the tournament tied for second place with Panama, Jorge Cayasso tied for first in hitting and finished second in home runs. But the team that became etched in the consciousness of Nicaraguans was the national squad in 1938—not so much for their performance at the Central American Games in Panama, but for the adventurous four-day journey that brought them there. The journey started by train then continued by ferry. But their ferry caught fire and sank off the north coast of Costa Rica. As a result, the squad had to travel by horse through the jungle to San Jose, and finally by train to Panama. Bayardo Cuadra, a noted Nicaraguan baseball historian, feels the journey created a sense of national pride and mythic identification with Nicaraguan ballplayers that still exists today. "That was the primitivism of baseball—the efforts of athletes with very little travel money," said Cuadra. "The country identified with their sacrifice to persevere and represent their country."

Pipeline to the Pros

On the sleepy grounds of Jackie Robinson Stadium, Calixto Vargas, a national hero, runs one of a handful of baseball academies for Nicaraguan prospects. Although I'd never heard of Vargas prior to my first visit to Nicaragua, his name had been brought up so often in baseball history conversations in 1988 that I felt honored fifteen years later to have the opportunity to interview him. Vargas had starred on the much-celebrated national team that defeated Team Cuba in the 1972

Amateur World Series. In 2000 Vargas set up the academy for the Houston Astros, but the club backed out two years later as part of cutbacks in their Latin American scouting operations. Vargas switched caps and now signs players, teaches them, and, when he thinks they're ready, invites a scout to watch them play. If they sign, Vargas takes 15 percent of the signing bonus (much less than the *buscónes* of the Dominican Republic). I watch him working with all positions, showing shortstops how to field, critiquing the pitchers' pick-off moves, refining the jumps ballplayers take for stolen bases. While youths are running laps under the intense mid-afternoon sun, Vargas sits down in the stands to talk with me. Beads of sweat run down his forehead. Butterflies are gliding over the field, cicadas are humming, a bulldozer on adjacent land is leveling trees for a new soccer field. To date, eleven of his students have signed on with Major League teams. Vargas points to a lanky youth who is long-tossing in the outfield. "This one, Lester Hernandez Espinoza, is about to sign with the Padres. I converted him from first baseman to pitcher, because he's tall and has the body for a pitcher."

Vargas whistles over Espinoza and tells him it will be good training to talk to me so he'll have experience when he has to deal with the baseball beat writers. The lanky seventeen-year-old tells me he's from Barrio 14 de Septiembre and played Little League for his neighborhood team. He dropped out of baseball for a while because he couldn't afford a pair of shoes and needed to help out his father, who owns a tailor shop. At age fifteen, his coach invited him to come back. The coach called Vargas and told him they had a tall youth with the body of a ballplayer. Two years later Espinoza had signed a contract. "My goal is not just to sign," says Espinoza. "I want to arrive at the dream of all Nicaraguans, which is to play professional baseball—to have money to help my family."

I thank him for his time, and Vargas walks over eighteen-year-old pitcher Ron Montierro, who sits with me and tells me that in his hometown, Diriamba, a small town about twenty miles south of the capital, many talented players don't know there is a baseball school. "Now I have the opportunity to improve," he says. "But there are many who don't have the opportunity and are very good ballplayers, too."

After Montierro jogs back to his workout, Vargas laments that he is one of the only individuals providing technical instruction to Nicaraguan youth. "This country can't advance, because by ourselves we can't elevate the level of baseball in this country," he says. "Thirty-eight Nicaraguan players are currently under contract with Major League organizations. This country needs a few hundred players signed for baseball to climb." Vargas travels all over to find his players. He hosts a national radio sports talk program and people often call in to invite him to check out a youth. He is known for stopping his car whenever he sees a teenager who is six feet or taller to ask if he plays baseball. Whatever the boy's response, he says, "Come to my camp and I'll teach you how to pitch so you will have a chance to play professional baseball in the States." Very rarely does a ballplayer refuse the offer. The typical signing bonus with a Major League club is more than they might make in a lifetime in Nicaragua.

Twelve Major League clubs employ Nicaraguan baseball stars or well-known journalists as bird dogs. Their job of convincing prospects is easy not only because signing may be a Nicaraguan youth's only way out of poverty but because it may give the ballplayer notoriety. Reaching AAA makes him a national celebrity. Players who have the proverbial cup of coffee in the Major Leagues are anointed as folk heroes. One can imagine Vicente Padilla's flight to stardom when he soared to the majors less than four months after his debut in the minors, never mind his breakout season three years later with the Philadelphia Phillies. Newspapers ran daily coverage: game highlights, reports on his condition the next day, quotes on his abilities, and speculation about his next pitching matchup. In Padilla's hometown of Chinandega, local radio personality J. J. Hernandez greets callers with "Where Vicente goes . . ." The caller responds, "The people go." I sat in the studio for Hernandez's popular local sports radio program *Ahi Deportivo*. During the course of an hour, several local Little League coaches popped into the studio to solicit donations on air for gasoline to take a team to a regional tournament, local anesthesia for a ballplayer, and gloves (the team only had three). Vicente Padilla's mother, Florentina Ordoñez, appeared in the studio later in the show with a cash donation to cover the requests. Her son is deeply admired in the community for donating medicine to hospitals and establishing scholarships for students. He grew up in the outskirts of Chinandega in abject poverty. By age seven, he was forced to work full-time cutting undergrowth with a machete on a banana plantation. Perhaps because Padilla hasn't forgotten the similar plight of fellow Chinandegans, Nicaraguans often praise his humility in the same sentence in which they extol his accomplishments.

"Vicente is an example for others in the community," says Gerardo Acuña Palma, Vicente's coach in Mayor A Ball (the Nicaraguan equivalent of Legion Post Ball). "He inspires the other youth, who see where he was born, how was his life, how he behaves, and wish to be just like him."

Enrique Armas, one of the country's most popular radio sports broadcasters, clearly demonstrated the grip that Padilla has on the country. As we were driving through the hilly southwestern outskirts of Managua toward the studios of Radio Nicaragua, past the jarring squalor of Barrio Hialeah, which seemed to stretch onward indefinitely, he turned on the radio, then switched from one FM station to the next. All stops on the dial were broadcasting that evening's Philadelphia Phillies–Atlanta Braves matchup, in which Padilla was starting. Armas explained that every station had its own team of broadcasters, who were watching the game on ESPN from their studios and rendering it in Spanish for their listeners. He added that on nights when ESPN did not broadcast games, the broadcasters re-created the game from telephone descriptions of the action by colleagues in the States.

On the air on Radio Nicaragua, Ivan Ruiz, a former manager of the national team, tells me, "Remember that Vicente is a star of Nicaragua and everyone follows him here. Wherever there's a radio signal, his games are transmitted." I sit in as a guest in the studio with Armas, Ruiz, and several other well-known Nicaraguan baseball personalities. And as they call the game with no pretension that they are anywhere other than in front of a television—although, to their credit, it sounds very much like they're in a broadcasting booth at Atlanta's Turner Field—they break down obscure stats such as the percentage of batters who reach base by bunting against Padilla, refer to the action in past Padilla outings, remind listeners of the probable date of Padilla's next outing, and occasionally ask me about my local team, the Boston Red Sox, displaying a knowledge of the roster and team statistics that would impress any Red Sox fan.

The journey to Padilla's hometown to see the baseball academy of Enrique Gasteazoro was one of the most poignant times of my return trip to Nicaragua. Gasteazoro, a thirty-seven-year-old banana plantation owner, had arranged for his personal assistant to drive me in his BMW. Riding in this air-conditioned, state-of-the-art vehicle, passing dusty dilapidated barrio entrances and hundreds of impoverished passersby, felt excessive and unjust. One observation I'd often made on this second visit to the country was just how the chasm between haves and have-nots seemed to have dramatically widened since my previous trip. Enrique Gasteazoro, Enrique Armas, Roger Taylor Mora, and several other *beisbolistas* lived in Barrio Villa Fontana, a walled-off neighborhood of elegant two-story homes with servants and pristine lawns overlooking the impoverished sprawl of Barrio Hialeah. The upper-middle class in Managua expanded after the Sandinistas lost power and factory owners returned from exile. The number of impoverished barrios in the capital also seemed to have increased exponentially, rendering my 1988 city map useless.

Tito Rondon, a former Los Angeles Dodgers broadcaster and retired managing editor of *La Prensa*, felt that class division has harmed the national pastime. As he spoke to me by phone from his home in Miami, he described baseball before the revolution as a sport loved by rich and poor. Some of the best-known players came out of the upper class, and the game was the only activity that united all the social classes, the two coasts, and different ethnic groups. "It was the cultural glue that was holding Nicaragua together," he said. "Now all the rich people have cable and the Major Leagues on ESPN and don't give a hoot about playing or following the [winter] league. And the only ones who follow the game are the poor kids who play because they want to go to the States, not for the love of it."

As Gasteazoro's car passed beyond the city limits, I reacquainted myself with the rural landscape that is the pride and joy of Nicaraguans. Along the Carreterra Norte is a world that, to the naked eye, global capitalism seems to have left untouched. One passes majestic volcanoes, jagged hills, mahogany tree farms, sugarcane fields, farms that produce thatch for roofs, people lingering in the yards of their shanty huts in the shade of *malinche* trees that line the road, and villages with ham-

10. *In a small, poor village outside of Matagalpa, Nicaragua, children use makeshift equipment to play baseball. During the 1980s aid poured in from around the world to help the people of Nicaragua. Along with medical supplies, school supplies, clothes, and farm equipment was an occasional baseball bat, ball, or glove.* (Photo by Paul Tick.)

mock shops and roadside stands that sell tortilla with queso de mantequilla. In these communities, soccer is only a game and baseball is still the center of the universe. In Leon and Chinandega, the ballparks fill nightly, *pelota de calcetin* (stickball with a homemade ball made from a tightly wound sock) is common, and the locals strongly believe that because most males work with a machete, they have forearm strength, which makes them far better ballplayers. In 2001 Gasteazoro parceled off a section of his *finca* Teresa to build a tropical field of dreams. The first rural-based academy challenged a popular mode of thinking that those born into poverty and farming remain impoverished farmers. At the inauguration of the field, the mayor of neighboring El Viejo announced that he hoped the ball field would help area youth abandon vices such as alcohol, drugs and gangs.

Befitting his role as the most accomplished ballplayer in Nicaraguan history, Dennis Martinez set up a more ambitious model for teaching baseball to children in May 2004. The academy was born out of an article the Granada native read in 2003 that the majority of Nicaraguan males between the ages of fourteen and twenty-five had dropped out of school. During the tryout session, Martinez asked prospects if they attended school. Many ballplayers told him that they had left school to help their parents survive. He decided at this point that the academy would assist students in attending school and university and require all ballplayers to attend school. "I came up with the idea to help in any way that I can," said Martinez. "We have to prepare them, because until now we have forgotten about our youth and they are our future."

Bringing Home Talent

One hope in Nicaraguan baseball circles is that the youth who are signing and going to the United States to play professional baseball will soon raise the standard of play and level of conditioning at home. Returning ballplayers are like returning migrants who bring back lots of new ideas about how to improve things. They also bring back capital, which gets invested or spent in the home country. Sometimes they have considerable capital if they've made it to the Big Leagues, which can result in an upgrading of the local baseball scene at home.

Nicaraguan baseball historians maintain that the winter league's absorption of players first from visiting Atlantic Coast teams and later from abroad greatly improved the quality of play. In the 1930s Cuban and Dominican players—many of whom had been visiting the country on barnstorming tours—stayed in the Pacific and shared their knowledge of the game. Nicaraguans suddenly found that they could hold their own in international play. During World War II, Albrook Field, a ball club consisting of U.S. soldiers stationed in Panama, came to Nicaragua to play a series of games against the local teams and the national team. Terry Moore, who had been an All-Star center fielder for the St. Louis Cardinals before the war, was the star attraction, and Nicaraguans were thrilled to have a flesh-and-blood Major Leaguer on their soil. Hundreds flocked to the airport to greet the Americans as they landed.

After a poor performance in the 1948 Amateur World Series, Nicaragua's baseball authorities decided to take the sport to the next level by hiring a North American to coach the national team. Andres Espolita was a young man with a modern vision of baseball. He strongly believed in scouting new talent and setting up training camps around the country to develop talent. The arrival of a second wave of talent from the Atlantic Coast was due in large part to the work of Espolita.

Many of these players were adopted by Cinco Estrellas (five stars), the National Guard's ball club, whose name was derived from the Anastasio Somoza Garcia's status as a five-star general. The National Guard hoarded some of the country's best players, hiring and paying them as privates and promoting them to a higher rank if they played well. While Somoza divorced himself from the day-to-day operations of the team, he was an ardent fan of the team and of the game in general. Years before entering politics he had organized his own youth league team. In 1948 he named himself manager of the Nicaragua national team to put a fire in the belly of the players, although he let his staff take care of the baseball. Noted for their tremendous discipline, Cinco Estrellas dominated the baseball scene from the 1940s through the 1970s.

The 1950s and 1960s ushered in a new era with the emergence of professional baseball in Nicaragua. The Liga Professional en Nicaragua was founded in 1956 under the premise that foreigners needed to be brought in as a gate attraction. Nicaraguan ball clubs made working arrangements with Major League teams and imported prospects who needed seasoning before making the leap to the big leagues. Before it folded in 1967, the league had hosted scores of ballplayers who had played or would go on to play in the Major Leagues. Among the notables were Ferguson Jenkins, Luis Tiant, Cookie Rojas, Bert Campaneris, Marv Throneberry, Lou Piniella, Phil Regan, Jim Kaat, George Scott, Zoilo Versalles, and Ron Hansen. "One would see lines of children in the hotels and at the practices watching the players," says baseball historian Julio Miranda. "It was a magical period for us and unforgettable."

Declining Popularity

Under a *malinche* tree on the disheveled sidewalk of a posh Managua side street, Efrain shares with me more of his thoughts on the current state of Nicaraguan baseball. Efrain is on duty as a night watchman for the private residence behind us. Bats are circling above and periodically knock small fruit off the *malinche* tree overhanging the street, and lightning is eerily flashing in the southwest night sky.

"The sport is almost dead!" says Efrain. "The state of baseball right now is like a house where the front is kept clean, but the inside is dirty. Vicente Padilla is pitching well for our country and there are many youths signing. But in the Little Leagues, there is no support, so players can't develop."

Efrain and I are grateful for the opportunity to catch up. He picks a beautiful pink blossom from the tree and tells me he recently planted a *malinche* tree in his yard. He says the fruit in his yard will eventually grow large and he will have to trim the tree with a machete.

Efrain says he understands why I follow baseball—because it's my career, because I write about baseball. I tell him that I also follow baseball because it's a beautiful sport. The field is beautiful, the action is beautiful, and there are so many stories and things to talk about. My first memory of baseball is of my father, who passed away recently, taking me to Fenway Park and pointing out Rico Petrocelli's footwork at third base between pitches. Efrain smiles and nods. "I understand that," he says. "In reality, it's not that I don't have interest. The truth is that it's just hard these days to follow."

Although I had a tight interview schedule and I was unable to revisit others I'd befriended in 1988, many of whom no longer lived in the same neighborhoods, it felt deeply meaningful to be seated again with Efrain. We speak of our futures. Efrain has recently divorced and vows he will soon remarry. He preaches to me that I need to settle down and get married. He also thinks I should write a book about the poverty in Nicaragua—about fatherless children selling food in the streets that was plucked out of the trash, about how some kids end up addicted to sniffing glue and fumes from the gasoline pumps. He says that one twelve-year-old girl from the barrio walks around naked to advertise herself as a prostitute. "It's the story of how we're living in Nicaragua," he says. "I have a plan to build three huts in my yard, which I could rent out to others," he says. "That might prevent me from dying of starvation someday."

Fifteen years earlier Efrain had been almost as pessimistic about poverty under the Sandinistas. The government supplied him with rice, but inflation had made other goods such as a bar of soap unaffordable. On countless occasions Efrain had waxed ecstatic about his childhood as a batboy in the Mayor A League on Ometepe Island, where the community gathered around the diamond on Sundays and picnicked afterward with food brought over in carts by the visiting team. Many islanders had told me that the peak year for Mayor A baseball on the island was 1972, the same year that the national team upset Cuba, the Nicaraguan equivalent of the U.S. Olympic hockey team's victory over the Soviets in 1980. Any Managuan who was around during that era would remember the hail of bullets fired in the air all over the city after the final out. For days after the game, Nicaraguans dragged tin cans through the streets. The celebration was short-lived however, as a few days later the city was shaken by a powerful earthquake that killed as many as 10,000 Managuans. Partially collapsed buildings still litter the landscape of downtown Managua more than thirty years later. Eight days after the quake, Hall of Famer Roberto Clemente passed away when his plane, which was carrying relief supplies to the Nicaraguan people, crashed off the coast of his native Puerto Rico. Clemente's altruism is memorialized in Nicaragua with eleven schools named in his honor and his uniform number retired. But when most people in Nicaragua refer to the year 1972, they speak glowingly of the victory over Cuba.

How could a country so in love with baseball grow weary of it? I posed the question to Carlos Garcia, president of the Nicaraguan Federation of Amateur Baseball (FENIBA), a private nonprofit that oversees all levels of Nicaraguan baseball, from the national team all the way down to Little League ball. Called strong-willed and stubborn, charismatic and shrewd, futuristic and old school, and a slew of other flavorful descriptives by fellow Nicaraguan *beisbolistas*, Garcia is one of the most accomplished and controversial figures in the history of modern Nicaraguan baseball. He began making waves in 1959 by spearheading an eventually successful movement to make baseball an Olympic sport. Three years after the demise of the 1967 professional league, Garcia breathed new life into the game by inaugurating an amateur league with Bob Feller throwing out the first pitch and Joe DiMaggio at the plate. When the

Sandinistas took power, Garcia was accused of treason and thrown in jail. Like so much of Nicaraguan political history, the truth behind his arrest is complicated. Garcia explains that the Sandinistas may have felt threatened by his ties to North American professional baseball and his stature in the international baseball community. Historians point out that his public criticisms of the policies of the Sandinistas and former ties with Somoza may have sealed the deal. After four and a half years in jail, Garcia was released from prison and moved to the United States, where he organized the Nica League, which Garcia refers to as "the Nicaraguan National League in Exile." The league consisted of municipal leagues of Nicaraguan Americans in Los Angeles, Houston, New York City, San Francisco, and Miami, and an annual national championship in front of a packed house at Bobby Maduro Stadium in Miami. Following a change of government, Garcia returned to his homeland in 1990 and was promptly elected president of FENIBA.

"I believe that baseball can sell, but here in Nicaragua there is a problem of sports culture," Garcia tells me. We're seated in his windowless office in National Stadium, where photos of Dennis Martinez and former president Ronald Reagan hang on the wall behind him. Occasionally, his attractive secretary walks into the office with a memo and as she leans over his desk each time he asks for a peck on the cheek. "Young people no longer want to play Little League—which not only teaches baseball, but how to think and learn better. Our main purpose is to develop ballplayers, but there's a cultural fence that impedes us from doing this."

Critics contend that responsibility for the disappearance of Little Leagues falls squarely on Garcia's shoulders. They argue passionately that the demand for Little League baseball has dipped slightly but still exists, and that FENIBA's resources are spread too thin and Garcia no longer earns the trust of investors. And the lack of investment is extinguishing baseball at all levels. The national team has had its most desperate budget shortfalls and the country's best players turn down the opportunity to play on the team because the salaries are well beneath their standard of living.

Nemesio Porras, who three years earlier had announced his "retirement" at the age of thirty-one from the national team, estimated that salaries for the team were half of what they were in the mid-1990s. Seated behind a desk enveloped by trophies in the back room of his Esso gas station in Barrio Altamira, the most accomplished first baseman in Nicaraguan baseball history explained that playing six months on the national team during the winter league off-season would leave him far worse-off than tending to his gas station. "I would have liked to have continued, but unfortunately one must work so that my family and I can build a future. Baseball is the most beautiful thing, but it's momentary."

Baseball officials often accuse the players of being anti-patriots, says Willie Wilson, a popular Costeño who starred for Boer and Cinco Estrellas in the early 1970s and now has his own daily sports talk radio program. When Carlos Garcia inaugurated the First Division league in 1970, the owners of the teams gave players jobs. Wilson and his teammates worked four hours in the morning at the brewery that owned Boer, then practiced from 2:00 to 5:00 p.m. Games were held on weekends—one game on Saturdays, a doubleheader on Sundays. Gradually the owners discovered they were turning a profit at the gates and by 1972 they had pulled players from the factories and said they would pay them just to play. But from 1972 to the present—with the exception of the Sandinista era—it has been an era of frustration for players. "Our problem is we are not amateur and not professional," said Wilson. "Carlos tells you you're only amateur and can't make more money. But the player lives off of baseball, and if you don't have money in this poor country, you have a lot of problems."

Nicaraguan sports journalists have hard-hitting theories on why the money is lacking. In 2003 many told me that Garcia's lessening stature at home and abroad has hurt his ability to raise capital for the league. With the high turnover of owners of Major League teams, Garcia no longer has the ties he once had with the big leagues. Garcia was close friends with the O'Malley family, longtime owners of the Los Angeles Dodgers. They would often visit the country and sponsor tournaments. In 1992 the ball club built Dodgers Friendship Stadium, a Dodger blue Little League ballpark on the grounds of the former Somoza mansion. But when the team changed hands in the 1990s, Garcia lost a funding source. In the 1990s Garcia also had close ties with President Arnoldo

Aleman, who helped invest in teams. And some in the media argue that the current administration of President Enrique Bolanos does not sympathize with the sports world simply because of Garcia's past loyalty to the former corrupt administration.

As for the scarcity of children's baseball, part of the blame also rests on the Sandinistas—or perhaps on the decade-long war that prevented the Sandinistas from achieving their most ambitious social policies. Tens of thousands of youth were sent off to the front lines, fled the country, or went into hiding out of fear of being scooped up and thrown unprepared into the war zones, facing rebels with advanced training and weaponry from the United States.[3] Likewise, leagues that were in the planning stages couldn't be implemented due to lack of funds. Attempts at stabilizing a weak cordoba sent inflation soaring, which suddenly made baseball an exorbitantly expensive game to play. In 1988 I had witnessed firsthand the cost of a baseball skyrocket to 600 cordobas, which at the time worked out to about one month's salary for the average Nica. Efrain's barrio team had owned only a few pieces of equipment and had no league to support it. Their plan to buy more equipment relied on placing wagers with opposing teams on the games they played.

Modeling the Cuban system, the Sandinistas abolished high school sports programs with the intention of setting up special high schools for top athletes that would train them in their respective sports. However, none of these schools materialized, perhaps again because of lack of resources, and high school baseball was lost and has little hope of returning soon, given the country's impoverished education system.[4]

By contrast, many veteran Nicaraguan baseball personnel yearn for their 1980s way of life. The Sandinistas supported national and local teams and sponsored winter and summer league teams (even an Atlantic Coast team for a gallant two-year stretch), ensuring that a significant number would stay afloat from one season to the next. They hired retiring athletes as physical education instructors, invested in Little Leagues and maintained them year-round, kept homegrown talent at home, and ensured health care for all, including athletes. If a player performed well in an international tournament, he would be given a house, and a new car might show up on his doorstep as well. Attendance was also higher, as fans appreciated the stability. "In the 1980s, the stadiums were full because baseball followed only one course," said Gerald Hernandez of *La Prensa*. "Nobody exited the league because it was prohibited. So there was more enthusiasm in the league and more interest."

I sat down to chat with Hernandez and his managing editor, Edgard Rodriguez, about the state of baseball in Nicaragua in their office at *La Prensa*. Being in the building brought back unsettling memories. Fifteen years earlier, the Sandinista government shut down the newspaper and deported three U.S. diplomats from the U.S. Embassy, with accusations that both institutions incited civil unrest. I had been visiting the remote town of Matagalpa, in the Central Highlands, on the day the events unfolded, and found myself panicking. Here I was in the middle of a war-ravaged country and the government was openly bearing down on freedom of the press, one of the most sacred civil liberties in the States, and although I suspected from past precedent that the U.S. Embassy was guilty as charged, I also knew it as a refuge for American citizens. Looking back on those events and remembering the routine news stories of deadly Contra ambushes of civilian vehicles and Sandinista use of civilians as shields reminded me that being in Nicaragua at that time was a frightening experience.

Rodriguez, who is a part-time scout for the New York Yankees, had been a sports reporter with the left-leaning major daily *Nuevo Diario* at the time. Hernandez had been in secondary school in the late 1980s and a sports beat writer since 1996. As Hernandez showed me on his personal Web site the baseball statistical discrepancies from year to year due to variations in the length of the season, Rodriguez chimed in that these inconsistencies are a longstanding problem in Nicaraguan baseball and reflect Carlos Garcia's disregard for the passionate baseball fan. Rules change from one year to the next, players and coaches involved in scandals such as fixing games are only minimally punished, teams do not market themselves and license their logos for caps, and statistics are not made public. As an example, he tells me that the national team had played in a tournament in Honduras three days before and the newspaper still didn't have statistics from this game.

Hernandez explained that soccer is on the rise because the sport caters to the interests of fans. For instance, they have already forwarded to the newspaper their schedule for the upcoming season, whereas baseball doesn't even know yet how many teams will be fielded. He adds that FIFA (the international soccer federation) recently presented to the Nicaraguan soccer federation a grant for one million dollars over four years to be used toward hiring instructors from abroad and building a new soccer stadium in Managua and a soccer academy in Diriamba. "FIFA gives money to help Nicaraguan sports," says Hernandez. "The international baseball community gives nothing."

Sports journalists are quick to point out that while most fans prefer baseball (seven out of ten fans, according to a 2003 *La Prensa* poll), they're attending soccer matches in droves. Cable television has positioned the game as stylish and in certain towns like Esteli, games are played before packed stadiums. "We are passing through a critical moment," said Willie Wilson. "You go to a soccer game and see four, five, six thousand people in the stadium, and the next day people are saying, 'Oh, soccer is knocking out baseball.' Baseball has a problem."

Baseball journalist Edgard Tijerino tells me it may just be a fad. He recalls that when the professional league ended in 1967, people followed soccer until the spectacular inauguration of Carlos Garcia's league in 1970. Tijerino tells me that the current dip in popularity is due to economics, the availability of cable TV, which allows fans to watch games from home, and the nation's uncomfortable ballparks. "The game is passing through rough times," he said, "but I think it will persevere."

For Jose Dolores Membreño Garcia the dip in popularity of baseball is a year-round worry. He's on the Little League board of directors for the small rural town of Nindiri, which is playing for a national Little League tournament title. "Williamsport," as the locals call this tournament, is a four-team competition. The winner moves on to the Dominican Republic to play in the Latin American championship—the winner there earns a spot at the Little League National Tournament in Williamsport, Pennsylvania. Membreno's son is a second baseman on the Nindiri squad. As I sit with the proud father in the stands of Dodgers Friendship Stadium, he tells me how area businesses used to give money to the league, but now they give only to the regional soccer league. The team has managed to scrounge the money for the tournament from donations by people in town. He tells me the kids nowadays have to practice with sponge baseballs, which are less expensive.

As we talk, it seems like the crowd is coaching the players, who are indeed listening to the crowd's instructions. About fifty people are in attendance, including a large contingent of women sitting together. Many are also advising the umpire: "He didn't touch home!" "Umpire, he's pitching without his foot on the rubber!" "Change umpires!" A man with an ice cream cart rings his bell from time to time. Another vendor sells plastic bags of water.

As the game comes to an end, the people in attendance file out, crossing two planks of wood that take them over a dried-up stream. Membreno and I stay in the stands watching many of the kids from both teams, who have decided that they would play another game for fun. The pitcher from 14 de Septiembre is kneeing the ball like a soccer ball as they hash out the rules. Several of the players are wrestling with a boy to keep him from running the bases.

"It's beautiful to watch the field," I say. Membreno nods and smiles.

As the pickup game starts, the kids argue and discuss each play. We chuckle at one point when it seems like all the kids on the field are talking at the same time. Membreno nods approvingly and says, "That's how they learn."

Notes

1. The number of teams in the league varies from year to year.
2. Ham, "Americanizing Nicaragua," 188.
3. An estimated thirty thousand people lost their lives during the war.
4. A 2003 poll by M&R and Associates found that 823,000 Nicaraguan children don't even have access to a school system, 32 percent of the schools that do exist don't have electricity, and 29 percent of schools don't have running water.

Bibliography

Arrellano, Jorge E. *El Doctor David Arellano*. Managua, 1993.

Garcia, S., Carlos J. *Resena de cien Anos de Beisbol en Nicaragua*. Managua, 1991.

Ham, Clifford D. "Americanizing Nicaragua: How Yankee Marines, Financial

Oversight and Baseball Are Stabilizing Nicaragua." *American Review of Reviews* 53, no. 2 (1916): 185–91.

Rondon, Tito. "Historia del Beisbol en Nicaragua: Aparecen en enscena Titan y San Fernando." *La Prensa*, February 21, 2000.

———. "Historia del Beisbol en Nicaragua: Los Comienzos." *La Prensa*, February 7, 2000.

———. "Historia del Beisbol en Nicaragua: Los Primeros Pasos; Nace el Boer." *La Prensa*, February 14, 2000.

———. "Historia del Beisbol en Nicaragua: La Primera Liga." *La Prensa*, February 28, 2000.

Ruiz Borge, Martin. *Records Victoria del Beisbol Nicaraguense de Primera Division*. Managua, 1993.

Tijerno Mantilla, Edgar. *El Mundial Nica*. Managua, 1993.

CARLOS AZZONI, TALES AZZONI, &
WAYNE PATTERSON

11 | Brazil

Baseball Is Popular, and the Players Are Japanese!

For the better part of its first century, Major League Baseball players were predominantly from the United States, with only a handful having learned their skills in a few neighboring countries such as Canada, Mexico, and Cuba.[1] Since the 1970s, however, one country after another has made its presence in MLB: Puerto Rico, Venezuela, Colombia, Nicaragua, Panama, the Dominican Republic, Curaçao, and, further afield, Australia, the Netherlands, Japan, South Korea, and Taiwan. Indeed, today's Major Leaguers come from nineteen different countries.

This chapter documents the emergence of a new country-Brazil—into the spectrum of professional baseball, one that is surprising in many ways. What is unique about Brazil's emergence in professional baseball can be expressed in three observations:

1. Baseball (*beisebol*) has developed in a country that is the leader in the world's most popular sport—soccer.
2. Baseball has developed into a major sport with almost no input from the United States.
3. Virtually all of the players from this country are of Japanese heritage; in effect the game has been imported from Japan.

Although baseball is a long way from becoming as popular as football (or soccer, as it is called in North America), the expansion of baseball has been an interesting cultural phenomenon. As one looks at the development of baseball throughout the world, often the introduction of the game can be traced to the presence of players from the United States. But we also see some evidence of baseball being exported to neighboring countries without the direct influence of U.S. baseball. As Michael and May Oleksak note in their recent study, *Beisbol: Latin Americans and the Grand Old Game*, "It was the Cubans' fight for independence from Spain during the last two decades of the 1800s that spurred the game's migration during this violent period. . . . Some [Cubans] went east to the Dominican Republic, while more headed west to the Yucatan Peninsula of Mexico."[2] In both cases, though introduced by immigrant Cubans, the game soon took root among citizens of the receiving country. (The first Mexican national to appear in the U.S. Major Leagues was Melo Almada in 1933. Dominican players were largely prohibited because of the color barrier, so that the first Dominican, Ozzie Virgil Sr., did not make his first MLB appearance until 1956.)

In Asia the emergence of baseball is largely attributed to the popularity of the game in Japan, going back over a century ago. Originally introduced by Americans, baseball spread from Japan to Korea and Taiwan.

In Brazil, as we will demonstrate, the development of baseball is tied to the immigrant Japanese. The game exists in Brazil primarily because of its popularity in the Japanese community; indeed in the early days of Japanese immigration, the community was held together in part because of its love for baseball.

Brazil the Country

It has often been said that people in the United States have a limited worldview and limited understanding of the nature of other societies. As U.S. president George W. Bush once said to the president of Brazil, "Do you have blacks, too?" Certainly knowledge of Brazil is limited in U.S. society.

The United States dominates the North American continent in much the same way that Brazil dominates the South American continent. Brazil is larger in land area than the 48 contiguous U.S. states and has a population of 182,032,604, only 31 percent smaller than the U.S. population. São Paulo is either the third or the fifth largest city in the world, depending on how one counts (either 17.7 million or 19.9 million).

Southern Brazil tends to be the economic engine of the country while the North is poorer and less industrialized. It is in the more affluent South that baseball has flourished.

First Appearance of Baseball in Brazil

The first record of baseball being played in Brazil was in the early twentieth century, about the same time that it appeared in Mexico and the Dominican Republic. It was originally played in Brazil by employees of U.S. companies who were in the country for short-term projects. Despite the interest of the U.S. visitors, the game did not take hold among Brazilian citizens, who were already enthralled by football (soccer). As Celia Abe Oi notes, baseball was introduced by

employees of American companies, particularly an electric energy company. The first recorded game was played in the city of São Paulo. In the 1913–14 season, the Mackenzie team of São Paulo was able to attract a number of soccer players to turn to baseball. There was still a baseball league in the 1920s, with American players, led by a director of the telephone company.[3]

In the 1920s–1930s the development of baseball in Brazil took a turn unlike that in any other country. Rather than taking root in the general population in this football-mad country, baseball survived in Brazil only because of the influx of immigrants from Japan, where baseball enjoyed enormous popularity.

The first wave of Japanese immigration to Brazil began in 1908 with a formal agreement between the Japanese and Brazilian governments. Brazil needed workers for its coffee farms, and Japanese farmers were eager to move to Brazil, believing they could escape the poverty in Japan. Immigration swelled in the period between the two world wars, and the immigrants brought baseball with them. The most popular destinations for Japanese immigrants were São Paulo and Paraná. São Paulo is now the second largest "Japanese" city in the world, after Tokyo. São Paulo and Paraná have remained the centers for the growth of baseball.

By 1929 a cultural and sporting association was formed in the Japanese community. Called Associações Japonesas Unidas de Presidente Prudente in Portuguese and Rengo nihonjin kai in Japanese, the association developed land in a community called President Prudente. This allowed for the construction of a sports complex with facilities for soccer, tennis, volleyball, basketball, and softball, as well as the first baseball diamond. At this time, there were more than thirty-five hundred Japanese immigrant families in the country, working primarily in coffee and cotton farming.

With the approach of World War II, fears about the allegiance of Japanese immigrants led to restrictive measures to weaken the links between the immigrant community and Japan. Unlike the measures taken in the United States, the restrictions in Brazil focused on the reduction of cultural links with the home country.[4] The Japanese language was prohibited, as were meetings of Japanese groups. Materials written in Japanese were destroyed. Thus, a permitted leisure activity such as baseball became a primary rallying point for the Japanese immigrant community. After World War II restrictions on the Japanese community were eased, but as in the United States there was very little return migration to Japan. The Japanese community gradually became more integrated into Brazilian life and culture. Today the ethnic Japanese population in Brazil is around one million with about 50 percent of the population employed in agriculture, 35 percent in commerce, and 15 percent in industry. There is also a growing presence of the ethnic Japanese in positions of leadership, including in the cabinet of the Brazilian government.

Post–World War II Baseball Development

With the arrival of peace, Brazil, along with other nations, was better able to promote leisure activities. As a result, by 1946 the Japanese community, though still disillusioned with wartime treatment in Brazil and with world affairs, became determined to develop culturally and socially. The first efforts in this direction were leisure and sporting diversions, including baseball. In September 1946 the São Paulo Federation of Baseball and Softball was formed under the leadership of a reporter from the *Gazette Esportiva*, Olímpio de Sá Silva, who served seventeen years as president. In February 1947 the first meeting of the federation was held. Twenty-eight teams and their representatives were present; 70 percent of the representatives had ethnically Japanese names.[5]

11. *Junior Interclub Brazilian Baseball Championship, 2005: Nippon Blue Jays (base runner) vs. Coopercotia (catcher). Ibiúna–São Paulo.* (Photo by Flávio Torres/Fotomídia.)

This year marked the first organized baseball competition in Brazil, with a league in São Paulo. The first champions were the EC Mailhense, who defeated Suzano 6–3 in the championship game. It is difficult in retrospect to judge the quality of the play, though two isolated narratives offer some clues. First, in 1951 the Columbia University baseball team came to play the Brazilian national team as the first international baseball presence in Brazil. Lou Gehrig notwithstanding, Columbia University had not been a powerhouse in U.S. college baseball.[6] In a batting demonstration, Anthony Mitcher, Columbia's left-handed first baseman, hit all of the available balls into a heath beyond the left-field wall, ending the event. Seven years later in 1958, a new stadium was dedicated in São Paulo, the Estádio do Bom Retiro. The inauguration was celebrated with a series between a São Paulo All-Star team and the team from Waseda University of Tokyo. The cumulative score in the series was Waseda 372–São Paulo 5, with the Japanese university team hitting 53 home runs. Brazilian baseball still had a long way to go.

In the mid-1980s the Confederaçao Brasileira de Beisebol e Softbol (the Brazilian Confederation of Baseball and Softball) was formed as a governing body for both sports. As with many national sports bodies, it has focused on player development, national team development, and youth baseball and softball. Under the leadership of Jorge Otsuka, the confederation has developed to the point of having an estimated forty thousand players in Brazil and over one hundred clubs participating in various levels of national championships.

Entrance of Brazilians into Professional Baseball

At present, all domestic baseball competition in Brazil is what is called semipro in the United States. Many of the teams or clubs have corporate affiliations, and the players are supported at least in part by work with supportive organizations. Though there is no professional baseball in Brazil, the quality of play has come a long way, and Brazilians are beginning to enter the professional ranks in the United States, Japan, Taiwan, and other countries. In the past four years, five to seven Brazilian players have gone abroad each year to play in high schools, colleges, or professional leagues in the United States and Japan. Several Brazilians now play on the minor league teams in the United States, including Rafael Motooka and Rafael Miranda with the Florida Marlins organization, and pitcher Rodrigo Hirota with the New York Mets organization.

The first Brazilian to be signed to a professional contract in the United States was José Pett, who in 1992 signed for $700,000 as a sixteen-year-old free agent with the Toronto Blue Jays. A 6'6" right-handed starting pitcher, Pett rose rapidly through the minors until 1996 when his performance worsened. In 1998 he made the Pittsburgh Pirates forty-man roster, though he never appeared in the Major Leagues. After a few years in AAA, he was released in 2000 by the Cleveland Indians. He appeared in 101 minor league games almost exclusively as a starting pitcher, with a win-loss record of 23-34 and a career ERA of 4.70.

Rafael Motooka of São Paulo was the second Brazilian to play professionally in the United States. He is currently playing for the Potomac Cannons, the Class A Carolina League affiliate of the Cincinnati Reds. He has been in the Reds organization for four years.

The current (2004) list of Brazilian professionals playing in the United States and Japan is as follows:

Table 1

PLAYER	TEAM	COMMENT
Tiago Campos	Cincinnati Reds (Dayton Dragons)	R-R outfielder playing for the Dayton Dragons in the Class A Midwest League in 2004. Batted .196 with 102 at bats in his first professional season
Adriano De Souza	Toronto Blue Jays	Assigned to play in Italy
Anderson Gomes	Fukuoka Daiei Hawks	Right-handed pitcher, signed by Fukuoka in 2002
Rodrigo Takeo Hirota Maciel	Seattle Mariners	Assigned to play in the Dominican Republic
Daniel Yuichi Matsumoto	Yakult Swallows	L-L outfielder, signed by Yakult in 1999. Has played parts of three seasons with the Swallows, batting .533 in limited play in 2004
Rafael Motooka	Cincinnati Reds (Potomac Cannons)	Right-handed hitting catcher, signed by the Reds in 2000. Has played five seasons in Rookie and Class A baseball, with a cumulative batting average of .217
Kleber Ojima	Makoto Cobras (Taiwan)	Right-handed pitcher, pitched several years in Japan.
Yoshimi Sakura	Chunichi Dragons	Infielder, signed as the number 3 draft pick by Chunichi in 2003
Reinaldo Tsuguio Sato	Yakult Swallows	Has appeared in 11 games in 2004 for the Swallows.
Henrique Shigueo Tamaki	Hiroshima Toyo Carp	Right-handed pitcher, signed as the number 3 draft pick by Hiroshima in 1996. Now in his ninth year with the Carp, appeared in 31 games in relief this season with a 2.73 ERA.

There are other encouraging signs of growth in the game in Brazil. The Brazilian Confederation now has a program with Japan and Cuba to exchange players and coaches. In addition, several Cuban coaches are hired from time to time by the confederation to spend a season in Brazil. In a partnership with the Japanese company Yakult, the confederation has built what it calls the country's baseball "headquarters." Built five years ago in Ibiuna, a city sixty kilometers from São Paulo, the facility is home to the confederation's baseball academy for young players. It has three official-size fields, and its training and housing facilities are spread across 220,000 square meters. The Brazilian national team uses the facility as a training camp before all international competitions. Brazil now has about 35,000 baseball players, 4,500 of them affiliated with the confederation. The majority live in São Paulo, Rio de Janeiro, and Paraná, where the Japanese communities prevail. There are about seventeen national competitions among one hundred clubs every year. Brazil finished seventh in the 2003 Baseball World Cup in Cuba and fifth in the 2003 Pan American Games in the Dominican Republic, the best results ever for Brazil in each of the competitions.

To better assess the development of baseball in Brazil and Brazilian ballplayers abroad, we conducted about a dozen interviews with professional ballplayers, the coach of the national team, the head of the Brazilian federation, scouts, and fans. Below are several biographical sketches that reveal the central characteristics of Brazilian baseball.

Rafael Motooka

Rafael began playing baseball at the age of six or seven. He joined organized leagues as a preteen, including Little League. He then made the club team in his home area, Guarulhos, and finally was selected for the Brazilian National Baseball Team. Guarulhos is best known to travelers as the site of the international airport in São Paulo. Rafael was not scouted until he played for the Brazilian national team, in an international tournament in Mexico City. Soon after a Cincinnati Reds scout offered Rafael a free agent contract. Rafael signed and began his professional career at the age of seventeen in Sarasota, Florida, for the Reds' Gulf Coast League team.

12. Junior Interclub Brazilian Baseball Championship, 2005: São Paulo vs. Gecebs (batting). Ibiúna–São Paulo. (Photo by Flávio Torres/Fotomídia.)

Only the second Brazilian ever to play professionally in the United States, Rafael did so as a catcher, the most demanding and skilled of all positions. When he arrived in the United States Rafael knew no English, though he did know what the McDonald's sign stood for. When we stepped up to the counter at a restaurant, Rafael detected that our server was Spanish-speaking. He quickly slipped into fluent Spanish, which he had learned from his Hispanic teammates. Now in his fourth season, his command of English is quite good. Like most Brazilians, Rafael is also a serious *futebol* (soccer) fan. He once aspired to play soccer, a wish shared by his father, but gradually shifted to baseball. Asked about differences in how baseball is played in the U.S. and Brazil, Rafael mentioned that in Brazil, if a team is ahead 10–0, they might still bunt. "Here in the United States, anyone who did that would be flat on his back at their next at bat." Rafael also believes that it is tougher to succeed in the United States than in Japan or Brazil because of the long path to the majors through the deep and very competitive minor league system.

Kleber Ojima

A right-handed pitcher, Kleber Ojima is one of Brazil's top players. The twenty-seven-year-old native of Campinas, São Paulo, Ojima was named the best pitcher in the 2003 Baseball World Cup in Cuba. In January 2004 Ojima moved to Taiwan to play for the Macoto Cobras. Previously he had been with the Mitsubishi of Hiroshima in Japan. He returned to play on the Brazilian national squad in the Baseball World Cup and in the Olympic qualifying tournament. Ojima started playing baseball at age eight, along with older brother Thiago (also a Brazilian national team player), after watching his father play in a veteran league.

When asked how the development of Brazilian baseball contributed to his success abroad, Ojima replied, "Last year, Brazil's adult team achieved great international results, attracting the attention of international managers. My contribution in the World Cup in Cuba [Brazil finished fifth] prompted the interest of clubs in Italy, United States and Taiwan."

We asked why he wanted to play abroad.

In addition to the financial part, what attracted me was the challenge to play in a professional league. I had always achieved good results in national and international competitions, especially last year, but always playing as an amateur. In Brazil, baseball still is a very amateur game. The tournaments are short and played only on weekends. In addition, players often have careers in addition to baseball. Those things don't happen in professional leagues abroad.

He believes his move to Taiwan may have been a very wise career choice:

I've been getting media exposure because of my good results. Because I play in the main league in Taiwan [where baseball is the top sport], all games are televised live. Thus, I started being recognized by people. Recently, a TV documentary about my life was conducted and I have been asked to give several interviews. I even have a fan club. [He has a Web site as well.][7]

Jorge Otsuka

A seminal figure in Brazilian baseball development, Jorge Otsuka is the longtime president of the Brazilian Baseball and Softball Confederation (CBBS). Otsuka is optimistic about baseball's future in Brazil, noting that Brazil is a country where sports in general are extremely popular—the country has numerous World Cup championships in soccer, as well as a growing world presence in basketball, volleyball, tennis, and auto racing. He also cited the recent adoption of a national baseball confederation and training program with international coaches. This latter approach has aided the development of baseball in other countries.

Otsuka credits the work of the confederation, with the help of the Brazilian Olympic Committee, in lifting the level of play in Brazil. "Now we are able to face traditional countries such as Cuba, Mexico, Panama and the Dominican Republic. In the last World Cup [played in Cuba] we finished proudly in seventh place. In the Pan American Games we finished fourth, and in the Olympic qualifying tournament we were eliminated in the quarterfinals by Cuba. Our biggest problem is that we need more people playing the game. Today, the majority of the players are concentrated in the most southern part of the country, and we need to change that."

Otsuka was also asked about the limitation on the growth of the game given its concentration in the Japanese Brazilian community. "Baseball began in an organized form in Brazil only fifty years ago, and now finally we are being able to break the [Japanese] barrier and include non-Japanese in the game. With this change, we have been able to bring baseball to schools and colleges, and from here we will be able to become a top contender internationally. We dream of a possible medal in the Pan American Games in 2007, and a berth in the 2008 Olympic Games. To keep improving, we feel the Brazilians need to play more among top-level teams. That's why we endorse the policy to send more and more players to foreign leagues."

We asked if Brazilians use the same training methods at the new training facility in Ibiuna as in Japan, knowing that compared to the United States, the Japanese do more physical conditioning, have longer practices, and very long repetitions of drills.[8] "The training methods used at the facility," said Otsuka, "are a mix between the Japanese and Cuban schools. The Brazilian coaches tend to follow the Japanese methods, but three Cuban coaches [all Olympic medalists] were recently brought by the Brazilian Confederation to add new methods."

We asked Otsuka to describe the atmosphere around the club matches and championship games in Brazil, and about attendance: "The atmosphere is usually upbeat, and the average attendance at the games varies between 500 and 1,000 people, depending on the cities where they are played. Because baseball is not widespread in the country, some parents are not familiar with the rules of the game and tend to cause minor disruptions when they believe a wrong call is made. There is very little advertisement, and the local games are not broadcast on radio or TV [MLB games can be watched by those who subscribe to ESPN International on cable TV]. Only the local Nippon newspapers and the Brazilian Confederation's Web site follow the tournaments closely, publishing news and results."

The Face of Brazilian Baseball

Clearly Brazilian baseball has a different face from that found in the United States and in Japan, where the professional level of the sport has influenced its development throughout all ranks. Although the Brazilian fan base is small, it is devoted. The players and their teams look much like their counterparts in other countries in terms of uniforms and equipment. However, the style of play, as noted by Motooka, is quite different. In the United States there is a great emphasis on the unwritten rules of the game, the understandings about what is acceptable or not in certain game conditions. For example, there was great debate surrounding the successful bunt attempt by San Diego catcher Ben Davis in the eighth inning of a 1–0 game (May 2001) when he broke up a no-hitter being pitched by Curt Schilling, then of Arizona. The unwritten rule is that one never breaks up a no-hitter in the late innings by bunting. This debate would have been incomprehensible in Brazil. In the Brazilian game, a base runner whose team is ahead 10–0 may even steal second base. In the United States the base stealer is likely to be knocked down on his next turn at bat.

The Future

With MLB's ever-increasing interest in finding new talent throughout the world, the opportunities for Brazilian ballplayers will increase. Discussions of a Baseball World Cup and the hope of someday expanding the Major Leagues beyond the United States and Canada make these opportunities more likely. Brazil has raised its profile in international play, and it is getting help from quality coaches from Cuba and Japan. The presence of this level of coaching may overcome the fears expressed by Mitsuyoshi Sato, the manager of the Brazilian national team, regarding the popularity of baseball in Brazil: "One of the reasons the interest in baseball is not widespread in Brazil is because of the complexity of the rules of the game, which are very different than the ones in soccer."

Nevertheless, with its enormous athletic talent and vast numbers, Brazil is poised to make a mark on the world stage in baseball. However, organized professional baseball is a curious enterprise. In one respect, it is the ultimate form of meritocracy: given the multitude of performance measures in the game, it is relatively easy to make decisions about cutting, say, a .200 hitter or promoting a .300 hitter. But in other ways the merit model breaks down. For almost seventy years, many of the greatest performers in the sport were not eligible to participate in the American game. And while Jackie Robinson broke the color barrier in 1947, baseball's racial bigotry toward African Americans and prejudicial judgments about other groups have not disappeared. Research has shown how prejudice has affected the advance of Caribbean players, Canadians, short right-handed pitchers, and African American players today who are not center fielders.[9] Japanese ballplayers have suffered in similar fashion. To wit, Masanori Murakami, the first Japanese-born player in MLB (1964–65), actually fed the impression that Japanese players couldn't cut it despite his outstanding MLB ERA of 3.43, which was even lower than his lifetime ERA in Japan. Thirty years later the same prejudice followed Hideo Nomo, who has won 117 games in the Major League over the last ten years. Americans grudgingly came to accept Japanese pitchers while holding onto the belief that they couldn't play a position. Then came Ichirō, who as a rookie in 2001 led the American League in hitting. But of course he is a singles hitter—there could never be a slugger—and then in 2003 Hideki Matsui succeeded on the MLB stage. In sum, we need to take into account how such judgments of talent, primarily by the international scouts who provide the initial talent assessments, will affect the rise of Brazilians, most of whom will be of Japanese heritage.

It is also worth observing whether Brazilian players will be attracted more to Japan than to the United States. Japan offers fewer steps in the minor league system, a more familiar style of game, possibly more recognition by Japanese scouts, and ethnic similarity. The United States offers the potential of higher salaries and greater recognition. Language does not appear to be a factor, since few Brazilians of Japanese heritage (of this generation) speak Japanese or English.

It is likely that a Brazilian will soon be in the Major Leagues, even if the sport is only played in certain parts of Brazil, and even if *futebol* continues to be the most popular sport. The sheer size of Brazil—soon to be the second largest country fielding Major Leaguers—will have an impact.

Notes

1. The title of this essay is the semi-facetious response from the first person who responded to one of the authors (Patterson) when he first asked about baseball in Brazil.
2. Oleksak and Oleksak, *Beisbol*, 17.
3. Abe Oi, *Beisebol*, 4.
4. The strength of their cultural ties to Japan is illustrated by the following. There was a broadcast on August 15, 1945 (called "Gyokuon-hoso" in Japanese), which announced Japan's surrender, that was unbelievable for Japanese immigrants in Brazil. Many of them didn't believe this news and some even said that emperor's boats would come "to bring them back to Japan." Some of them heard of the surrender by way of the Brazilian media, and in 1946 Japanese extremists murdered some of their countrymen who recognized the truth; for the extremists it was inconceivable that Japan, the Divine Country, could be defeated. This quote is translated on http://www.fukuokalatina.com/uk, a Web site that explores the Japanese cultural presence in Latin America, from original Japanese-language sources "Kaigai ni Yuhi Shita Fukuoka Kenjin Koryushi" (Dai-4-kai Kaigai Fukuoka-kenjinkai sekai taikai jikko iinkai, 2001) and "Nikkei Brazil Iminshi" (Yukiharu Takahashi, Sanichi Shobo, 1993).

5. Associação Esportiva Linense, Massayoshi Muto; Esport Clube Jundiaí, Ta-
   ketaro Mita; Dragão Esporte Clube, Kango Kamijo; São Paulo Gigante Base-
   Ball Clube, Roberto Saito; Universo Base-Ball Clube, Mauricio Loureiro;
   São Paulo Futebol Clube, Rivadal Mota Marcondes; Santo André Base-Ball
   Clube, Kenji Orie; Pereira Barreto Base-Ball Clube, Tomotsu Ishi; Associan-
   ção Prudentina de Base-Ball, Seny Oguido; Coopercotia Atlético Clube, Vin-
   cente Monteiro; Piratas Baseball Club, Durval Vieira Pinheiro; Diamante
   Baseball Clube, Mario Sato; Araçatuba Baseball Clube, Tsunehiro Koroki;
   Martinópolis Baseball Clube, Sussumu Imamura; Lizzitada Baseball Clube,
   Hiroshi Iwama; São Paulo Baseball Clube, Ossamu Yoshi; Alvares Machado
   Baseball Clube, Ichiji Tsuji; Canam Baseball Clube, Shiguero Homa; Esporte
   Clube Mariliense, Haruo Ikeda; Pompéia Baseball Clube, Masanobu Takeda;
   Lima Canto Baseball Clube, Julio Baba; Tigre Baseball Clube, Issamu Kata-
   yama; Associação Desportiva Floresta, Olímpio Sá e Silva; Atlético Clube de
   Registro, Eiji Matsumura; Itaquera Baseball Clube, Renato Teruo Tanaka;
   Oratório Baseball Clube, Yocio Nakamura; Indiana Baseball Clube, Tadashi
   Okamura; Clube de Esportes Americanos, Alexandre dos Santos Amaral.
6. Lou Gehrig left Columbia in 1923.
7. See http://home.kimo.com.tw/maddogbone/kleber.html.
8. "Yakult's baseball training facility was built by Yakult Brazil, not Yakult Japan. Yakult Brazil's current president, Massahiko Sadakata, built the baseball
   complex because he wanted to give back to the nippon community after the
   profits made by his company in the country. Sadakata and Yakult Brazil gave
   the training facility to the Brazilian Baseball and Softball Confederation and
   still help finance its maintenance." Jorge Otsuka, president of the Confedera-
   ção Brasiliero de Beisebol e Softbol, private conversation with the author.
9. Oleksak and Oleksak, *Beisbol*; Williams and Patterson, "Trois Balles, Deux
   Prises"; Corbett and Patterson, "The Social Significance of Sport." Other examples of scouting prejudice arise in the re-segregation of African American
   players in the Major Leagues. Corbett and Patterson note that in 2002, 75
   percent of Major League center fielders were African American, while there
   was no African American third baseman or first baseman, only one catcher,
   and only three out of 150 (2 percent) were starting pitchers.

References

There are, unfortunately, no writings on Brazilian baseball available in English.
The citations below by Célia Abe Oi, director of the Museum of the Japanese

Immigration History in São Paulo, written in Portuguese, are the only known publications on Brazilian baseball in any language. There is a fleeting reference to Brazilian baseball in Maarten Van Bottenburg, "Global Games," trans. Beverley Jackson (Urbana: University of Illinois Press, 2001).

Abe Oi, Célia. *Beisebol, História de uma Paixão*. São Paulo: Federação Paulista de Beisebol e Softbol, 1996.

———. *Guia de Cultura Japonesa*. São Paulo: Fundção Japão, 2004.

Corbett, Doris, and Wayne Patterson. "The Social Significance of Sport." *Proceedings of the 14th Annual Cooperstown Symposium and Baseball and Society*. Jefferson NC: McFarland, 2003.

Der Speigel, May 19, 2002.
    Available at http://www.spiegel.de/panorama/0,1518,196865,00.html.

Http://espn.go.com, ESPN Network, 2003.

Lewis, Michael. *Moneyball*. New York: W. W. Norton, 2003.

Miami Herald, March 7, 2004, C1.

Oleksak, Michael, and May Adams Oleksak. *Beisbol: Latin Americans and the Grand Old Game*. 2nd ed. New York: McGraw-Hill/Contemporary Books, 1996.

Reaves, Joseph A. *Taking in a Game: A History of Baseball in Asia*. Lincoln: University of Nebraska Press, 2002.

Wendel, Tim. *The New Face of Baseball*. New York: HarperCollins, 2003.

Williams, Savanah E., and Wayne Patterson. "Trois Balles, Deux Prises: The Influence of Canada on Baseball, The Influence of Baseball on Canada." Paper presented at the Fifth Annual Cooperstown Symposium on Baseball and Society, 1993.

12 | Canada

Internationalizing America's National Pastime

Although baseball in Canada today is flourishing at the youth, amateur, semiprofessional, and professional levels, most people tend to consider it a marginal extension of American sporting life. Admittedly, the country has a Major League franchise in Toronto and more than a dozen Canadian players, including Larry Walker, Eric Gagné, Paul Quantrill, Rheal Cormier, Matt Stairs, Corey Koskie, Aaron Guiel, Rich Harden, Ryan Dempster, Jeff Zimmerman, Chris Reitsma, Jason Bay, Justin Morneau, Erik Bedard, Cody McKay, and Pete LaForest, play big league baseball. It is fair to say, however, that none of these stars of the diamond has been accorded the national recognition and adulation of hockey players such as Wayne Gretzky, Mario Lemieux, or Bobby Orr, or of golfer Mike Weir, who has recently become a national sporting icon. It is thus tempting to regard the history of baseball in Canada, from the mid-nineteenth century to the present, as part of the natural diffusion of America's national pastime beyond the borders of the United States, just as Canadian hockey enthusiasts frequently talk of the internationalization of what they regard as "Canada's game."

Among sport historians a diffusion model is often applied as a way of explaining the globalization of twentieth-century sporting culture and games of all types. According to Joseph Arbena, Allen Guttmann, Steven Riess, and others, modern sporting forms originated in highly developed metropolitan societies, spread outward into hinterland or colonial territories where they were first introduced at the elite level, and then percolated downward to the masses. The British game of soccer provides a classic illustration of the process. Developing out of unruly and relatively unorganized "folk football" play, the game was regulated, codified, and modernized in the nineteenth century, exported to all corners of the British Empire and ultimately to the world, and has assumed the status of the "people's game" from FA cup matches at Wembley Stadium to street football in the barrios of Rio de Janeiro.

In some ways, however, the diffusion model obscures more than it reveals about the complicated history of the development of baseball above and along the 49th parallel. In Canada the diffusion process is uncertain, given that games of townball and variations of the British game of rounders were being played as early as the 1820s. In fact, baseball in Canada may have developed simultaneously with baseball south of the border, and given the porosity of the border and movement across it in both directions this is hardly surprising. Two Canadian historians, Bob Barney and Nancy Bouchier, have even suggested a Canadian origin of the game, based on a set of rules and diagrams drawn up by Adam Ford for a game in Beachville, Ontario, in 1838, a year before the mythical "invention" of baseball by Abner Doubleday in Cooperstown, New York. Of course, as Stephen Gould has pointed out, claims of the invention or origination of sports that evolved out of more traditional games are often dubious and suggest a "creationist" rather than evolutionary state of mind.

Whatever the game's beginnings, baseball was widely played in Canada at mid-century, albeit with varying rules. During the 1850s and 1860s, baseball clubs in Ontario communities such as London and Woodstock followed the rules of the eleven-a-side Canadian game, while in the Maritimes the New England version held sway. Around 1860 teams in London, Hamilton, Toronto, Woodstock, and Guelph all adopted the New York Knickerbocker rules so that they could challenge baseball clubs south of the border, and by the end of the decade the standardization of the game's rules was virtually complete. By that time teams in New Brunswick and Nova Scotia had abandoned the New England game in favor of the New York rules as well. On the Pacific Coast baseball clubs were springing up in Victoria and Vancouver during the 1860s, largely as a result of the close connections between British Columbia and American states to the south.

In many cases it is hard to decide who was influencing whom. If the reliance on Americans to ensure a sophisticated level of play is any indication of a process of diffusion, there is little evidence to suggest that Canadian baseball was especially derivative of American influences. In the 1860s the *New York Clipper* warned readers that "the Canucks are not to be trifled with, and unless better teams are pitted against them in the future, the laurels may pass from the American boys to them." In 1874 the Guelph Maple Leafs won the world semiprofessional baseball championship with a lineup of Canadian players. Less than a decade later young Canadian-born players from Ontario and the Maritimes such as Mike Brannock, Bill Reid, Charles "Pop" Smith, and Bill Phillips were playing in the National Association in the United States. Between 1870 and the end of the century sixty-four Canadians played in the National and International Associations.[1] Perhaps the best of all of them was James "Tip" O'Neill of Woodstock, Ontario, who captured the first Triple Crown in big league history, playing for the St. Louis Browns in 1887.

Of course, some of these players had left Canada at a young age as their parents sought work in the mill towns of New England or employment in the bigger cities of the United States. For example, Toronto-born Art Irwin, who revolutionized fielding by padding a buckskin driving glove and sewing the third and fourth fingers together, moved to Boston with his family at the age of fifteen. John "Chewing Gum" O'Brien and Bill Phillips both moved with their families from New Brunswick to the United States as children, O'Brien to Lewiston, Maine, and Phillips to Chicago. By the first quarter of the twentieth century, moreover, many American-born players with family ties to Canada were toiling in the big leagues.

Among the more notable were Franco-Americans such as Nap Lajoie, Del Bisonette, and "Frenchy" Bordagaray, and such recognizable stars as Pie Traynor, Stuffy McInnis, and Harry Hooper, who had family roots in the Maritimes. Known for diving catches, headlong slides, and confrontations with umpires, Bordagaray flaunted his French heritage, at one point taking up fencing and sporting a D'Artagnan-style beard in Three Musketeer fashion. Then there was big Larry McLean, whose birthplace is usually listed as Cambridge, Massachusetts, but who grew up in Fredericton, New Brunswick. A catcher with a bullet arm and pro-verbial bent elbow, McLean was known for biting off enormous chaws of Brown Mule tobacco and washing it down with a pint of corn whis-key. McLean was constantly in trouble with his managers. In 1906, for example, St. Louis manager Kid Nichols sent McLean to the minors af-ter a drunken escapade that included his jumping in the fountain court of the Buckingham Hotel. Said Nichols, "I can pitch to Larry real good, but I can't manage him worth a dime." McLean later returned to the majors with the Cincinnati Reds, but his drinking kept him in trouble and was responsible for his death at the age of forty in a bar fight in Boston.

Despite its rough edges and reputation for rowdiness, baseball had pushed other team sports in Canada aside in the last quarter of the nineteenth century. This was particularly true of British team sports such as cricket, soccer, and rugby, which the Anglo-Saxon bourgeoisie thought would encourage a respectable social order and a deeper al-legiance to nation and empire. Despite the elite's hopes for respectable sport, however, British games were often resisted, especially in Quebec, and quickly gave way to North American sports such as lacrosse, hockey, and baseball.[2] Even in parts of the country with strong imperial connec-tions—in the Maritimes, for instance—baseball was the summer sport of choice for most people by the 1880s. By that time, too, the game was rapidly spreading into newly settled regions in the west.

Baseball moved west from Ontario to Manitoba soon after the latter joined the confederation in 1870. A Winnipeg baseball club was formed in March 1874, led by A. G. Bannatyne, a wealthy merchant and the city's first postmaster, and a decade later there were three clubs operat-ing in the city: the Hotels, the Metropolitans, and the Canadian Pacific Railway clubs. For the most part the game developed without the influ-ence of the United States.[3] As Bill Humber has noted, of the 12,000 in-habitants in Manitoba in 1870 only seventy were Americans, suggesting that Manitoba's early baseball owed little to the influence of the United States.[4] The game prospered outside of Winnipeg in places like Brandon and further west in Battleford and was well enough established that by

1880 teams from the province were seeking out competition in Minneapolis and St. Paul. In Saskatchewan, Alberta, and British Columbia, settlers from the United States would contribute more significantly to the growth of the game. Baseball thus came to the Canadian west from two directions: east from Ontario through Manitoba and along the rail line, and north from the United States.

In the few decades leading up to World War I baseball in Canada was embroiled in commonplace Victorian discourses about respectable behavior, and embellished with class, race, and nativist prejudices. For some snooty members of the Anglo-Saxon elite, baseball seemed a crass and disreputable sport, representing the worst characteristics of American culture. When the University of Toronto fielded a baseball team in 1885, a correspondent to the student newspaper warned readers that "the associations of the game . . . are of the very lowest and most repugnant character . . . degraded by Yankee professionalism."[5] Implicit in this, of course, was a critique and fear of the influence of American culture on Canadian life. The commentator's remarks were likely motivated as much by concerns about baseball's popularity among the working class. Unlike curling, cricket, tennis, or golf—sports that appealed to the social elite—baseball attracted the support of all social classes and gave vent to vigorous class, ethnic, and community rivalries. Concerned about professionalism, gambling, alcohol consumption, and the frequently rowdy behavior of fans and players alike, proponents of "respectable" sport and of "gentlemanly amateurism" remained ambivalent about baseball's social value.

At the same time there were those who thought that baseball could teach recent immigrants "appropriate" North American social values. This was particularly the case in Saskatchewan and Alberta, which by the turn of the century were attracting hundreds of thousands of immigrants, many from eastern Europe, Scandinavia, and Ukraine. According to Donald Wetherell and Irene Kmet, sports such as baseball were important in securing Anglo-Saxon hegemony in the west. For the most part, however, the immigrants were involved in establishing farms and had little time for leisure pursuits. Rather it was in the urban centers such as Calgary and Edmonton where baseball developed around the turn of the century.

Discourses about baseball's respectability were dissolving by World War I in the face of the game's emergence as a marketable form of mass entertainment. In his study of the prewar Vancouver Beavers of the Northwest League, Robin Anderson found the sport to be unencumbered by debates about respectability. Baseball in Vancouver "was all about money. . . . [O]wners, players, and fans eagerly sought monetary rewards from the game. Of course, none of this would have appeared out of character in the frantic acquisitory climate that coloured the boom years of pre-war Vancouver."[6] Vancouver was hardly unique, however, since these years witnessed the acceptance of professional sport as a legitimate form of mass entertainment.

After the war virtually every city, town, and village across the country sported a ball team, and baseball entered a new golden age. Amateur leagues, youth teams, semipro community baseball, and itinerant barnstorming teams flourished. A number of Canadian cities and towns also operated successfully in baseball's minor leagues. Most successful was the Toronto Maple Leafs club, which operated from the beginning of the century until 1912 in the Eastern League, and then the International League where it continued to toil through the 1960s. Montreal had teams in a number of different leagues, but like Toronto became a fixture in the International League in the 1920s. Professional minor league franchises also operated between the wars in Vancouver, Winnipeg, Hamilton, London, Ottawa, Quebec City, and Trois-Rivieres. The Cape Breton Colliery League, which operated from 1937 through 1939 at the Class C level, had teams in Sydney, New Waterford, Glace Bay, and Dominion.

Baseball might have been a unifying community activity, but not all social divisions evaporated as baseball games became highly desired marketable commodities. Invidious judgments about respectability still plagued African and Asian Canadians, recent immigrants, native peoples, and women as they took up the sport. After the Great War some black players occasionally found spots on semiprofessional town teams, but for the most part they were confined to playing for all-black clubs like the Halifax Coloured Diamonds, the Saint John Royals (who won the New Brunswick Intermediate Championship in 1921), the Amber Valley team from Edmonton, and the Chatham, Ontario, All-Stars whose roster included Ferguson Jenkins Sr. All of these clubs were capable of beating the best senior teams in their respective provinces. Of the ethnic-based teams, none was more successful than the Vancouver Asahi baseball club. Organized in 1922, the Asahis played in Vancouver's Terminal League at Oppenheimer Park in so-called Little Tokyo. Known for their slick fielding, speed on the base paths, and bunting prowess, the Asahis were prominent throughout the interwar period, winning five Pacific Northwest championships in a row beginning in 1937. The club disbanded as a result of the internment of Japanese Canadians in 1942. The Asahis were recently inducted into the Canadian Baseball Hall of Fame.

The interwar period was also the heyday of barnstorming black ball teams crossing the border to play exhibition games for a guaranteed portion of the gate. Chappie Johnson's Colored All-Stars, the Philadelphia Colored Giants, the New York Black Yankees, the Cuban Giants, the Boston Royal Giants, and other aggregations drawing on players from the so-called Negro Leagues thrilled Canadian audiences with their skillful play. One of the finest of these touring clubs was a semipro team from Bismarck, North Dakota, with both white players and Negro League stars Satchel Paige, Double Duty Radcliffe, Hilton Smith, Chet Brewer, and Quincy Troupe in tow. The Bismarck club, which won the 1935 National Baseball Congress semipro championship in Wichita, Kansas, played a number of exhibition games in Canadian prairie communities. Occasionally these clubs resorted to clowning, and sometimes played on racial stereotypes in order to attract an audience. In the same year 55,000 people in Montreal watched the Zulu Cannibal Giants play a trio of games in wooly headdresses, stripped to the waist, their faces and chests painted. When Mussolini invaded Ethiopia, the club changed its name to the Ethiopian Giants.

Certain players were particularly well-known for their clowning routines. Barnstorming provided a supplement to salaries in the Negro Leagues for many black players, and in a few cases Canadian semipro teams offered contracts to black stars. Independent leagues like the Quebec Provincial League, Ontario's Intercounty League, and, before 1937, the Cape Breton Colliery League offered employment to black players. In 1935, for example, the Granby, Quebec, club signed African American pitcher-outfielder Alfred Wilson, and Cape Breton's Dominion Hawks

signed George "Whitey" Michaels of the Boston Royal Giants as playing coach. Both were dropped the following year as their leagues affiliated with organized baseball and accepted its prohibition against black
ballplayers.

The interwar years also witnessed the steady development of women's
baseball in Canada. Prior to World War I women were largely confined
to the role of spectators, except for the traveling Bloomer Girls teams,
or variations of the same, that had been touring Canada since the 1890s.
The few women who played had to overcome suggestions that those
who entered male terrain were "unnatural" and that playing a man's
game would subject their supposedly frail bodies and temperaments to
unnecessary stress. Women's baseball developed rapidly, especially in
Toronto and western Canada, during and after World War I. In 1914, for
example, the Toronto Playgrounds Baseball Leagues introduced organized baseball for girls in two divisions. By 1920 more than fifty teams
were registered. Women's baseball also flourished on the prairies and
the Pacific Coast, and the Saskatchewan ladies league was probably the
most competitive women's league in the country after the war. Although
women in the Maritimes had fewer opportunities to compete, Edna
Lockhart, a five-sport star from Avonport, Nova Scotia, was recruited to
pitch and play third base for Margaret Nabel's New York Bloomer Girls
during the 1930s.

In 1943 chewing gum magnate P. K. Wrigley established the All American Girls Professional Baseball League (AAGPBL), and in his search for
talent drew heavily on the experience of young Canadian players. Since
the AAGPBL initially used a ball whose dimensions were somewhere
between a fastball and softball, the fact that most Canadian girls had
played softball was by no means a liability. Of all the players in the
AAGPBL between 1943 and 1954, about 10 percent were Canadians, the
majority of whom were from Manitoba and Saskatchewan. Among the
more notable were Helen Callaghan of Vancouver, whose son Casey
Candaele went on to play Major League baseball, Helen "Nicki" Fox of
Ardley, Alberta, Gladys "Terry" Davis of Toronto, and Evelyn Wawryshyn
of Tyndall, Manitoba. The Canadian women who played in the league
were inducted into Canada's Baseball Hall of Fame at St. Mary's, Ontario, in the summer of 1998.

The coming of World War II altered the baseball landscape, weakening the organized baseball system and diverting many high-quality players into the service where they often suited up for military teams. According to Paul Thompson, then scout for the Chicago Black Hawks of the NHL, the strongest clubs in the country outside of the Toronto Maple Leafs and Montreal Royals in the International League were those in Vancouver and Halifax, where troops were congregated before going overseas. In Halifax, for example, Major Leaguers Dick Fowler, Joe Krakauskas, and Phil Marchildon, as well as a number of players from AAA baseball such as NHL star Bob Dill, played for their respective service clubs in the Halifax Defense League. Marchildon had played three years for Connie Mack's Philadelphia A's, winning 17 games in 1942, before joining the Royal Canadian Air Force. Shot down on a bombing run, Marchildon finished out the war in a German POW camp, but made it back to the majors and along with Dick Fowler became a mainstay of the A's pitching staff. Fowler remains the only Canadian pitcher to throw a no-hitter in the Major Leagues. Playing for the lowly A's, who finished last in the American League three times between 1945 and 1950, Marchildon and Fowler combined to win 104 games against 91 losses over that five-year stretch.

The years immediately following the war were ones of significant adjustment for baseball across North America. In the first place, the pent-up demand for entertainment that accompanied the war stimulated baseball's development at all levels, from community and youth baseball to the minor league system and the Major Leagues. Finding themselves with a surfeit of players, big league clubs were faced with the enormous challenge of evaluating players in their organizations who had been on their way up through the minor leagues before the war, and comparing them with the younger players they had signed in the interim. The result was the expansion of the minors from 23 leagues in 1946 to 42 the following year and 59 by 1949. New circuits such as the Border League, the Can-Am League, the Northwest League, and the Western International League located franchises in mid-level Canadian cities such as Kingston, Sherbrooke and Trois-Rivieres, Quebec City, and Victoria. Toronto and Montreal remained fixtures in the International League.

After a stint in the Western International League, Vancouver joined the Pacific Coast League.

The oversupply of baseball talent after the war kept player salary levels low—even at the Major League level—and provided an incentive for independent leagues to challenge the organized baseball system. The most celebrated of the postwar "outlaw" leagues was Jorge Pasquel's Mexican League, which offered lucrative contracts and lured a number of front-line Major Leaguers south of the border. Among those who jumped their existing contracts were Sal Maglie, Adrian Zabala, Alex Carrasquel, Max Lanier, Freddie Martin, and Danny Gardella. Curiously, the Mexican League experiment had a significant impact on the postwar baseball scene in Canada, partly because of the influence of Brooklyn Dodger pitcher and Quebec native Jean Pierre Roy. After winning 25 games for the Montreal Royals in 1945, and having been called up to the Dodgers late in the season, Roy was unhappy with the contract offered him the following year. He thus joined a number of players from the Dodgers' organization, among them catcher Mickey Owen, Roland Gladu from the Brooklyn squad, and pitcher Bucky Tanner, and Canadians Roger and Stan Breard off the Montreal Royals roster, who decided to sign in Mexico. All were banned from organized baseball as a result. After the collapse of Pascual's Mexican League experiment, Sal Maglie, Freddy Martin, Danny Gardella, and the others made their way to independent leagues in Canada. Most played in Roy's Quebec Provincial League, which was now considered an outlaw circuit. Mickey Owen was invited to play in Ontario's Inter-county League, and Bucky Tanner made his way to the Maritimes to play in the Halifax and District League, where he caught the attention of fans by regularly wearing a Mexican sombrero to the ballpark.

The province of Quebec also played a crucial role in "baseball's great experiment," the dropping of the color barrier in organized baseball. In 1945 the Brooklyn Dodgers signed Jackie Robinson to a contract with the Montreal Royals of the International League. The following year the Dodgers signed four more African American ballplayers to play in their organization, and the Cincinnati Reds a fifth. The Dodgers considered Montreal an ideal location for Robinson to break in, assuming that in Canada he would escape the racial taunting that would likely take place elsewhere. Of the other Dodger signees, pitcher Johnny Wright and Roy Partlow spent the 1946 season at Trois-Rivieres in the Class C Canadian American League, while Roy Campanella and Don Newcombe played for Nashua in the New England League. The Cincinnati Reds signed infielder Vincent "Manny" McIntyre of Fredericton, New Brunswick, that same year, and assigned him to Sherbrooke, Quebec, in the Class C Border League. McIntyre would later suit up as Minnie Minoso's replacement with the Negro League Cuban Giants.

Robinson took the city of Montreal and the International League by storm, leading the 1946 Royals to the league pennant, batting .349 and stealing 40 bases. Montrealers and Canadians elsewhere embraced Jackie as their hero. When the Royals defeated the Louisville Colonels of the American Association to win the Little World Series, Robinson was mobbed and chased by adoring Montreal fans. According to one newspaper, this "may have been the first time in history that a white crowd chased a black man with loving, not lynching on its mind." The following year Robinson became the first black ballplayer of the modern era to play in the Major Leagues. "Jackie has been one of the greatest ambassadors of goodwill," wrote African Canadian journalist Cal Best. "He has proven to all concerned that a member of the race can conduct himself with all the decorum and dignity that is necessary in the face of the greatest obstacles."[7]

During the 1950s and early 1960s Canadian baseball became more closely intertwined with the game in the United States than it had ever been. The lifting of the suspensions of Mexican League jumpers in 1950 not only meant the return of Maglie, Martin, Gardella, and others to the Major Leagues but paved the way for the eventual return of the Quebec Provincial League to the organized baseball fold as well. At the same time independent leagues in the Maritimes, Ontario, and the West provided fans with high-level competition. The cross-border Man-Dak League of the 1940s and 1950s drew heavily on players from the old American Negro Leagues, while others relied largely on collegiate and seasoned semipro players from the United States. These leagues also provided a context in which Canadian players Ted Bowsfield, Vern Handrahan, Ken Mackenzie, Claude Raymond, Reno Bertoia, Glen Gorbous, Frank Colman, and others prepped themselves for future big league careers. The most accomplished Canadian player of that era, of course, was Ferguson Jenkins of Chatham, Ontario, who went on to win 284 games in the majors from 1965 to 1983. A Cy Young Award winner in 1971, Jenkins was the first Canadian to be inducted into the National Baseball Hall of Fame at Cooperstown during the 1991 induction ceremonies.

The face of Canadian baseball changed dramatically at the end the 1960s with the awarding of a Major League franchise to Montreal. Playing in matchbox size Jarry Park, the Expos were an instant hit, and players such as red-haired Rusty Staub, "le grande orange" as he was affectionately known, Quebec native Claude Raymond, and infielder Ron Hunt became heroes overnight. A decade later the Expos moved from Jarry Park to Olympic Stadium. In this cavernous structure, with less than ideal sight lines for baseball, the Expos experienced a period of stability and success on the field, led by catcher Gary Carter, outfielder Andre "the Hawk" Dawson, and pitcher Steve Rogers. But the successes of the 1980s were replaced by declining fortunes of the club in the 1990s. Disillusioned as the club began to sell off its young star players, including Canadian native Larry Walker, fans began to stay away from the increasingly decrepit Olympic Stadium in droves. The 2004 season was the last for the Expos franchise in Montreal, and the club relocated to Washington DC in 2005.

When the Expos franchise was awarded to Montreal in 1969, Canada was experiencing the flush of nationalism that surrounded the centennial celebrations and Expo 67. In addition, the Liberal government of Pierre Trudeau was committed to building a national sporting edifice that would encourage nationwide competition for athletes in various sports including baseball. In 1964 the federal government incorporated the Canadian Federation of Amateur Baseball, now known as Baseball Canada, and under its auspices national competitions at all levels have been established. Made up of eleven provincial and territorial associations, Baseball Canada now represents over five hundred thousand players, sixty-two thousand coaches, and eleven thousand umpires. The national team program has flourished under Baseball Canada's leadership. In 1991, for example, the Canadian eighteen-and-under youth team, led by future Major Leaguers Stubby Clapp and Jason Dickson, won the country's first baseball gold medal at the World Youth Championship held in Brandon, Manitoba. Clapp also starred for the Canadian club in the Pan-American Games, which won 6 of its 7 games including a victory over the United States.

The final success story of the modern era is that of the Toronto Blue Jays. Toronto was awarded its Major League franchise in 1976, and under the effective management and player development tandem of Paul Beeston and Pat Gillick gradually built a contending team during the 1980s. As they entered the 1990s under field manager Cito Gaston the Jays had assembled a talented squad led by Joe Carter, Dave Winfield, Dave Stieb, Jimmy Key, Pat Borders, and Tony Fernandez. In 1992 and 1993 Gaston's charges were world champions. Over the past decade, however, escalating costs and a weak Canadian dollar have contributed to changes in ownership and have made it difficult for the Jays to compete against wealthier organizations in the free agent market. Now in a rebuilding phase, Toronto is trying to blend youthful players into a club that can once again compete with those at the top.

Whatever the fortunes of the Jays, and despite the loss of the Montreal Expos, the future of baseball in Canada is bright. More and more Canadian players are being drafted by Major League teams, and a solid nucleus of Canadians playing at the AA level and above suggests that the numbers of Canadians in the big leagues will continue to grow. At the international level Canada is perhaps more competitive than it has ever been. In part this is a product of the influence of the United States on the development of Canadian sporting culture over the years. But this is by no means the whole story. Canadian baseball was a product of local circumstances and conditions, growing side by side with the American game over the years, though never separate from it.

Notes

1. On the history of baseball in Canada, see Humber, *Diamonds of the North*; Howell, *Northern Sandlots*.
2. Howell, *Blood, Sweat and Cheers*, chap. 2.
3. Stubbs, *Shoestring Glory*.
4. Humber, *Diamonds of the North*, 83.

5. *The Varsity* (University of Toronto), November 14, 1995, 44–45.
6. Anderson, "'On the Edge of the Baseball Map.'"
7. Cal Best, *The Clarion*, November 1, 1947.

Bibliography

Anderson, Robin. "'On the Edge of the Baseball Map' with the 1908 Vancouver Beavers," *Canadian Historical Review* 77, no. 4 (1996): 573–74.

Bouchier, Nancy. *For the Love of the Game: Amateur Sport in Small-Town Ontario.* Montreal: McGill-Queen's University Press. 2003.

Elliot, Bob. *The Northern Game: Baseball the Canadian Way.* Toronto: Sport Classic, 2005.

Howell, Colin. *Blood, Sweat and Cheers: Sport and the Making of Modern Canada.* Toronto: University of Toronto Press, 2001.

———. *Northern Sandlots: A Social History of Maritime Baseball.* Toronto: University of Toronto Press, 1995.

Http://histoirebaseball.150m.com/lpi4749 (Quebec Provincial League).

Http://www.athletepage.com/wcbl/index.html (Western Canada Baseball).

Http://www.baseball.ca/eng_home.cfn (Baseball Canada).

Humber, William. *Diamonds of the North: A Concise History of Baseball in Canada.* Toronto: Oxford University Press, 1995.

Humber, William, and John St. James. *All I Ever Thought About Was Baseball: Writings on a Canadian Pastime.* Toronto: University of Toronto Press, 1996.

Menary, David. *Terrier Town. Summer of '49.* Waterloo: Wilfrid Laurier University Press, 2003.

Prentice, Bruce, and Merrit Clifton. "Baseball in Canada." In *Total Baseball*, ed. John Thorn and Peter Palmer. New York: Warner, 1991.

Shearon, Jim. *Canada's Baseball Legends: True Stories of Canadians in the Big Leagues since 1879.* Kanata, Ontario: Malin Head, 1994.

Stubbs, Lewis St. George. *Shoestring Glory: Semi-Pro Ball on the Prairies.* Regina: Turnstone, 1996.

Turner, Dan. *Heroes, Bums and Ordinary Men: Profiles in Canadian Baseball.* Toronto: Doubleday, 1988.

Wetherell, Donald, and Irene Kmet. *Useful Pleasures: The Shaping of Leisure in Alberta, 1896–1945.* Regina: Canadian Plains Research Center, 1990.

3 | Europe

13 | Italy

No Hotdogs in the Bleachers

Known for Renaissance art, fabulous opera, and unparalleled cuisine, Italy has far less illustriously fielded professional baseball teams for over fifty years. Following the introduction of the game by American servicemen during World War II, small numbers of young Italians began forming teams in various cities up and down the boot. By 1948 league play began with five teams from Milan and one from Bologna each playing a game a week. The following year two leagues emerged, the Federazione and the Lega di Baseball Italiana, with teams from Rome, Milan, Bologna, Firenze, Modena, and other cities. By 1951 these evolved into the Federazione Italiana Baseball Softball (FIBS), which is still in existence and governs men's pro baseball and women's softball from its central offices in Rome and several regional offices. Throughout the 1950s and early 1960s, eight to twelve teams competed in FIBS, playing a game a week through an eighteen-week season. Though a few players received a small fee for their services, the league in those years likely resembled a recreational or semipro league more than the professional organization of teams playing today. By the 1970s each team's schedule increased to 30 or so games a year, and by the 1980s teams played between 50 and 60 games, usually with a 3-game series each weekend.

Despite this heritage, professional baseball attracts minimal attention in Italian sporting culture, with crowds counted in the hundreds attending regular season games in ballparks about the size of college or spring training facilities. The game receives scant coverage in local newspapers; in the country's national sports daily, *La Gazzetta dello Sport*, it is often easier to find scores of American MLB. This lack of popularity can to some degree be attributed to Italy's status as a single-sport nation, with soccer as the undisputed center of every sports fan's consciousness. Nearly all Italian men (and many women) support a soccer team with the same passion they have for their families. The popularity of soccer, however, does not fully account for baseball's failure to gain a foothold in Italy. Auto racing (meaning Ferrari on the F1 circuit), basketball, boxing, and even volleyball garner more media coverage and fan interest than baseball, though all lag well behind soccer.

Some signs of progress are evident. In 2002 the Federazione entered into an agreement to have a "Game of the Week" broadcast through a paid package to fans in cities with "major league" level teams. In addition, the league has begun holding national baseball camps for youth. Nevertheless, baseball in the *bel paese* remains a "boutique sport," about as popular as professional lacrosse in the United States. As such, it attracts few casual fans. The fans who do follow the game tend to be *appassionati* (die-hards). They are knowledgeable about the rules and zealous about their team. While the quality of play certainly falls short of that in the United States, Latin America, or Asia, fans enjoy a game that boasts a strong history of native-born players and teams, attracts a small group of foreign players, and offers a richly satisfying experience at the ballpark.

La Lega Maggior

In FIBS the men's "major league" is divided into levels A1 and A2. The A1 league, the higher level, presently fields ten teams, but over the years the number has risen as high as twenty when A1 assimilated several A2 teams during the early 1990s. In the past ten years or so, the A1 league has settled on eight teams playing a 54-game regular season, with single games on Friday nights and doubleheaders on Saturdays during the months paralleling the American professional season. Games are not scheduled on Sunday to avoid competing with soccer in April, May, and late September. To a U.S. fan the use of the designation "A" is unintentionally appropriate because the play in these leagues approximates that of the A-level minors in the States. Still, the A leagues offer exciting baseball.

Each year the top four teams of the A1 league enter the playoffs (two best-of-seven series) to determine the winner of the championship, called the *scudetto*, which literally means shield or escutcheon and describes the shape of the patch the champions wear the following year. The awarding and wearing of the *scudetto* originated in soccer and has been adopted by other Italian team sports as well as baseball. Following the A1 playoffs, the champion and runner-up enter into another series with the top two teams from A2, called the Coppa Italia (Italy Cup). Rather than a battle for recognized national supremacy, the Coppa, though its name sounds prestigious, is more an exhibition, akin to the various "city series" that used to take place in the United States between teams in the same city, for instance, the White Sox and Cubs. Rarely does a team from A2 win, although if one does it usually cashes in on the bragging rights and often becomes a contender in A1 the following year. A much more important series for A1 teams is played each June or July among the top professional teams from the various European leagues. In Italy the A1 league shuts down for two weeks while the two best teams from the previous year play for the coveted European Cup against counterparts from countries such as Holland, Spain, Germany, Russia, France, and, more recently, some Eastern European nations.

The A2 league has twenty-four teams divided evenly into two divisions, playing a 44-game schedule. Though A2 is considered a major league, the level of play falls a cut below A1, and teams rarely employ higher-priced foreign players as is common at the higher level. Nevertheless, the best A2 teams in any given year are roughly equal to the weakest in A1. In fact, A2 squads compete to advance to A1 with the A2 champion and runner-up advancing to A1 the following year, while the bottom two teams in A1 drop to A2. To clarify, imagine that the teams with the worst record in MLB, say Milwaukee and Tampa Bay, would drop to AAA ball, while the teams with the best record in AAA, say the Buffalo Bison and Norfolk Tides, would move into the majors the next year. Such an arrangement might force tight-fisted MLB owners to spend more to keep their teams competitive.

Below the A-level league there is a minor league system of sorts, with levels B and C. This is not to say that all teams at these levels are directly affiliated with A clubs, as in the American system. While a young player can use these lower levels to make a name for himself and perhaps garner a contract from an A-league team, most teams at B and C are independent. Like the higher-level teams, they can advance with a strong year or drop to a lower level with a poor one. Theoretically, a c-level team could eventually advance to A1 with several good years in succession. The B-league game is about equivalent to play at the lower divisions of college ball; C teams would probably be challenged by good high school teams in the United States. The players are paid, but they also have other jobs. At the C level there are several divisions, arranged geographically to save time and money on travel. These teams also have sponsors, often local, to help meet expenses. But like all pro teams in Italy, no matter what the sport, B and C teams, as well as those in A level, are subsidized by the weekly millions from the government-sponsored soccer lotteries, such as Toto Calcio and its many variations. These lotteries generate so much money that all pro teams—from soccer to women's volleyball—receive some kind of subsidy. For baseball, an unpopular sport, these subsidies can provide a sizable piece of a team's budget.

Legendary Players and Teams

Italian baseball, like its American counterpart, marks its history in statistics and legend, with the Federazione maintaining an archive of records in Trieste. Until recently the league statistician was Enzo Di Gesu of Turin, who compiled weekly box scores and stats and forwarded them to regional league offices. He also maintained a league home page, providing a wealth of statistical information.[1] Di Gesu also edited the Italian magazine *Tutto Baseball e Softball*, though finding this magazine on Italian newsstands is harder than finding an ERA under 3.00 on the Colorado Rockies' pitching staff. At one time it was difficult to compile career statistics of individual players, but the latest FIBS Web site lists player records back to 1960, championship winners, league leaders for each year, career leaders, records of the national team in competition, and complete records of the previous season. These stats provide a strong sense of the history and character of the Federazione, its legendary players, and the place of foreign players in it.

While there is no Babe Ruth of Italy, there are players who might be called the Cy Young and Ty Cobb of the Federazione. Giulio Glorioso fills the former role, but since he pitched in the early (and less developed) years of the league it is difficult to determine the scope of his talent. Dominating Italian hitters from the early 1950s to the late 1960s, Glorioso played most of his career with teams from Rome and perennial powers Parma and Nettuno, except for three years from 1960 to 1962 when he led the Milan team to three *scudetti*. In fifteen seasons from 1953 to 1967, Glorioso topped the league in strikeouts eleven times, averaging over 150 in seasons that averaged only 18 games. His most phenomenal year had to be 1961, when he whiffed 218, won each of Milano's 18 games, and posted a microscopic ERA of 0.23. In nine of his phenomenal prime of fifteen years, Glorioso led the league in wins, averaging fifteen a season when his teams were playing an 18-game schedule. In the heart of his career, 1961–67, he went 108-8-1.29. Only in the last three years of Glorioso's prime, when the Federazione increased the season to 32 games, was he not responsible for all of his team's wins. As might be expected, Glorioso dominated the ERA statistics, winning the crown seven times, and five times averaging less than one run a game. Following his fifteen-year prime, the glorious Giulio pitched seven more years, posting a record of 49-44, with over 803 strikeouts, pushing his career total over 2,500. Add to these numbers Glorioso's five no-hitters, and it is easy to see why he was contacted by the Cincinnati Reds for a possible tryout.

As if pitching were not enough, Glorioso played both infield and outfield and won two batting titles, with a .432 average in 1960 and a .444 average in 1961. Despite his prowess at the plate, Glorioso clearly must be measured by his pitching, for his statistics become even more phenomenal since the Federazione has always been and still is a hitter's league. From 1952 to 2002, only eight times has the batting champion hit under .400, and twice the leader has cracked the .500 mark. Indeed, it is not uncommon, even today, for teams to bat over .300. In 2002 second-place Bologna hit .306, and three other teams hit above .270. A few years earlier, league-leading Danesi Nettuno and runner-up Parma weighed in at .355 and .329, respectively. As for pitching, the cellar-dwelling Paterno team had a team ERA of 7.75, bad but well below that of hapless Verona's 11.15 in 1997. Scores in double figures are routine, and scoring over twenty runs in a game is not the anomaly it is in the United States. Some of this output may be attributed to the Federazione's use of aluminum bats in recent years, but even in its first decades when wooden bats prevailed, Federazione hitters put up astronomical numbers at the plate.

Among the most prolific of these hitters have been catcher Giorgio Castelli and outfielder Roberto Bianchi. If Glorioso is Italy's Cy Young, Castelli is its Ty Cobb. Castelli was scouted by American teams and after his rookie season in 1968 was offered a contract to be groomed as a backup for Johnny Bench, but the deal fell through when the Reds signed talented prospect Bill Plummer. Castelli remained in Italy, playing all his seasons with Parma, where he won eight of eleven league batting crowns from 1968 through 1978. His first was shared with another player at, for Castelli, an aberrantly low .324. But then it was his rookie year, and he was seventeen. The remaining seven were won outright with averages consistently well over .400, two over .500, and a high of .540. In 1974, his best year and maybe the best year ever by a professional player, Castelli won a triple crown, hitting .515, with 26 *fuori-campi* (home runs), 79 RBI, and a staggering 1.010 slugging average in a 44-game season. Castelli's prime years were 1968 through 1978, but he played until 1984, remaining one of the Federazione's most potent hitters and finishing with 1,064 hits, a lifetime average of .423, 163 home runs, and 696 RBI in 605 games.

Through there may not be a Babe Ruth of Italy, outfielder Roberto Bianchi, who retired in 1999, has been the Federazione's most consistent power hitter. As an eighteen-year-old rookie outfielder for Bologna in 1981, Bianchi served notice on Italian pitchers that he would be a force for years to come, leading the league with 43 RBI in a 40-game season. This marked the first of Bianchi's seven RBI titles, among which are a record 102 over the 66-game schedule of 1985. Though Bianchi has led the league in home runs only three times, he is the Federazione's career leader with 288. Six times he has been the league's most potent *bombardieri*, or leader in slugging average. Of his six leading figures, the lowest is .741 in 1990, the highest 1.051 in 1987, the year he also won the triple crown with 27 homers, 72 RBI, and an average of .474. This league-leading average is the highest of Bianchi's three batting crowns, with the others at merely .460 and .466. Retiring at age thirty-six, Bianchi remained a potent hitter throughout his career, for fifteen years the biggest bat in the lineup of the always contending Bologna squad, before splitting his last three years with Rimini and Modena. His career line astounds: .384-288-1,170 in 949 games.

In addition to legendary players, the Federazione boasts some storied teams. Nettuno, a small seacoast town about forty kilometers southwest of Rome, is home to one of the charter members. Along with three European Cup Championships, Nettuno has won fifteen A1 *scudetti* to lead the pack, including several in the 1950s with Glorioso on the mound, and six of the last thirteen. Nettuno's introduction to baseball began with the formation of softball teams after the game was introduced by the U.S. Marines, who landed at nearby Anzio during the campaign from Sicily to Rome. In fact, Nettuno became the site of a cemetery for fallen American soldiers. The softball teams quickly developed into baseball teams, and today the town is one of the few hotbeds of the game in Italy, hosting teams at various levels of competition. Another strong squad hails from Rimini, an Adriatic resort town known more for its nightlife and beaches. Rimini has won ten *scudetti* (three of five from 1998 to 2002). Other storied teams in the Federazione's annals are Parma, where Castelli played, and, in the early years, Milan. Though Milan no longer fields an A1 team, it dominated in the 1960s. Parma and Milan rank third in number of *scudetti*, each claiming eight, but Parma also boasts the distinction of winning a remarkable thirteen of the thirty European Cup tournaments.

Nettuno might be called the Yankees of Italy; however, Italian teams are not identified by nicknames but by city and sponsor. In the last few years, for example, Nettuno is listed as Danesi Nettuno; Danesi is the name of the coffee company that sponsors the team. These sponsorships are necessary to help cover players' salaries and expenses because gate receipts are small and there are no lucrative TV contracts. Sponsors also may change from year to year, so while important financially, rarely do they become part of a team's identity. Oddly, many Italian teams will integrate the name of the sponsor with the uniform and logo of a team in American MLB without adopting the name of either. For example, Nettuno dresses like Cleveland, complete with Chief Wahoo logo on the hat, but is not known as the Indians. On the back of the Nettuno jersey, the player's number is imprinted in white against the brown backdrop of a coffee cup labeled "Danesi." Parma mimics the Angels and recently Bologna the Mariners, but fans refer to teams by town or city, rather than sponsors or MLB nicknames. This is fitting given the Italian people's fanatical, at times irrational pride in their hometowns. Unlike in America, where Major League teams are located in large cities, because of sponsorships and subsidies Italian teams may hail from small towns as well as great metropolises, little Castenaso in the Emiglia Romano region as well as Florence or Rome. Thus a team in A1 can be a source of great pride for a small, lesser-known locale.

Americani e Stranieri, or Americans and Other Foreigners

While it is difficult to assess the quality of play in Italy, one measure is the performance of foreigners who have played in the Federazione, particularly those who have played in the majors. Until recently Italian teams were limited to two foreign players on the roster, but a lawsuit brought by foreign basketball players against their league has relaxed the quotas in all sports. Some teams do not have any; others will carry three or four. These *stranieri*, usually from the United States or Latin America, are expected to be stars.

Among the most recognizable of the non-Italian players listed in the Federazione's records are former Pirate and Tiger utility infielder Jim Morrison; Lenny Randle, a solid infielder whose best years were with the Rangers and Mets; and Jorge Orta, who played most of his sixteen years in the bigs with the White Sox and Royals. In roughly one hundred at bats a season during a twelve-year big league career ending in 1988, Morrison averaged .260 with a high of .304 in 1983. He also hit 112 home runs, belting a career-best 13 in 1985, his only year as an everyday player. In 1990 Morrison turned up in the Federazione, putting up numbers of .390-12-75 in 62 games. Randle is one of a few recognizable position players who spent more than a season in Italy, playing four from 1983 through 1986. In his first year, at thirty-four, Randle won the batting title with an average of .475. In 1986 he led the league in *basi rubati* (stolen bases) with 32. After only 27 home runs in twelve years and 1,138 games in the American majors, he hit 47 in four seasons and approximately 200 games abroad. Clearly the success of these two average players, at an advanced age, illustrates the gap between MLB and the Federazione. Not every American, however, has been successful. Jorge Orta, probably the best of the three with MLB career numbers of .278-130-715, signed with Parma during the stretch drive of the 1994 campaign but was a disappointment, batting only .222 with only 1 homer and 4 RBI in 14 games. Perhaps Orta did not have time to acclimate himself to the pitching; then again, he was five years removed from his MLB career and forty-three years old.

Other players with much briefer big league service or time in the minors only also crop up in FIBS records. Among the briefest but most illustrious tours in Italy is Brad Komminsk's two years in 1994-95. Never fulfilling the potential hoped for by the Braves and Indians, this hulking outfielder smashed 38 home runs for Rimini in 89 games over two seasons, topping all sluggers with 19 in 1994. In 1994 Komminsk also led the league with 61 RBI and posted the best slugging average in both years with .804 and .848. One of the more interesting short-timers (no pun intended) is Harry Chappas. Other than Eddie Gaedel, Chappas, at five-foot-three is usually recognized as the smallest man ever to play in the majors. A shortstop signed by Bill Veeck, Chappas averaged .245 in 72 games over three years with the White Sox. Four years later he hit .319 with 8 homers in 56 games with Grosseto, a long-established and always competitive Tuscan squad.

More than a few pitchers have also tried their hand in FIBS. Jason Simontacchi's recent success with the Cardinals brought more attention to Italian baseball than it has ever received in the United States. The publicity, however, was not always positive as commentators used his experience in Italy to underscore that he had seemingly "come out of nowhere" and miraculously learned to pitch all of a sudden. True, Simontacchi had dominated FIBS hitters in the 2000 season, going 15-1 with a miniscule ERA of 1.56 and 136 strikeouts in 133 innings as he pitched Rimini to a *scudetto*. But he himself said that he had learned a change-up in Italy that improved his pitching beyond the mediocrity he had shown in a couple of minor league seasons prior to going there.[2] Like Simontacchi, Ed Vosberg spent a year in Italy early in his career. A journeyman reliever in the 1990s, Vosberg is perhaps best (or worst) remembered for scalping his complimentary All-Star Game tickets when he played for Texas. In 1992, pitching for Novara, an also-ran, he won 9 and lost 5, giving up only 2.34 runs per nine innings and striking out 145 in 123 innings, before returning to the United States to put in eight seasons with five teams. The versatile Vosberg also played 35 games at first and in the outfield, putting up good numbers: .319-9-37.

Unlike Simontacchi and Vosberg, other MLB players surfaced in Italy looking for a last hurrah and a nice paycheck rather than a steppingstone to the majors. Journeyman starter and Italian American Pete Falcone enjoyed probably the most spectacular of these seasons in 1990. Having retired in 1984 with a 70-90 career record with the Giants, Cards, Mets, and Braves, Falcone went 17-2 with 183 strikeouts in 143 innings and a 1.19 ERA but faltered in the playoffs, losing 2 of 3 with an ERA of 3.48 as his Rimini team was edged out by Nettuno for the championship.

Though not as dominant as Falcone and Simontacchi, other single-season pitchers fared well. In 1997, after a respectable but less than stellar big league career, Canadian Kirk McCaskill was signed to anchor the pitching staff of Sarti Firenze, the Florence team that had just advanced into A1 after winning the A2 championship in 1996. McCaskill pitched well but in bad luck. Though posting an ERA of 2.01 and striking out over 100 in 107.1 innings, the thirty-six-year-old former Angel and White Sox southpaw finished an unremarkable 6-6 as 19 of the 43 runs scored against him were unearned. Les Straker, who had only two years with the Twins but two starts in the 1987 Series, cobbled together an 8-8 record for Bologna in 1991 but redeemed himself with a playoff win in which he yielded only 1 run and fanned 10. After twelve years and a 79-92 record, mostly with Cleveland, Rick Waits won 40 games, lost only 11, and amassed 347 strikeouts in three years (1987–89), though he never led the league in any category. More recently, Jaime Navarro, a veteran of twelve seasons with Milwaukee and three other Major League clubs, led Grosseto's dominant pitching staff with a 15-2 record. Joining with two young Italian pitchers, who were a combined 26-2, Navarro helped

Grosseto edge out perennial contender Bologna for the regular season championship and the league playoffs.

Few American players have found long careers in Italy, but there have been exceptions. Craig Stimac, a catcher and third baseman who appeared in 29 games in 1980–81 with the Padres, played significantly longer than most ex–Major Leaguers. With 533 hits and 95 career home runs but never winning the Italian home run crown, Stimac's career in Italy spanned six years. His first, 1984, was also his most notable when he nearly won the triple crown with a .436 batting average and 74 RBI. Though he also led the league in slugging at .855, Stimac was beaten out for the home run title 23–18 by fellow American Mark Funderburk. Funderburk, who had batted .200 in 2 games with Minnesota in 1981, would return to the Twins in 1985 to hit .314 and poke 2 dingers in 29 games before dropping into baseball obscurity.

Several Americans who likely spent time in the minors or on college teams but did not have the talent to reach the majors chased their baseball dreams to Italy. Career records indicate that though often briefly successful, they returned home after a season or two. The most notable exceptions are Danny Newman and Dave Sheldon, whose career stats, ages, appearances among career leaders, and continued presence in the league indicate they have made the *bel paese* home. Both Sheldon and Newman pitch as well as play in the field. A native of Cleveland, Newman was still playing at thirty-nine in 2003, after fifteen seasons as an outfielder, first baseman, and pitcher. Though never leading the Federazione in an offensive category, his career batting average following the 2002 season was a lofty .354, and on the mound he had won 107 and lost 86 with an ERA of 2.89. Sheldon, a Californian, had amassed numbers of .323-125-625 when at forty he entered his twentieth season after joining Newman on the Bologna team for opening day 2003. Primarily a hard-hitting shortstop, Sheldon has been less distinguished as a pitcher. Working mostly in relief after two lackluster seasons as a starter early in his career, Sheldon owns a meager lifetime record of 21-20 with an American Leaguesque ERA of 4.01. Both Sheldon and Newman obtained Italian passports in the late 1990s and were members of Italy's Olympic team at the 2000 Sydney Games.

Quality of Play

Given the success of these players, it is surprising that more aging stars or failed minor leaguers have not chosen to play in Italy. Aside from offering the opportunity to develop or extend a career, Italy is a thoroughly modern nation with all the amenities found in the United States, beautiful beaches, and breathtaking landscapes, as well as matchless traditions in culture and the arts (though these last two are not always at the top of most athletes' list of priorities). But there are likely several reasons American players have not flocked to Italy as they have to Japan. First, the Japanese leagues pay far more. In Italy the average player makes only about the equivalent of $3,000 a month, though he also receives a car and a rent-free apartment. While a former Major Leaguer with solid credentials might earn significantly more, playing in the Federazione is not the way to riches.

Second, the aluminum bats, the lack of depth on most pitching staffs, the resultant prolific hitting, and the sometimes wide gaps between the strongest and weakest players and the best and worst teams detract somewhat from the character of the Italian game when compared to its American or Japanese counterpart. High scores, for instance, result from the fact that the quality of pitching drops significantly from a team's two best starters to its bullpen. Thus, if a starter falters, the middle- or late-inning relievers lack the talent to prevent the game from degenerating into a softball-like slugfest. The gaps between the best and worst teams are larger than one finds in American professional leagues. While the league champion often wins 70 or even 80 percent of its games, teams in last often lose the same percentages of games. In 2004 Grosseto's pitching so dominated the league that Navarro set a record for winning percentage at .879, finishing 47-7, but just 4 games ahead of Bologna's 43-11, .796, second-place effort. In the league basement, Saim Rho went only 6-48, for a percentage of .111. Other recent years have seen similar gaps between the best and worst squads. Rimini, 2002 champs, posted a .722 winning percentage while cellar-dwelling Paterno won only 7 of 53 for a percentage of .132. In 1997 the Verona team far exceeded the futility of the 1962 Mets, losing all of its games to finish 0-54.

Despite its problems, Italian baseball may eventually produce Major

League talent. In 1997 and 1998 three of the Federazione's stars played in the American minors. Claudio Liverziani, then a young outfielder from Juventus Torino and now one of the biggest stars of FIBS, was signed by the Mariners and posted a respectable .262 average with the single-A Wisconsin Timber Rattlers. Lauded for his fundamentals and attitude, Liverziani was projected to move into AA but started slowly and put up meager numbers—.248-3-33C—before returning home. The same year, another Italian player, Davide Rigoli, fared less well. Signed to a single-A contract by the Expos, he hit only .178 in limited duty and returned to the Grosseto club for 1998. Andrea Castri, a power-hitting third base-man, signed by the Yankees and assigned to low-A Oneonta, hit .241 with a couple of homers and 14 RBI in 1998 in 141 at bats. The next year, at high-A Greensboro, he was released after dropping to .195-4-24.

That all three of these players continue as stars in FIBS today does not appear to reflect well on Italian baseball. Nevertheless, their experiences indicate that Italian players are beginning to be competitive. Developing players of the quality of those in the Americas or Japan will take time, but increased MLB interest in Italy could hasten the process. Recently the Mariners and Dodgers, two teams with an eye for international talent, have entered into informal agreements with Italian teams. Such accords provide Italian coaches access to knowledge that can help them develop young players. Furthermore, in 2003 MLB had representatives measuring Rome's Olympic Stadium in hopes of scheduling a regular season series there, as has been done in Japan.

Though not comparable to American or Japanese baseball, Italian baseball compares favorably with that of other European nations, and even internationally the Italian national team, Gli Azzuri (the Blues), as they're called, have managed to win some games.[3] In the European Championships, a biennial tournament of national teams, Italy has won eight times, finished second fourteen, and third three in the twenty-five tournaments played. In short, they have finished in the money in each one. Only Holland, finishing first seventeen times and second seven, has done better. In the European Cup, the annual tournament of profes-sional rather than national teams, the Italians have won twenty-six of the thirty-nine years the Cup has been contested to Holland's ten. Like other European teams, the Italian nationals have had less success off the

13. *Italian National Team playing in the 1978 World Championship. Parma, Italy.* (Photo by Maurizio Bonazzi.)

continent, compiling a 45-71 mark in international World Championship tournaments and going 8-23 in Olympic matches. While these international records are hardly impressive, they are respectable in view of the limited popularity of baseball in Europe.

Portarmi Via Allo Stadio, or Take Me Out to the Ballpark

Though to an American Italian baseball probably looks about as good as Major League soccer would to an Italian, the game offers any fan a pleasant experience at the ballpark. While the 1997 FIBS home page optimistically listed the average turnout between 500 and 2,000, with sellouts during playoffs, crowds are generally closer to the low end of this average. The small crowds, though detrimental to league coffers, ensure that everyone has a great seat. In addition, the crowd size promotes camaraderie among fans that leads to conversation about the game and allows children to roam freely, never far from their parents' eye. Most fans are very knowledgeable, and though scorecards are not available for sale at the park, usually someone is keeping score in a score book brought to the game. While fans root passionately, often creatively cursing umpires and opposing players, conspicuously absent is the rowdy behavior that mars European soccer and increasingly threatens sporting events in the United States.

The lack of rowdyism is likely attributable to the fact that no one at the game is drunk. Italians may be famous for producing wine, but they drink it largely with meals or by the single glass when taking respite in a bar or café. For most people, to become conspicuously drunk is considered a social disgrace and would not be tolerated in the social space of a ballpark. Alcohol is not sold in the stands, but then neither is anything else. No hot dogs, peanuts, or Cracker Jacks. When Italian fans want refreshment or respite, they repair to the small bar in each park. While an Italian bar serves beer, wine, and a full line of liquor, its resemblance to an American bar ends there. People in Italy do not sit in a bar and drink for hours. They may take a drink or two and chat with friends, but bars are usually small cafés with a stand-up counter and limited seating. Even in the larger bars, most patrons stand at counters, or if there is a lot of seating it is outside at sidewalk tables. Along with alcoholic drinks, bars offer espresso, cappuccino, fruit juices, mineral waters, a variety of pastries and sandwiches, and often candy and ice cream. Children are welcome, drunks are not. At the ballpark, fans may wander down to the bar for a quick *apertivo* or *panino* (small sandwich), but the most they will carry back into the stands is a bottle of water or an ice cream cone. This behavior likely results from cultural attitudes toward eating. Italians tend to view food more seriously than most people do. It is something to be savored *a tavola* during leisurely meals, not eaten on the run or in the steady snacking that Americans practice in U.S. ballparks.

The ballparks themselves, as mentioned, are about the size of older A ball or spring training parks, with capacities ranging from one to seven thousand. As would be expected, the parks consist of a main grandstand behind the plate, usually covered, with uncovered bleachers extending down each baseline. The grandstands are made of concrete but without the ballpark chairs common in U.S. parks. One sits on the concrete, or at best a small plastic seat without a back. Some fans, however, bring lawn chairs and set them up in the stands. Though small, the parks often have distinguishing characteristics. At Bologna, for instance, a ceramic baseball about three feet tall holds a plaque honoring Gianni Falchi, a baseball pioneer in the city and the man for whom the park was named. Nettuno boasts an impressive entryway, with "Nettuno Baseball" in large black lettering contrasting with the white façade of the circular home plate grandstand. Florence's park offers a Lilliputian charm, sitting in the massive shadow of the nearby home of A. C. Fiorentina soccer, a stadium befitting an NFL team. At Grosseto, though the stadium is a rather shabby concrete affair, it sits in a beautiful city park, and adjacent to it is a café with expansive outdoor seating under bright Cinzano umbrellas. Fans congregate here before and after games, to socialize not just with each other but with the players. One such night when I was there, Jaime Navarro, not long out of the American majors, was there hanging out with teammates and chatting with fans. To any tourist unfamiliar with baseball, the players would be unrecognizable as they enjoy a pre- or postgame snack.

More striking than the parks themselves are their settings, with postcard views behind the outfield fences. In Florence the Tuscan hills rise above the tiled roofs of the small palazzi of the tidy middle-class neighborhood beyond the outfield fence. Down the left-field line at Bologna's Stadio di Gianni Falchi, the fan can see high-rise apartments, symbols of modern Italy, above a line of lush greenery, while beyond the fences in center and right, olive trees growing on the hillsides evoke the nation's agrarian roots. B-level Macerata in the Marche region plays in a small park on a hillside. Above is the walled medieval town the team calls home; below is a wide valley of green fields ending against the rugged horizon of the Apennine mountains. At Livorno's home field, "I Mori" via Sommati, fans smell the salt air as they look beyond the outfield fence to see the trains of the Roma-Torino line wending their way up and down the Tuscan coast.

Transplanted to Italian culture, baseball ultimately suffers a lack of popularity but enjoys a strong commitment from a coterie of devotees. Unlike MLB, which constantly woos the casual fan that Italian baseball lacks, Italian baseball appeals only to the knowledgeable core who truly care about the game. In other words, professional baseball in Italy has exactly the status American owners fear: it is a game appreciated and supported by the knowledgeable few, a group of what we call "purists" in America, but it has not achieved the status of sport as business or industry, as baseball has in the United States. Though FIBS will continue to develop and improve, with soccer by far the nation's dominant sport, baseball will likely remain a sport for only the passionate fan, and therein, perhaps, lies its beauty.

Italian Baseball Terms

batting average: *media battuta*
catcher(s): *recevitore, recevitori*
center fielder: *esterno centro*
fan(s): *tifoso, tifosi*
first base player: *primo baso*
home plate: *casa* (literally "house," since the Italian language does not distinguish between house and home)
home run(s): *fuoricampo, fuoricampi* (literally "outside field")
infielder(s): *interiore, interiori*. Players are identified specifically by base: *primo baso*
left fielder: *esterno destra*
outfielder(s): *esterno, esterni*
pitcher(s): *lancitore, lancitori*
player(s): *giocatore, giocatori*
pitch: *lancia*
right fielder: *esterno destra*
run: *punti*
runs batted in: *punti battuti in casa*
second base player: *secondo baso*
shortstop: *interbaso*
single, double, triple: all resonate with English, *singoli, doppie, tripli*
stolen bases: *basi rubati* (bases robbed)
strikeout: no translation; Italians use the English word
third base player: *terzo baso*
umpire: *arbitro*
wild pitch: *lancia pazza* (literally "crazy pitch")

Notes

1. FIBS statistics are taken from http://www.baseball-softball.it, the official Web site of the league. Other stats come from the former league home page run by Di Gesu, which is now defunct. Other useful places to find information on FIBS are the Baseball Italian site at http://www.baseballitalia.com, and Baseball News, an on-line weekly magazine at http://www.anteprima.net/baseball.

2. Mike Dodd, "Perseverance Pays Off for 'Greybeard Rookies,'" USA Today, July 7, 2002, available at http://www.usatoday.com.

3. Records for international play are assembled from the Web site of the Confederation of European Baseball: http://www.baseballeurope.com.

14 | Holland

An American Coaching *Honkbal*

I remember walking to the mound with a runner on second base and the left-handed hitter coming to the plate. I had every intention of walking the batter with first base open, in a 1-run game, and facing the right-handed hitter following him. However, Jan Hijzelendoorn, the righty pitcher, and my catcher, Paul Smit, felt we could get the lefty from Team USA out with off-speed pitches away. I reluctantly let Hijzelendoorn pitch to Barry Bonds. We did get him out on a grounder to the second baseman. That fall of 1984, I was coaching the Dutch National Team. Would I be the last manager to decide to pitch to Barry Bonds with a base open?

That was not the only major decision I had to make as the Dutch head coach. My role went way beyond calling pitches, making lineups, and giving signs. A more important job was to change the approach and strategies of the Dutch baseball players and baseball community.

Dutch baseball, called *honkbal*, got its start in 1910 and two years later the Royal Dutch Baseball and Softball Association (KNBSB) was founded. During World War I, when American soldiers visited Holland, the game began to grow. The American soldiers stationed in Europe played games in Holland, and the Dutch took a liking to baseball. Holland is a small country, and although its favorite sport is soccer, the Dutch people who played and followed baseball became dedicated and passionate about the sport. Today, there are an estimated 30,000 baseball and softball members of the KNBSB.

Wanting to improve their status and baseball performance, the Dutch Baseball Federation has long encouraged baseball teams from America to visit and play against Dutch players and teams. My Dutch baseball experiences began in just this way, in spring 1975 with the Springfield College baseball team. Just after I finished my third year as a graduate assistant at Springfield College, working with the legendary college baseball coach Archie Allen, we were invited to Holland to play exhibition games and put on clinics. The Kinheim Baseball Club of Haarlem and their members hosted the trip. Kinheim played baseball in the *hoofdklasse* (head class) of Holland, which is the highest level of baseball. The Springfield College players and coaches stayed with club members during our visit.

The baseball system in Holland, like other countries in Europe, is quite different than that of the United States. In the United States, sports such as baseball are played at the interscholastic and intercollegiate levels. However, in Holland, there are no interscholastic or intercollegiate teams, though occasionally Dutch schools would have "fun" games between city schools. These games were informal with no qualified coaches to teach or coach baseball. Instead, physical education teachers organized them. In addition, there were no public parks with baseball fields where kids could go out and play pickup or informal baseball. The only way a youngster could play baseball would be in a family club that sponsored baseball. These were private clubs in which a family paid a membership fee to belong.

There were various leagues based on the teams' abilities, with the top league level being the head class. The organization of the leagues was such that every game was significant no matter where a team was in the standings. At the end of the year, the last two teams in the head class were demoted to the first class for the subsequent season. The best two teams in the first class were promoted to the head class. It was a great approach to keeping player and fan interest throughout the season. Since the goal of a team was either to move up in a league classification or stay at the same level, it did not matter if the two best or two worst teams in the league were playing. No one wanted to be demoted to a lower class.

There is a national champion in each class of baseball. After the

Dutch baseball playoffs end, a European tournament, made up of the champions from the various baseball-playing countries in Europe, is held every two years. Each club team is allowed to have two American or foreign players on its team. Usually the most financially sound clubs would sign Americans in order to put the best possible team on the field. Occasionally, there would be an American coach, and I was later fortunate enough to become one of these coaches.

Our Springfield College team spent approximately three weeks in Holland in 1975, and we traveled all over the country to play different clubs. The Dutch teams did not have a large number of pitchers on their teams and that made for high-scoring games for us. We played clubs from the different classes, and we went through the competition pretty easily, undefeated at 7-0, until we lost our last game against the Dutch National Baseball Team 3–2.

We played several games in the rain until we finished the game or until it was impossible to play. The Dutch were used to rainy conditions, and the weather did not seem to affect them. The attitude was that the weather could be worse tomorrow, so why not play today.

One significant difference between American and Dutch baseball is the small size of the playing fields. Since Dutch land is at a premium, and the people building the baseball fields did not envision baseball growing in popularity the way it has, the majority of baseball fields are quite small compared to college fields or town fields in the United States. A typical Dutch field may be just 270 feet down the foul lines and 320 to 330 feet to center field. Most fields are not symmetrical because the baseball facilities must be stuffed into the available space.

Compared to American players, the Dutch players were not as strong. Many of our student-athletes played other sports, including American football and basketball, and were involved in strength training. Though many Dutch players were tall and athletic, they lacked upper body strength. Most Dutch kids play soccer and cycle for exercise, which do not build the upper body. Charley Urbanus, a Dutch player who did graduate work at Springfield College in 1980, took weight training and brought it back to the baseball establishment in Holland where others followed his example.

The Amstel Tigers

After my first trip to Holland I thought it would be nice to coach there sometime in the near future. In 1979 I got that opportunity when the Amstel club wanted an American coach. The Amstel Tigers were located in Amsterdam, along the Amstel River, and were one of the strongest clubs in the head class. Two of their board members, Han and Charlie Urbanus, were among the most knowledgeable baseball people in Holland. A very notable baseball player was "young" Charley Urbanus, Han's son.

When I arrived in Amsterdam, I went to the Urbanuses' home and met with Han, old Charlie, and young Charley. We discussed the team's strengths and weaknesses, and evaluated all the Tigers players. It became apparent during this meeting that I had been brought to Holland to win a championship. The Tigers were one of the most talented teams in the head class with several players on the National Team, but the team had not yet won a league championship. The club promoted Dutch baseball and its players, and was the only club in the league that did not have American players on its squad. The administrators believed the Dutch players' development would be hurt by having Americans in the lineup. The majority of Americans who played in Holland were normally the key positional guys—pitchers, catchers, and shortstops. As I later found a lack of quality Dutch players at these positions, I could understand the Tigers' philosophy. Yet they believed that an American coach was necessary to win a championship.

At the first practice session with my new team, I tried hard to put names to faces. I was surprised by how much batting practice players received. We batted for one and one-half hours, which I later found out was normal in Holland. The Tigers did, however, spend time practicing offensive and defensive situations, which most Dutch clubs did not emphasize. This was the influence of old Charlie Urbanus.

My first baseball game was two days later, a Saturday, and I was very excited to begin my coaching experience. We won on both Saturday and Sunday. However, there were a few situations during the weekend that made me realize that coaching Dutch baseball was going to be different than coaching in America.

The Dutch players' approach to the game was more laid back and less structured than that of my American college players. It was common for the Dutch to have tea or coffee and sandwiches before they took the field for pregame practice. Some smoked a cigarette in uniform, even when walking around the field. I could not believe that the players would fill themselves up with food and caffeine before a game. During the seventh-inning stretch the players would have a snack and drink, such as tea, cola, or coffee for energy. I wanted to change these "bad" habits, but I realized it would take time and much convincing.

After Sunday's game I was feeling pretty good about our two wins. Therefore, I was surprised to be called to an emergency meeting with the team's administrators. It seems they were concerned that I did not start the backup right fielder in either game of the weekend. They thought he might quit the team if I did not give him one start on the weekends. I reminded the group that they had emphasized how important it was for the Tigers to win. It was the proverbial conflict of "social/fun vs. winning." Oh well, maybe it was not that different from college coaching.

The league schedule was 36 games spread out over eighteen weeks with 2 games per week. Most teams did not have much pitching, but you needed at least two starters. Later, when I coached the National Team, I convinced the Dutch Baseball Federation to play a third league game on Wednesdays. I believed that for the Dutch players to improve, they needed to play more games. After all, it was normal for American college players to play 50 games or more in the spring and another 40 to 50 games in the summer.

The baseball development of Dutch youngsters, ages eight to fifteen, was similar to that of children in the United States. However, after that, American baseball players develop more rapidly than the Dutch because they receive much more exposure to the game. I really believed the number of games played per year made a significant difference in how a player improved. The Dutch are three or four years behind the Americans. Since there are no collegiate or high school sports in Holland, the only baseball experience for the Dutch players was the league format. It would take a Dutch player three years to play as many games as played by a Division I player in the United States, since a U.S. player typically plays fall and spring baseball on campus and a series of summer league games.

In spite of their limited playing experience, some Dutch players have succeeded at the highest levels of professional baseball. Wim Remmerswall, a right-handed pitcher, played for the Red Sox organization and was with Major League club for two seasons in 1979 and 1980. Ultimately he had a hard time adjusting to American baseball, and he left the Red Sox to return to Holland. He later played in the Italian professional baseball league. Another Dutch success was Bert Blyleven, a pitcher with one of the best curve balls in the Major Leagues. Blyleven was a Dutch native, though he moved to the United States with his family as a child. He is still considered a possibility for the U.S. Baseball Hall of Fame.

Umpiring was another strange facet of Dutch baseball. Many of the umpires there had not grown up playing baseball and did not have a real feel for the game. In club baseball, the umpires were basically volunteers, and, as a result, it was difficult to criticize them. They made some of the games an adventure. Some umpires felt they were as important as the players. I really thought some bad calls were made by the umpires to bring attention to themselves. The Dutch players would get very upset and emotional over the bad calls, but there was not much you could do. Like the weather, the umpires were just part of the normal baseball landscape in Holland.

That first season, 1979, our Amstel Tigers won their first championship. We finished the season with a 30-6 record and a 14-game winning streak. Considering that games were only played on weekends, we went seven weeks without losing a ball game. My club was ecstatic, and I got a traditional dumping in a dirty Dutch canal. In the spring of 1980 my family and I returned to Holland and again we were the champions of Holland.

Despite our success, the Dutch media could be annoyingly negative. In the United States I was used to reporters being generally positive in their analysis, reporting the outcome and key happenings in the game. At home, reporters seemed to realize that my college baseball players were pure amateurs and they did not analyze them like professional athletes. However, the Dutch media dealt with their players and teams like we do in the tough media cities of New York and Boston. The Dutch players attend school or maintain regular jobs as teachers, doctors, businessmen, and so forth, and they play baseball as a hobby. They are amateurs, not professional ballplayers. Yet the sportswriters were mercilessly critical. I later found that it was easier for our team to play in baseball tournaments abroad, where there was less scrutiny and less pressure on everyone.

The Dutch National Team

In 1983 the Dutch National Baseball Organization (KNBSB) was looking for an American baseball coach because the Dutch were going to host the World Baseball Championships for the first time. I felt honored when I was hired to coach the Dutch National Team.

The KNBSB thought we should develop a three-year plan geared toward success in the World Championships in 1986. The format of international baseball competition is similar to American football and Major League Baseball playoffs and World Series. International baseball tournaments are short-term affairs, like a World Series, with each game taking on more significance, resulting in a lot of pressure on the players and coaches to perform well.

As I reviewed the results of the previous international tournaments, I noticed the Dutch teams were competitive in most games, but consistently gave up a big inning of three or more runs that took them out of a ball game. The starting pitchers seemed to go too long. I did not think we would have starting pitchers who could last six or seven innings against countries like the United States, Cuba, Taiwan, and Japan. I thought we should use more pitchers for fewer innings. Bart Volkerijk was probably the best Dutch pitcher with the most international experience. My thought was to make Bart our closer and use the younger pitchers as starters and middle guys so that they would have less pressure on them. I believe it is easier to start a game than to close a game; the toughest outs are in the seventh, eighth, and ninth innings. Next I had to convince Bart to embrace this new strategy. Bart agreed to give my idea a try. However, I did not anticipate the uproar over this decision—Dutch baseball people, media, and fans thought that Shapiro was crazy or stupid. Take the best pitcher and make him a reliever, what nonsense!

14. *The Dutch National Team in 1986 in Haarlem. Manager Harvey Shapiro in the fore-ground.* (Photo courtesy of Harvey Shapiro.)

I spent many weekends watching Dutch club baseball in order to se-lect the best players for the National Team. I held practices on Wednes-day nights with an elite group of Dutch players until the final group of players was selected. The first major event for the National Team was the Haarlem Honkbal Week in mid-July. Other than the European Championships, it is the most notable baseball tournament in Europe. The stadium in Haarlem is like an old American minor league ballpark with seating for approximately 7,000.

The tournament is a weeklong, round robin event with the best teams meeting for the championship on the final day. I was anxious to see how my team would perform. I tried to instill a philosophy of unselfish teamwork in the players and encouraged them to play "National League" (American) style baseball—be aggressive on the bases, steal bases, use the hit-and-run, and generally play "small ball." I did not want to sit back and wait to score with just base hits, as I did not think we would hit enough against our international competition. I was especially curious about my new pitching philosophy—using two or three pitchers a game with Bart Volkerijk closing for us. The whole team was very young, and I had to be patient, reminding myself that we were looking to the future. I told the players that we wanted to improve with each game and that we had to play the process (nine innings) and not just play for the win. Yes, we wanted to build our team confidence, which comes with winning, but it was more important that we improve and set the stage for the future.

After the festive opening ceremonies, with all the teams parading on the field, we opened the tournament against Taiwan. After a Taiwanese home run in the second inning, we scored three runs. My starter and mid-reliever pitched well, and I could have finished the game without using Bart. However, I wanted to see how he would handle the closer role. Well, he had an easy one-two-three ninth inning, and we won the first game 3–2 in front of 5,000 enthusiastic Dutch fans.

We finished the round robin play in first place, putting us in the Haarlem Championship game against Team Canada. My first coaching experience with my National Team was going well; even the Dutch press seemed to be impressed with the team, though that would soon change. In the final game, the score was tied 1–1 going into the top of the seventh inning when we fell apart. Canada scored ten runs after two were out and nobody on base. After such a successful week of playing good baseball, that one inning devastated us. In the press conference after the game, the media really gave me a tough time—they wanted to know how I let it all happen. My six-year-old son, Scott, was with me in the pressroom, and he whispered to me that his tee ball team did not always win either.

In October we traveled to Curaçao for my team's first competition outside of Holland. With a gambling casino in our hotel, I put a 2:00 a.m. curfew on the team. Since this was the beginning of our trip, I stayed up and oversaw the casino area. I was more exhausted than the players, but the curfew was kept, though my players did not like having any restrictions placed on them. I reminded the players that there would be no smoking or drinking in uniform. I wanted the players to play and act like national athletes representing their country. I encouraged them to take a light swim in the morning to relax before the tropical heat set in.

In our game against Panama, a fight broke out. A Panamanian runner tried to steal second and was going to be out. The runner stopped and put up his hands, signaling that he was giving up. He then elbowed my second baseman, knocking out a tooth and sending him to the ground. I sprinted out to second base, and the Panamanian team ran out as well. As I approached the bag, I realized that I was the only member of the Dutch group out there. Fortunately, nothing happened other than lots of yelling by both sides. However, I came to realize that the Dutch are not physical people and not interested in protecting their own teammate.

From Curaçao, we departed for Cuba. Because of Cuba's tight security, flights arrived and departed from the country only at night so that nobody could see their military installations. Consequently, we arrived in Cuba in the middle of the night. During the two hours we spent in Cuban customs, we experienced the most meticulous inspections of our luggage. The customs officers spent more time with my belongings. Was it because I was an American or was I just a little paranoid?

Throughout our visit, there was a constant military presence. Even on the trip to the practice field, our bus was escorted by military police. During practice, there were soldiers stationed at the field and on each dugout; one was positioned with a machine gun. About one hundred Cubans watched us practice.

As the Twenty-eighth Amateur Baseball World Championship began, Cuba was the favorite. Cuba had long been the strongest baseball country in the world, and there was no reason to believe that their dominance would not continue. They had several players who were not only professional baseball prospects but could probably then play in the Major Leagues. At this time, Cuban ballplayers had not yet started to defect to the United States.

The opening ceremonies were held at Guillermon Moncada Stadium in Santiago. The beautiful stadium, which reminded me of an American minor league park, was filled to its capacity of an estimated 25,000 Cubans. On the following day, we won our first game against Taiwan. It was a great win for the Dutch in the World Championships, and I was treated like a celebrity in the postgame press conference. For one day, we were tied for first place in world competition, but it did not last. Though we played well at times, my Dutch team finished with a record of 1-8, losing eight straight heartbreaking games. Nevertheless, I was happy with the performance of my younger players in their first year of international baseball. Holland is a small country and will always be short on talent in world competitions.

The Cuban team showed its superiority and won the World Championships again. In the final game, they easily handled Team U.S.A. The young American collegians could not compete against the highly skilled Cuban veterans. The Cuban team played an aggressive, intimidating, free-swinging type of baseball, reminiscent of the old St. Louis Cardinals, the Gashouse Gang of the 1930s. They were also similar to the Oakland A's in their championship years in the 1970s, taking the extra base and often sliding with their spikes high. The Cuban pitchers threw inside and sometimes appeared eager to throw at hitters early in the game, to set the tone, not unlike Roger Clemens. The Cuban players had a swagger and cocky nature—they believed that they were the best players and the best team. However, I thought that if you could keep the score close and make the Cubans compete for the full game, they could become emotional and vulnerable to defensive and mental lapses. They are just not used to playing close games. From the World Championships I learned a good deal about how other cultures approach the game. It seemed that most Latin American countries tried to copy the Cubans but did not have their dominating talent.

The Latin teams played a very emotional style of baseball. When things did not go well, the players and coaches were vocal, and not afraid to yell at each other, the umpires, or the opposing team. The players were somewhat unpredictable and could change their moods from inning to inning. It was very difficult to read the opposing team and determine how they were going to compete. Our game against the Netherlands Antilles was a good example—the Antilles players did not seem to be in the game, and we were ahead 7–0 in the seventh inning. Then all of a sudden, with one hit, the Antilles Team got excited, and we could not get them out.

The Americans, who are noted for their good pitching, sound defense, and power hitting, were easier for me to coach against because of their predictability and my own U.S. heritage. One major adjustment players and coaches of American teams have to make when they compete internationally is to the intensity of the international tournaments. U.S. players are accustomed to playing long college seasons without great pressure until tournament time. In contrast, each international game is more magnified in importance. Also, international teams are normally made up of older, veteran players, while American teams are college-age players with little or no international experience. It can be intimidating for young Americans playing on foreign soil to go up against the Cubans and other good baseball countries. The American teams are also selected and play together for short periods of time compared to foreign teams, which have years of experience competing together against other countries.

I found the teams from Asia—Taiwan, Japan, and South Korea—fundamentally sound both at the plate and in the field. Seldom did the Asian players make mental mistakes. Their practice sessions were fun to watch because the teams were so structured and spent far more time practicing than non-Asian teams. No matter how hot, cold, or rainy, the coaches staged long workouts until they were completely satisfied with the details of skills and fundamentals. Offensively, the Asians played a more conservative style of baseball and tended to play for one run at a time. With no outs in the inning, you could bet that the hitter would bunt to advance a base runner or runners. If there were a runner on third base with one out or no outs, the batter was likely to execute a suicide squeeze. Only if their team were a few runs ahead would they be more aggressive in their offensive style, such as stealing with one runner on base or double stealing.

One area that really set the Asians apart was the unorthodox style of their pitching, as most threw sidearm and submarine. Also, Asian pitchers tended to be economical with their pitches and did not walk many batters. Their coaches were quick to pull a pitcher from the game if control was a problem. On the other hand, if an Asian pitcher were throwing well, his coach would let him continue to pitch, without concern for pitch count. In addition, if a pitcher were hot, you might see him pitch on consecutive days regardless of the number of pitches or innings he had recently thrown. The health of the player did not appear to be paramount, although it is easier for a sidearm or submarine thrower to recover and come back the following day. While the Asians were not as physically big or strong as the American players, their teams were tough to beat because of their discipline and sound fundamentals. They were always fun to watch.

The European Championship

As I readied myself for another summer with the Dutch National Team, our main goal in 1985 was to beat Italy and win the European Championships. Reflecting on my first year with the National Team, I was deeply concerned about the mentality and work ethic of some of my players. I believed that it was an honor for a player to be selected for the team, and he should play and conduct himself accordingly. From now on, we would select players based on both ability and mental makeup.

The European Championships in 1985 included six national teams—Belgium, Italy, the Netherlands, San Marino, Spain, and Sweden. In reality, only two countries would be competitive, Italy and the Netherlands. The others were not yet strong enough to beat us or the Italians.

For our first game against Italy, 6,000 fans arrived early to our ballpark in Haarlem and were singing and chanting in unison. They were loud and hostile to the opposition. I thought that their presence might make my players anxious since we could understand what was being said, while the opposing Italians could not. With a home run by my DH and a porous Italian defense (five errors), we went out to an early lead and won the first game 5–4. I felt it was important for us to win the first game from a psychological standpoint. Our starter, Jan Hijzelendoorn, pitched six strong innings, giving up four runs, and Bart Volkerijk came in the seventh and shut down the Italians. With Bart we had probably the best pitcher in the tourney coming out of the bullpen when we needed him. We tried to put a lot of pressure on the Italian pitchers and their defense as we planted the seed in their heads that we were going to run at every opportunity.

In the second game with Italy, in front of 7,500 fans, we jumped out to a four-run lead in the first inning and never looked back. The final score was 6–4. We knocked out their starting pitcher in the first inning. One more win and the Dutch would regain the European Championship.

The next day we were back at it. I sensed that the Italians were down—their players had the look of guys who did not want to be at the ballpark. If we could take an early lead it could be an easy game. The stadium was packed with 7,000 excited fans. We were ahead 3–2, going into the bottom of the fifth inning, when our team scored seven runs and routed the Italians 12–4. We were the European champions again!

In the press conference after the game, the Dutch newspapermen appeared confused about what to ask in such a positive setting. However, they still downplayed our achievements by saying the Italians were much weaker this year because, for the first time, their team used only "real Italians" to play. I tried not to mind the Dutch media and just enjoy our victory.

Conclusion

Let me close with a few words about the 1986 Baseball World Championship, which Holland hosted and for which the Dutch National Baseball Organization had initially hired me three years earlier (to build the national team). The event, played in four Dutch cities—Haarlem, Eindhoven, Rotterdam, and Utrecht—was a two-week, round robin competition with eleven other qualifying countries (Belgium, Columbia, Chinese Taipei, Italy, Japan, Netherlands Antilles, Puerto Rico, South Korea, United States, Venezuela, and Holland). A new baseball park with lights was built in Eindhoven just for the event, while two other stadiums got new lights.

I knew playing eleven games in a two-week period would really test my Dutch players physically and mentally. I was also concerned about the stress on my team playing at home. Although it is normally advantageous to be the home team, the pressure on the Dutch players before a critical hometown media could be difficult.

We completed the play with a 5-6 record, tied for seventh place. Cuba was the champion with an 11-1 record. Overall, I was pleased because before the tournament my goal was for our team to place in the middle of the group. In Cuba two years before, we finished in last place, and now we showed that we could compete. From the viewpoint of the Dutch people, our seventh place was disappointing because we were one game behind the Italians.

In Europe today, Holland and Italy continue to dominate the baseball scene. The Dutch players are still some of the strongest on the continent. There are a small number of players who are in America playing professional baseball at the minor league levels. In 2004, with professional players now allowed to play, the Dutch baseball team qualified for the Olympics and finished sixth in the tournament of eight teams. Some of the Dutch players were actually pros from the Netherlands Antilles.

In future international competition, how will the Dutch fare? Since I coached the National Team, the Netherlands has continued to be competitive in world competition. Since it is a small country, with a limited pool of baseball players from which to choose, along with inclement weather and the dominance of soccer, Dutch baseball will be hard-pressed to reach higher levels. The availability of Antilles players with professional baseball backgrounds can significantly improve the team's tournament stature. However, it would not be realistic to think that baseball in the Netherlands could reach the echelon of a world baseball power. Nevertheless, those involved in the "American pastime" in the Netherlands have embraced the charm and excitement of baseball.

Bibliography

Enders, Eric. "El Pasatiempo Nacional." May 2001. Available at http://www.eri-cenders.com/cubaball.htm.

Fisher, Robert I. C. *Fodor's Holland.* New York: Random House, 2004.

"History of Baseball Outside the United States." *Wikipedia: The Free Encyclopedia.* Available at http://en.wikipedia.org/wiki/History_of_baseball_outside_the_United_States.

Http://www.knbsb.com (Royal Netherlands Baseball and Softball Federation).

Stoovelaar, Marco, and Organizing Committee Haarlem Baseball Week. "Haarlem Baseball Week History 1961–1998." Available at http://home.planet.nl/~stoov/hhwhis.htm.

15 | Great Britain

Baseball's Battle for Respect in the Land

of Cricket, Rugby, and Soccer

British baseball. It sounds like an oxymoron. Having grown up in the United States, I asked the obvious question when I heard those two words uttered together for the first time in 1996: "Don't the British just play cricket?" In the intervening years I've learned that not only do a small group of dedicated baseball players compete in Great Britain, but they've also added their own unique British ethos to the way the game is played.

In America baseball players have a certain attitude. Whether it's quiet confidence or overt ego-thumping, most ballplayers in the United States have an unwavering belief that they should always be in the starting lineup or should be the man on the mound at a crucial time in a game. This was certainly true once I got to the Division I college level and in the professional ranks. But the British take a slightly different approach.

I joined the Great Britain National Team in 1996 just weeks before the European (B-pool) Championships—I was eligible to play on the team by virtue of having been born in England. The squad had practiced together on ragged makeshift fields all summer, as Britain lacks more than one or two fields that would pass for high school–level diamonds. I arrived just before the tournament began, never having met my teammates. There were two catchers (my position) already on the team, but I was installed as the starter. Back in America that would have led to chemistry problems. Even if I was better than the other catchers, they would have complained that I hadn't "paid my dues." But my teammates welcomed me and we went on to win the championships. Maybe it is the country's long history of dedication to such tenets of amateur sports as sportsmanship and teamwork over all other sporting values that led to these players not putting themselves above the squad. (The amateur ethos has been so pervasive in British sport that rugby, one of the country's top games, did not go professional until the late twentieth century.)

Regardless of the reason, this experience led me to develop an enduring devotion to British baseball. Since my introduction in 1996, I've spent a season competing in the country's top domestic league and represented Great Britain in nearly every major competition. While the players still struggle to compete with traditional baseball powerhouses, the esprit de corps I encountered on the first team I played for remains along with a tremendous enthusiasm for the game.

Unfortunately, though, most people involved with British baseball have no sense of its history. In fact, very few can tell you the British baseball stars from ten years ago let alone a hundred years ago. Again, this may be a product of culture. The American baseball obsession for statistical history is not prevalent in Britain. While Britons are rabid soccer fans and can recall dates of goals from the 1940s, they aren't as slavish to stats as, say, your average Boston Red Sox or New York Yankees fan. This is particularly true for sports with smaller followings—like baseball. British baseball has also had too many low tides of interest when there was nobody to carry the tale of the British game from decade to decade. But to examine the history is to learn a century-old story that includes kings, Major League Baseball players, great captains of industry, and periods of some excellent baseball.

You don't have to look any further than a blustery day more than a century ago to get a taste of the British game's intriguing history. On March 12, 1889, the prince of Wales settled into his seat at the Kennington Oval, one of England's most famous cricket grounds, to watch baseball. The game between teams of American professionals was part of a tour set up by the great baseball entrepreneur, manager, and player A. G. Spalding, and featured, among others, future Hall of Famer Adrian "Cap" Anson. By all accounts, the man who would become King Edward VII watched every move intently, staying until the last out as the

Chicago White Stockings beat the "All Americans" 7–4 in a muddy, rain-soaked game.

Following the contest, the future king of England began to stroll away when a newspaper reporter caught up to him and asked for his impressions of the game. The prince of Wales looked the journalist in the eye, thought for a moment, and then asked for the reporter's notebook. He jotted down a note and walked away. The next day, the prince's statement was printed as part of the game account: "The Prince of Wales has witnessed the game of Base Ball with great interest and though he considers it an excellent game he considers cricket as superior."

For more than a century since, the British royal has, for the most part, seemed to speak for an entire nation. Like a ball game itself, baseball in Great Britain has had ups and downs—dramatic moments of success that include a world championship and professional baseball and wholly forgettable periods. British baseball has faced daunting obstacles, including a sports culture that can be inhospitable to games that aren't seen to be entirely British; world events that stunted baseball's biggest growth periods; regional disputes; and sporadic lapses in funding and vision. Nevertheless, inherent characteristics that have helped Britons through the ages—namely resilience and an abiding optimism—have also assured that in down times, British baseball has persevered.

In the Beginning

It all started in 1874, when the Boston Red Stockings, winners of America's professional championship the summer before, and the Philadelphia Athletics traveled to England to introduce baseball to Britons. Curious crowds attended these events (July 31–August 25) in such cities as London, Dublin, Liverpool, and Manchester. Regrettably, the format was unusual. In most of the exhibitions, the Americans would play some baseball and then compete in cricket against a local team. The odds were in favor of the Americans, who would field eighteen players to the customary eleven playing for the British teams. This undermined the exhibitions. Newton Crane, a British baseball organizer and former U.S. consul in Manchester, England, wrote in 1891 that the tour failed to spark interest because "the game of baseball was not understood, and in the short hour or two devoted to the exhibition matches but little idea of it could be acquired by the bewildered spectators."[1]

It took fifteen years and one of baseball's great early visionaries, A. G. Spalding, to bring longer-lasting attention to the sport in the British Isles. Spalding, who played every role in the world of baseball—player, manager, owner, sports equipment manufacturer—organized a world baseball tour in 1888. Spalding took two teams of baseball players—the Chicago White Stockings, the team he ran back in the United States, and a mixed squad of players dubbed the "All Americans"—around the globe to the Sandwich Islands, Australia, New Zealand, Ceylon, Egypt, Italy, France, and finally to Great Britain. Baseball writer Patrick Carroll, who has done considerable research on Spalding and refers to him as "a Gilded Age archetype," describes the venture as "a typical mixture" of Spalding's "passionate missionary zeal for the game, go-getting business 'push,' and his often Machiavellian politicking."[2]

The Americans arrived in England in March 1889 and played 11 games throughout the country, drawing considerable crowds. Some 8,000 spectators showed up for the game in London, which was attended by the prince of Wales, and 4,000 watched a match in Bristol later in the tour despite the weather being "exceedingly unpropitious," according to British baseball organizer Crane. "Most of the games [were] being played in fog, rain, and snow, and on grounds which were wet and slippery." There was another serious problem from the fan's perspective—rather than put on the best show possible, the American teams took each game very seriously, playing to win. This apparently decreased the crowd's enjoyment, as the duke of Beaufort, who helped host the baseball party, noted.

Of course, the jealousy between All America and Chicago, while it kept all the players up to mark and made them do their best to prevent their opponents from scoring, made the game dull to on-lookers, who did not understand it. If they could have played a few games not to be counted in their wins and losses against each other, in which the pitchers would give easy balls and enable the hitters really to make fine hits and give a chance to the field to make the splendid catches they are able to make, the game would have taken the fancy of the British public much more, as it would have thoroughly astonished them.[3]

The British reaction to the tour was, in the words of author Peter Levine, "lukewarm."[4]

The tour might have failed like the one in 1874 if it hadn't been for a group of young collegians who followed up the Spalding extravaganza by spending their 1889 summer vacation in England. Instead of just playing, they actually taught the game. They also set up matches throughout the country, establishing teams of both American and British players—a marked difference from the previous approach. As there is no substitute for playing, the Britons who got a taste of baseball were hooked. In October 1889 a group of enthusiasts formed the National Baseball League of Great Britain and, with the help of Spalding and his associates, planned a professional league to commence play the following season. The organizers found that "the football [soccer] clubs . . . whose efforts were confined to the winter months, were disposed to encourage the movement," according to the 1890 edition of *Spalding's Official Base Ball Guide.* Four of England's top soccer clubs—Aston Villa of Birmingham, Derby County, Preston North End, and Stoke—decided to start franchises in the new professional baseball circuit. There was one big hitch: very few British athletes had played more than a game or two of baseball before. With that in mind, the organizers advertised for six to eight young Americans to serve as instructors. They received nearly a thousand applicants. The teachers were given a round-trip ticket from New York to London and three to four guineas a week (the equivalent today of between £200 and £270 per week).

When play began in May, the performance of the players was "gratifying," "[t]he novices being experienced football players, finely trained in hand, limb and eye," noted *Spalding's Official Base Ball Guide* of 1890. While the Spalding guide couldn't be considered an unbiased publication, considering Spalding's involvement, it's worth pointing out that Jack Devey, a British native who also played for Aston Villa's soccer team, beat out all the foreign imports to win the batting title with a .428 average. As for attendance, the Spalding guide claimed it was "satisfactory, and toward the close of the season, especially at Preston, [the crowds] were quite as large as the average Minor League cities in the United States."

But there were problems. Many in the media were not keen to accept

DERBY BASEBALL CLUB.

FRANCIS LEY, President.

T. President, F. Booth, D. Allsopp, J. P. Reisenback, W. C. Bryan, Capt., S. D. Bullas, H. M. Middleton, W. North, J. Mellors,
Left Field. Centre Field. Third Base. Pitcher. First Base. Catcher. Second Base. Right Field. Short Stop.

1890.

15. In 1890 Derby was the British baseball team to beat. Run by industrialist Sir Francis Ley, Derby was poised to become the first champion of British baseball, but a controversy with other teams in the league led Ley's club to withdraw. Perhaps the club's greatest legacy was that until 1997, Derby's soccer team played at the Baseball Ground, the home of the baseball team. (Photo courtesy of the National Baseball Hall of Fame.)

baseball, fearful that the sport might encroach on cricket's dominance in the summer months. Some reporters did not believe that there was genuine interest in the game. "The baseball business is being 'boomed' with a vigour of which is a little too obviously artificial for the average Englishman," said a June 16, 1890, article in the *Birmingham Daily Post*. "The phlegmatic Briton does not care to have a pastime which has considerable amount of the advertising element about it foisted upon him."

There was also on-field controversy. The Derby team, which was run by leading industrialist Sir Francis Ley, had more foreign players (three) than any other club. As a result, within the first month of the season, Derby won enough games to clinch the championship. The other teams protested and Ley agreed to use only his ace American pitcher against Aston Villa, the league's second-best team. When Derby reneged on that promise, however, the other team leaders were furious and Derby pulled out of the league. Aston Villa was then named the league's champion, while Preston North End won the separate Baseball Association of Great Britain and Ireland Cup competition. Preston is regarded by today's British baseball organizers as the first English champion.

Off the field, the league had financial problems, losing an estimated $25,000 in 1890, according to William J. Harr, a former American diplomat who managed the Aston Villa team. The tremendous costs included advertising, recruiting players, and maintaining an office in London. While Spalding appears to have bankrolled much of the endeavor, one of his representatives did not provide all of the promised financial aid, which upset the British teams. A Spalding agent who was in England to promote baseball left the country with more than £300, which had been designated for the players, according to one newspaper account. Perhaps because of the high cost and no immediate attendance boom, Spalding never fully invested in British baseball again and the circuit folded after just one season.

Still, the league was not a complete failure. In at least one place—Derby—baseball proved that it could make money. Derby took in about £150 from the gate and had expenses that didn't exceed £100. Moreover, as a result of the initial attention generated by the league, the sport made substantial progress as an amateur game during the next twenty years. A number of the country's top soccer clubs followed the lead of the teams from the 1890 season and developed baseball teams for the short summer off-season. Along with Derby County, which continued to be a force in baseball and even played soccer, until 1997, at a stadium called the Baseball Ground, such soccer powerhouses as Arsenal, Tottenham Hotspur, and Nottingham Forest also took up the game. Many top soccer and rugby players took up baseball including Steve Bloomer, who represented England in soccer twenty-three times and played for

Derby, and John Kirwan, who played soccer for Tottenham Hotspur when it won the prestigious Football Association Cup in 1901.

By the start of the twentieth century, baseball had a place in British society. In 1906 the British Baseball Cup attracted around twenty-five hundred fans to White Hart Lane soccer ground to watch the home team, the Tottenham Hotspur Baseball Club, win the national championship. The following year, a baseball season ticket for Tottenham baseball games cost five shillings (about twenty dollars today).

In the official history of British baseball, there are no national champions listed between 1912 and 1933. But during this period, in 1913 and 1914, Major League Baseball did try to spur international interest in baseball with its first world tour since Spalding's 1889 effort. If the Americans had hoped to woo the British public on their London stop, their actions did just the opposite. The London leg of the four-month tour between the New York Giants and the Chicago White Sox was booked for mid-February. The great sportswriter Grantland Rice presciently wrote in the October 27, 1913, issue of the *Chicago Record-Herald*, "Now we are far from being endowed with a gambling disposition, but any citizen who wishes to wager that the Giants will be able to edge in one-third of their February London schedule will be accommodated up to our ultimate kopeck."[5] As Rice suggested, the weather held the tourists to a single game in London on February 26, 1914. This limited what the group, which included some of baseball's greatest players of the day including future Hall of Famers Tris Speaker, Sam Crawford, and Urban "Red" Faber and Olympic hero and baseball player Jim Thorpe, could exhibit.

Even worse, American hubris overshadowed any on-field action. Before the single contest occurred, one of baseball's greatest all-time managers, the Giants' John McGraw, did little to ingratiate baseball to the British public. In an interview with the *Pall Mall Gazette*, McGraw said that "American soldiers are superior to the British because of the athletic discipline in the United States and because every American soldier has learned to play baseball and through that game has benefited his mind as well as his body."[6] The game itself, which was held at Chelsea Football Club's hallowed Stamford Bridge Grounds, was a success as the White Sox won 5–4 in an exciting eleven-inning affair. After the game, King George V, who was in attendance, asked the U.S. ambassador to "tell Mr. McGraw and . . . [White Sox owner Charles] Comiskey that I have enjoyed the game enormously." Still, the words of McGraw probably resonated more than any goodwill the game produced. The *London Sketch* wrote following McGraw's outburst, "The impudence of the Yankee knows no limits; and their baseball visit has afforded another opportunity for the display of it."[7] In fact, some newspapers had called for a boycott of the game based on McGraw's statements.

Not surprisingly, baseball appeared to lose momentum during this period. Another key factor for this diminished interest was World War I. As would later be the case during World War II, baseball did not have deep enough roots to sustain interest during wartime. The influx of Americans into the country during the war did lead to extensive play, but it was almost exclusively among American and Canadian soldiers. In 1918 the Anglo-American League was set up in the London area for the entertainment and recreation of the American and Canadian forces. The biggest baseball event took place on July 4, 1918, at Stamford Bridge. The clash between the U.S. Navy and the U.S. Army attracted a crowd of 38,000, including King George V, Prime Minister David Lloyd George, and future prime minister Winston Churchill.

But following the war, the game had difficulty getting going again. In the fall of 1924, baseball supporters set up a series of exhibition games between the Chicago White Sox and the New York Giants in London, Liverpool, Birmingham, Dublin, and Paris. Unfortunately, the games did not get a full welcome. In Dublin, for example, an exhibition was scheduled for an afternoon start but was played instead at 11:00 a.m. so as to not conflict with a key cricket match. Overall, the media was dismissive of the tour, although the games did receive at least one positive review. The British playwright George Bernard Shaw, who, though not a sports fan of any sort, remarked after a Giants–White Sox game in London, "To go back to cricket after baseball is like going back to Shakespeare played in five acts with fifteen-minute intervals after seeing it played through in the correct Shakespearean way."[8] Ultimately, though, the sport was diminished by the war.

The Golden Age

It took a man who had made his fortune in the world of gambling to facilitate baseball's golden age in Great Britain. Sir John Moores founded the Littlewoods Football Pools Company in 1923. His pools remain a legalized form of gambling and—although the Moores family no longer runs it—the Liverpool-based company has grown into a powerful organization with a mail order business and 189 stores by 2002. Moores first became involved with baseball in 1933, when he formed the National Baseball Association in response to a challenge by the president of Major League Baseball's National League, John A. Heydler, to spur British baseball growth. Within a few months eighteen amateur baseball teams in two leagues had been formed in Moores's Liverpool, according to William Morgan, a publisher of British baseball periodicals. Heydler was so impressed that he donated the league trophy—a silver cup.

With Moores's business acumen and financial backing, baseball began to flourish. In 1934, for instance, a match between Scotland and England in Edinburgh drew fifty-three hundred spectators.

Moores became more ambitious with his baseball interests, and in 1935 he decided to form a professional league called the North of England Baseball League, based around Manchester.[9] The reaction of some in the baseball community was trepidation. "This is a daring move," wrote the *Liverpool Echo*, on the eve of the pro circuit's debut. "I know that sound judges would have liked such a development to have been deferred until [British baseball was at] a more mature moment. The time was not quite ripe."[10] Undeterred, Moores barreled ahead with the new venture. The players were mostly Americans and Canadians with solid baseball credentials and respected athletes from other sports like soccer and rugby such as Jim Sullivan, who is regarded as one of the greatest Rugby League players of all time. Typical of the foreigners was Stanley Trickett, a player for the Belle Vue Tigers, who previously was the captain of the baseball team at University of Kentucky. So could these guys play? Players with little baseball experience certainly attacked the sport with gusto. Benny Nieuwenhuys, for example, a South African soccer player for the famed Liverpool Football Club, was lauded after his baseball team, the Hurst Hawks, won because "his headlong dives for the bags were very effective if not spectacular."[11]

16. *A baseball game in the Liverpool area, ca. 1930. Under the stewardship of business-man Sir John Moores, baseball grew rapidly in Liverpool in the 1930s. Moores started three professional leagues throughout Great Britain, including one league that was made up of teams in and around Liverpool. Note the netting to separate fans from the playing field and the distance at which the catcher positions himself behind the batter.* (Photo courtesy of the National Baseball Hall of Fame.)

But it was clear that mastering the rules of baseball would not happen overnight. During the 1935 season officials were concerned that excessive base stealing was leading to bloated scoring (a team scoring twenty runs in a game was not uncommon). The promoters considered banning stealing altogether, but the Americans and Canadians protested vigorously. The reason for the high number of steals was not a flaw in the rules, said one experienced player, but the result of English pitchers not being able to effectively hold the runners on. The English pitchers were throwing out of the windup—a no-no with runners on base—instead of the stretch. Players also often faced inhospitable playing conditions as some teams competed in soccer stadiums, which were too small, while ground surface, torn up by football boots, was too bumpy, causing the ball to often bounce head high.[12]

Despite these problems, most teams in the league drew between one and 3,000 spectators with games between front-runners getting 5,000 or more. "Clubs produced remarkably large profits and gates were surprisingly big," crowed one paper after the season.[13] Founder Moores was elated by the performance of the first season and in an interview with the *Ashton-Under-Lyne Reporter* boasted that the National Baseball Association had "already gone ahead of the five-year plan originally set out."[14]

The next year Moores formed two new professional leagues—the Yorkshire League and the London Major Baseball League—to go along with the North of England Baseball League.[15] With three pro circuits throughout the country, Moores was now covering a tremendous amount of territory.

In its second season, owners in the North of England League became more aggressive in their recruiting. The expansion Liverpool Giants had six members with American playing experience and—between the North of England League and the nascent Yorkshire League—every decent ballplayer in the northern part of the country seemed to be a pro. The *Liverpool Echo* lamented that this meant that amateur leagues, the lifeblood for sustained growth of the sport, were suffering. The professional leagues were "claiming (top players), but at much too rapid a pace to allow their places to be filled adequately. . . . [T]hat has been a big defect of the early introduction of professionalism in baseball ranks." Despite the local British talent, top foreigners dominated early in the 1936 season. The Ashton Hawks, for example, were battling to stay out of last place in the North of England league when the team brought over a Canadian pitcher named Ross E. Scott. The results were immediate. In his first 4 league games, Scott struck out 58 batters (an average of 14 per start) and the Hawks finished the season well clear of the cellar.

While the Yorkshire and North of England Leagues were competing for players in the Midlands, which is in central England, and the north, the London Major Baseball League had its pick of top talent in the south of England. In 1936 there was little doubt that the London league was the best in the country. London's star player was West Ham's Roland Gladu, a French Canadian who had previously played minor league baseball for the Montreal Royals. Gladu, dubbed "the Babe Ruth of Canada," would eventually go back to North America and play in the Major Leagues with the Boston Braves in 1944. Unlike many of the contests up north, London Major Baseball League games tended to be low-scoring affairs. Also, when teams in the league did compete against their rivals from up north, the London clubs dominated. The London league was so strong that following the Olympics in Berlin, the U.S. Olympic baseball team traveled to the British capital to play two teams, White City and West Ham. (Baseball had been an exhibition sport at the 1936 Games.) Although the Americans prevailed against White City, West Ham beat the Olympic squad 5–3.

Both the London and Yorkshire leagues matched—and in some cases surpassed—the North of England Baseball League in interest. In London West Ham could draw crowds in excess of 4,000 and the Romford Wasps attracted 3,000 for some games. In the Yorkshire League, Hull brought out 9,000 for marquis matchups, and Sheffield's first home game attracted 6,000. Financially, the Yorkshire League topped the other two leagues. Hull, which had an average gate of £70 a game, and Sheffield, with an average of £50 to £60 a game, were particularly successful. These matches did have a mood that was quite different from American contests. "The big difference over [in the United States] is in the shouting," the *Scarborough Evening Post* wrote on May 16, 1936. "The Yanks make such a hubbub, both on and off the field, that it's like listening to a wagonload of escaped baboons." Ellis Harvey, who attended Romford games in 1936 and 1937, found that British baseball fans were also more reserved than those who attended soccer matches at the time. One reason for this difference could have been the British fans' relatively limited knowledge of the game. Harvey says that he went to games because "British folk tended to dismiss it" and he wanted to see what attracted so many thousands of Americans.[16] He was a cricket fan and although his knowledge of the game grew with each game he attended, it took a while before fans got to the point where they felt comfortable badgering the umpires about bad calls. (Today, although the number of spectators at most games is minuscule, fans are far better educated about the sport.

Major League Baseball games are telecast on British network television twice a week during the summer, and with the Internet, it's relatively easy to become familiar with the game.)

In 1937 the Yorkshire League became the top circuit, replacing the London Major Baseball League as the place to play. The Yorkshire teams heavily imported American and Canadian players to enhance their squads, and they poached some of the London league's best foreign players, leaving few British athletes on the field. Yorkshire's Leeds franchise, for instance, had only one English player. The money was pretty good for these professionals with an average salary, according to British baseball historian Ian Smyth, of £2 per week, a solid wage for the era.[17] A star player would make even more and would receive accommodation and additional employment. But Smyth points out that the influx of excellent foreign talent—particularly on the mound—led to some complications up north with low-scoring games becoming the norm. For the uninitiated baseball spectators, pitchers' duels—like the ones played in the exhibition games in 1889—were relatively boring. Nonetheless, many fans still came out, as evidenced by the 11,000 who watched Hull win the National Baseball Association Cup against the Romford Wasps 5–1.

Down south, baseball was beginning to fail as a professional sport. Stadium operators in London grew restless when the sport didn't quickly produce sizable dividends and only the Romford Wasps and the West Ham Hammers had top-caliber players in 1937. After that season, the league folded and teams like the Wasps became amateur clubs. Moores's rapid expansion left too few good players to go around. With some top players defecting, the London league suddenly had a marginal product.

But even in the north where interest was much stronger, the sport was also beginning to stumble as organizers began purging foreign players with dire consequences. In 1938 the Yorkshire Baseball League and the North of England League merged to become the Yorkshire-Lancashire League. The major difference with the new circuit: each club was limited to only two professionals. This was done to allow British players to develop, and it effectively dropped the top level of baseball from professional to semiprofessional. (An ill-fated renegade league called the International League tried to start up that year but went out of business after only a few weeks.) By 1939 attendance appeared to be waning. The loss of professional teams, which certainly lessened the quality of play, probably helps explain the drop-off in interest.

The professional leagues aside, perhaps Britain's greatest success in the global baseball community took place in 1938 when the country won the first-ever World Amateur Baseball Championship. The story began in August 1938, when the U.S. Olympic Baseball Team arrived in Plymouth for a 5-game "test series" against England. At the time there was no talk of a world championship. The U.S. squad was prepping for the Olympic Games that were planned for Tokyo in 1940. The team was made up of high school and college players who had been picked the month before at the USA National Amateur Baseball Trials in Lincoln, Nebraska. Former Major Leaguer Leslie Mann coached the team.

The English team was made up almost entirely of players born in Canada. England's top player, Ross Kendrick, was described in a game program as a "pitcher with a very clean style of hooks, speed and endurance." Kendrick would become a legendary fixture in British baseball, playing well into middle age; one eyewitness claimed seeing sixty-year-old-plus Kendrick pitching a game many years after the world championship triumph.

The series was set for August 13–19 in Liverpool, Hull, Rochdale, Halifax, and Leeds and attendance was impressive. In front of 10,000 fans in Liverpool, Kendrick defeated curve ball pitcher Virgil Thompson to lead England to a 3–0 first-game victory. Kendrick threw a two-hitter, striking out sixteen. Two days later England won 8–6 in front of 5,000 spectators in Hull. The Americans took the next game 5–0, in Rochdale, but England won the next 2 games. In Halifax Kendrick returned to the mound, shutting out the United States for the second time, 4–0, and then England won again, 5–3, in Leeds.

Following the series, the International Baseball Federation designated the contests as the first World Championships and named Great Britain the inaugural World Amateur Champions. To this day, that bureaucratic decision may be Great Britain's greatest baseball victory.

We'll never know whether British baseball players would have ever reached the levels of their North American counterparts because World War II ended the Yorkshire-Lancashire League as players of all nationalities went off to war. During the war Allied soldiers set up recreational baseball. The London International Baseball League was a highly competitive eight-team circuit that played in front of large crowds of primarily Allied soldiers. Unlike during the previous war, British players were at least marginally more involved with baseball; a British team called the Hornsey Red Sox played against North Americans throughout the war years. In addition to league games, many exhibition games were played during World War II. On August 7, 1943, for example, the U.S. Air Force played the U.S. Ground Forces at Empire Stadium, Wembley, before 21,500 spectators. Still, the game lost its hold on the British consciousness and a British championship would not be contested again until 1948.

Postwar Baseball

After the war baseball tried to reclaim its place in the British sports landscape. With a huge number of North American soldiers still in the United Kingdom, the sport had enough experienced players to return to minor prominence. In London baseball received solid coverage in local newspapers, and teams up north—most notably in Hull and in Stretford near Manchester—were also developing very capable baseball teams. But the quality of the leagues depended on foreigners. Andy Parkes, who played for the Stretford Saints in the postwar era, recounts that the team leaders would run over to local factories and firms whenever they heard an American or Canadian had joined. One of the Saints' (and northern England's) top players in this period, Wally O'Neil, was recruited through this very approach. O'Neil, a Canadian, had come to England to work as an electric control engineer but soon was enlisted to play baseball and went on to lead the Saints to numerous championships. If North Americans weren't joining in with the British, they were running their own teams. The Burtonwood Bees, for example, was a squad from a U.S. Air Force base that dominated in the 1950s. But financial support and general interest from Britons was limited. George Livsley, an organizer of the Stretford Saints, recalled that by the end of the war there was very little equipment available for British teams and that in some cases the cost often was prohibitive.[18] Chuck Cole, a player from that era, recounted how baseball was included at the Festival of

MERSEYSIDE NATIONAL BASEBALL LEAGUE

STRETFORD

Saints

Baseball club

CONDENSED RULES AND REGULATIONS

1.—The OBJECT is to win the game by scoring the most runs in nine innings.
2.—A RUN is scored when a batter becomes a baserunner and makes a complete circuit of the bases—First, Second, Third and Home.
3.—An INNING is composed of a time at bat and a time in the field for each team, having three outs while at bat, and making three putouts in the field. The visiting team bats first in the (top of) the inning, the home team last.
4.—A BATTER is out if: caught out; thrown out at first base; struck out; touched by a fairly batted ball; or if he bats from outside the batter's box. The batter MUST TRY to reach first base on any fairly batted ball.
5.—A BATTER may become a baserunner by a safe hit (single, double, triple, or home run); base on balls; being hit by a pitched ball; error; fielder's choice; or catcher interference.
6.—A BASERUNNER may advance: on a fairly batted ball; by stealing a base during the pitch; after a fly ball is caught; on a balk committed by the pitcher; or through interference.
7.—A BASERUNNER is OUT if: forced out; tagged with the ball while off base; touched by a fairly batted ball; or declared out for interference.
8.—A pitched ball is a STRIKE on the batter if: he swings; if it is in the STRIKE ZONE (across home plate between batter's knees and shoulders); or if he hits a foul ball except for the third strike. Three strikes and you're out.
9.—Four balls (which the batter does not swing at) outside the strike zone constitute a BASE on BALLS or a WALK to first base.
10.—A baserunner is FORCED OUT if a fielder with the ball touches the base the runner is obliged to reach because of another runner behind him.
11.—A pitcher commits a BALK when he breaks the rules on legal pitching procedure; baserunners advance one base.
12.—The complete and official Rules of Baseball are complex, multifarious and constantly open to reinterpretation and revision. Even though they are apparently comprehensive, nearly every day umpires are called upon to make decisions not directly covered by the rules.

OFFICIAL PROGRAMME PRICE 3d.

HOME GROUND—Turn Moss Field
Edge Lane, Stretford, Lancs.

17. Formed in 1947, the Stretford Saints, based in the Manchester area, was one of Britain's top post–World War II clubs. The Saints team featured a combination of British players and North Americans and won a national championship in 1966. (Photo courtesy of George Livsley and David Allen.)

Britain exhibition in London in 1951. While baseball was demonstrated in an exhibition for some four to five weeks during the summer, he only remembers "one or two inquiries" from potential players interested in taking up baseball.

U.S. and Canadian military games could still draw big crowds of mainly other soldiers, but audiences for British contests were much smaller. For example, a game in 1954 between the USAF Cowboys and RCAF Langar attracted more than 4,000 while a team in the northern city of Leeds, which could easily draw 1,000 spectators to a game before the war, had only 300 watch them lose to the Kingston Diamonds.

The fact that baseball's modest success in the 1950s was largely due to foreign players was not lost on British baseball pundits. The July 16, 1953, issue of *Baseball News*, a British baseball periodical, ran an editorial revealing the concerns about non-British involvement.

The scarcity of "home-produced" players has led to an increasing demand for the services of visitors to this country who are "ready-made" ballplayers. Whilst U.S. Servicemen are in England it is natural that there will be a large number of them competing in British baseball, . . . [but] there will naturally be a difference should there be a future decline in the numbers of "guest stars" available. It is for this fact alone that all teams should concentrate on building up "local talent" side by side with the experienced men.[19]

A decade later little had changed. The Stretford Saints' Parkes said to a newspaper reporter in the mid-1960s that the "Americanism" of baseball was inevitably hindering the game's growth. "I think it's bound to put some people off," he said. "But the game is American. All the terms are American. There aren't English words for them."

But organizers were unwilling to let British baseball go quietly. Although some companies offered sponsorship to individual teams (e.g., Ford Motor Company), gone were the days of substantial financial support from the likes of A. G. Spalding or John Moores. Nevertheless, in 1963, the National Baseball League was formed with teams from all areas of the country—Stretford, Hull, Nottingham, Coventry, Manchester, Birmingham, and London. The league aimed to start competition at the end of the soccer season and play until soccer started up again. The league survived until 1972, but the game was strictly amateur and any hopes of reclaiming a professional place in the British sports world seemed remote.

With the departure of Americans, the quality of baseball also diminished during this era. Jeff Archer, in his book *Strike Four*, writes about his efforts to develop baseball in Great Britain in the mid-1970s and early 1980s. He describes the sport as being in a sad state of affairs. Archer recounts an incident in 1975 in which his team, leading by a large margin, lost a shutout in the eighth inning. After the run was scored, the opposing manager, who was apparently drunk, staggered onto the field and apologized to the starting pitcher on Archer's team for breaking up the shutout. Archer later tried to set up a league in London that would draw paying customers, but his efforts ultimately failed and he moved to Holland, where baseball was more developed.[20]

One factor that probably contributed to baseball's stagnation was that the sport had become regionally fragmented. Signs of this appear as early as 1952. In June a squad from England traveled to the Netherlands to play and was criticized by London's *Evening News* for having a bias against southern players. According to the paper, the Sutton Beavers, which was a particularly strong team in the London area, sent the names of its three top players, but they were rejected. In the end, only one player from the south was named to the team. Later in the summer, southern organizers retaliated by forming their own squad—dubbed an England team—to play an international game against a Canadian All-Star team.

By the late 1960s, organizers in the north (centered in Hull) and the south (with teams mainly in London and the surrounding "home counties") clearly appeared to be focusing on their own areas. Despite winning the silver medal at the 1967 European Championships in Belgium, the country had difficulty putting together a consistent, cohesive national squad. International play in 1969 was emblematic of the factional nature of the game in that period. Representative teams from both South Africa and Zambia traveled to Great Britain to play separate series. Instead of British baseball's governing body forming a single squad, various regions put up All-Star teams against the foreign competition. Four areas emerged as baseball centers between the late 1960s and mid-1990s: Hull, Nottingham, Liverpool, and greater London. During this period, teams from in and around these cities won practically every national championship.

There have always been cultural differences between the regions, which sometimes spill over into baseball. As a player on the British squad at the 1999 European Championships, I remember a few of the London-based players returning to their room at the end of the tournament to drink a bottle of wine. I couldn't imagine the players from the north doing the same; a pint of lager suited them. Nevertheless, everyone got along, though there was some gentle joking about regional accents—the players from Birmingham in central England got it the worst. However, the cultural divide between players was shed on the diamond. If only the best players from across the country could have been brought together in one All-Star team, the standard of national play would have certainly been enhanced. It was the organizers who were the biggest impediment. Mike Carlson, who was Major League Baseball's representative in Great Britain between 1990 and 1994, believes the distinct regional power bases ultimately hurt the overall growth of the game. "To a certain extent, the problem [in Great Britain] is the club structure," he said. "You can't get to a wider area; you can't disseminate the sport beyond small areas. There were a lot of little fiefdoms. People liked running their small program. They'd rather be a big fish in a small pond."[21] In fairness, another obstacle was the cost of travel. The lack of funding often made team travel up and down the country every week too costly, and to this day, teams from the north and the south rarely meet—except in major events.

British Baseball in the New Millennium

As everything in the world is speeding up, so has the cycle of optimism and despair in the future of British baseball. In 1987 Scottish Amicable Life Assurance Society, a British-based insurance company, agreed to sponsor British baseball. The three-year sponsorship was said to be worth £300,000. With the funding, the British Baseball Federation formed the Scottish Amicable National League. Its purpose, according to the organization's official newsletter, was to provide British baseball with a "'Shop-window' that gives [the] sport credibility by staging games for the sporting public to the best possible standards."

Many involved with baseball at the time said that the sport was gaining ground on other sports. It also helped that Major League Baseball was being televised by the national network, Channel 4, and by Sky Sports. British baseball leaders staged several high-profile events to draw attention to baseball. The British National Team took on a traveling All-Star team of ex–Major Leaguers including Hall of Famers Bob Feller, Willie Stargell, and Billy Williams called "The Legends of Baseball" in Manchester. Alas, in 1990, the one hundredth anniversary of organized baseball in Great Britain, Scottish Amicable pulled out. The reasons are unclear. Some suggested that British baseball's leadership misappropriated funds, while others insist that the sponsorship just ran its course. Whatever the case, future sponsors of Great Britain's National League—including Coors and Rawlings—were not as generous as Scottish Amicable.

British baseball has also been marred by controversy. In 1991 entrepreneur Malcolm Needs organized a new league—the National League—to play in large stadiums and hopefully attract British fans back to the game. But a disagreement between Needs and British Baseball Federation (BBF) president Mike Harrold caused the National League to break away from the BBF and its players, who were among the country's best. BBF-related teams were banned from playing National League teams and players in the National League were barred from playing on the Great Britain National Team. In 1994 baseball's governing body in Europe got involved and Needs left British baseball, while the National League players were welcomed back into the BBF fold.

British baseball was also hurt by the foreign player limit put into place in 1988. The restriction, which followed a long history of fear that non-British players would dominate the domestic game, seriously curtailed participation, according to Alan Smith, a longtime British player and organizer. More specifically, the limit on foreigners caused the demise of the Surrey Baseball Association and the dismantling of three major adult teams: the Oxshott Orioles, the Woking White Sox, and, most important, the Cobham Yankees, which had been founded six years earlier and had won the All-England Club championship four times. "It caused David Brown, the man responsible for the Surrey Association, to lose interest in the sport here and affected the future of the six junior teams that he had created," Smith said.

To counterbalance British baseball's declining popularity, Major League Baseball has given it considerable support over the past decade. In 2000 the BBF joined with the British Softball Federation under the umbrella BaseballSoftball UK (BSUK) banner. Starting with just Mike Carlson and a single assistant in 1990, MLB's operation in London, which is now run by Clive Russell, a former aide to Prime Minister Tony Blair, offered BSUK considerable support. In 2002 a half dozen full-time employees and a host of part-timers and interns worked in MLB's London branch. Although the office is responsible for both game development and TV and merchandise licensing for MLB in Europe, the Middle East, and Africa, it also has worked closely with British baseball. In 2002 Frubes, a yogurt dessert for children made by Yoplait, became the first-ever title sponsor of MLB and BaseballSoftball*UK*'s Play Ball! program, which gives kids a chance to play baseball and softball during and outside of school (that deal ran its course by 2005). Along with MLB's efforts, BSUK now has a paid professional staff where, in the past, unpaid part-timers did the work of developing the game. The hope is that a handful of full-time employees will increase the profile of both baseball and softball in the United Kingdom. To that end, in 2005 baseball and softball together received a £300,000 grant from Sport England, a public entity that supports athletics in the country. This is the largest amount of public funding these sports have ever received in the United Kingdom.

The use of foreign players is no longer as controversial in Britain's domestic leagues as it was in decades past. The problem today is a dearth of experienced players. In 2003 British baseball organizers created a program to lure American collegians to play in the country's top league. Although that program has struggled financially, the organizers continue to look for ways to lure solid foreign baseball players to Britain to supplement local talent. While some still worry that too many non-British players may stunt domestic player development, they now understand that a core group of good foreign players are needed as role models, since there are relatively few American and Canadian soldiers still stationed in Britain. Only the military personnel in Menwith Hill up north and in the Cambridge base still actively play baseball.

But it's hard to tell if baseball is finally ready for sustained growth in Britain. Major League Baseball games are shown twice a week on Five, one of the five television networks in the country. A televised game on Five can attract hundreds of thousands of viewers. But there has not yet been a connection between a robust viewing audience and people willing to take up the game. Britain is not a "sporting nation" in the same way the United States is, where not only children but adults flock to play organized sports. More Britons watch than play. However, although the number who actually play baseball in Great Britain is small, their passion is huge. Some of the best players have begun going to America to play at U.S. universities. One British pitcher played two seasons in the Frontier League, an independent professional league in the Midwest.

On July 6, 2005, baseball's small band of organizers rejoiced at news that London would host the 2012 Olympics. For younger members of the Great Britain National Team, this meant an opportunity to be an Olympic athlete, as Britain would get an automatic bid in the Games' baseball tournament. More important, baseball would get much needed new infrastructure. A temporary baseball field was to be set up in Regent's Park in the heart of London. In addition, a permanent "legacy" facility would be set up in the Leah Valley outside London. Finally, there would be a state-of-the-art facility for British-bred players looking to hone their skills for years to come.

The rejoicing was short-lived. Two days later baseball was taken off the program for the 2012 games. No new fields, no additional financial support from the government, and no domestic buzz for baseball would occur. (At the time of publishing there was a still a sliver of hope; a re-vote for baseball is expected in February 2006.)

With the Olympic support no longer in the offing, to prosper baseball in Britain will need new benefactors—like John Moores and A. G. Spalding. Now more than ever, English culture appears determined to protect traditional English sports. A popular anti-baseball chant among detractors is that baseball is "glorified rounders," a child's game that bears a resemblance to baseball. Alas, this comparison hasn't changed in more than a century.

Notes

1. Crane, *The All-England Series*, 13.
2. Carroll, "Baseball in Graceland."
3. Crane, *The All-England Series*, 16.
4. Levine, *A. G. Spalding*, 105.
5. Elfers, *The Tour to End All Tours*, 227.
6. Elfers, *The Tour to End All Tours*, 229–30.
7. Elfers, *The Tour to End All Tours*, 229.
8. From Wilson Cross Scrapbook, courtesy of Mike Ross and SABR. The article from which the quote was taken was published in the *Evening Standard*, November 4, 1924.

9. The teams in the 1935 North of England Baseball League were the Oldham Greyhounds, Bradford Northern, Rochdale Greys, Salford Reds, Manchester North End Blue Sox, Belle Vue Tigers, Hurst Hawks, and Hyde Grasshoppers.

10. *Liverpool Echo*, May 4, 1935, 7.

11. *Ashton-under-Lyne Reporter*, June 15, 1935, 15.

12. This problem would be somewhat stemmed later as most professional teams ultimately played on the better kept grass of greyhound stadiums.

13. *Ashton-under-Lyne Reporter*, May 2, 1936, 18.

14. *Ashton-under-Lyne Reporter*, August 10, 1935, 19.

15. The inaugural teams in the Yorkshire League were the Greenfield Giants, Hull Baseball Club, Wakefield Cubs, Bradford City Sox, Sheffield Dons, Leeds Oaks, Scarborough Seagulls, and Dewsbury Royals. The 1936 London Major League teams were White City, West Ham, Hackney Royals, Harringay, Romford Wasps, and Catford Saints. The Streatham and Mitcham Giants was also a founding team but folded weeks into the first season.

16. Ellis Harvey, interview by the author, February 1, 2003.

17. Smyth, "History of Baseball," 23.

18. George Livsley, interview by the author, August 11, 2002.

19. "The Overseas Influence" (editorial), *Baseball News*, July 16, 1953, 2.

20. Archer, *Strike Four*, 19.

21. Mike Carlson, interview by the author, December 2, 2002.

Bibliography

Archer, Jeff. *Strike Four: Adventures in European Baseball.* Lafayette CO: White Boucke, 1995.

Bedingfield, Gary. *Baseball in World War II Europe.* Charleston SC: Arcadia, 1999.

Bloyce, Daniel J. "Booming Baseball." *Brit Ball* (January 1994).

Carroll, Patrick. "Baseball in Graceland." *The SABR (UK) Examiner* 12 (July 2001): 5.

Chetwynd, Josh, "Do You Remember When . . . Great Britain Were the First Baseball World Champions?" *Observer Sport Monthly*, August 2002.

Crane, Newton. *The All-England Series: Baseball.* London: George Bell & Sons, 1891.

Elfers, James E. *The Tour to End All Tours: The Story of Major League Baseball's*

1913–1914 World Tour. Lincoln: University of Nebraska Press, 2003.

Levine, Peter. *A. G. Spalding and the Rise of Baseball*. New York: Oxford University Press, 1985.

Morely, Patrick. "19th Century Baseball Tours Visit England." *The SABR (UK) Examiner* 5 (January 1995).

Morgan, William. *First Base Magazine* (Summer 1987): 38–39.

Price, Ronald. "Way Down South." *The SABR (UK) Examiner* 12 (July 2001).

Smyth, Ian. "The History of Baseball in the North of England." Master's thesis, Leeds Polytechnic Faculty of Cultural and Education Studies, 1992.

4 | The Pacific

16 | Australia

Baseball Down Under

Baseball was first played in Australia in the 1850s when newly arrived Americans played with English and Australian cricketers in Melbourne. Meeting on the cricket grounds in the old Carlton Gardens on Saturday afternoons, the first Australian games took place in the shadow of the great Exhibition Hall, a replica of the original in London. The first recorded baseball match, played at Sydney's Moore Park on July 9, 1878, was a pickup game, with both teams drawn from members of the Surrey Cricket Club. For the occasion they called themselves the Surrey Base-Ball Club.[1]

Just one year later, baseball games were organized in Melbourne when the St. Kilda Baseball Club wanted to give some competition to a touring American Negro music troupe, the Georgia Minstrels. Other American baseball players visited Melbourne during this period, coming from ships in port and other minstrel groups. Local cricketers and ex-patriot Americans sometimes obliged by organizing a game, but interest in baseball seemed to vanish once the minstrels sailed away. Off and on there was talk of forming baseball clubs, but nothing came of it until 1882 when a group of men from the United States and Canada got together and formed the Union Base Ball Club. In keeping with the trend of playing against visiting groups, the "Unions" played several matches, including a series against another American minstrel troupe known as the Lewis Mastodon Minstrels. Soon the local team disbanded, only to be reorganized in 1886, when former members of the Unions living in Sydney organized the New South Wales Baseball Association (NSWBA).

It consisted of two teams, the Sydney and the Union Base Ball Clubs. The NSWBA soon scheduled a series of exhibition games in which Union and Sydney played each other for many weeks before the "big" game of May 1, 1886. Sydney beat Union 24–21.

When the American ship *Mariposa* visited Sydney in 1887, the NSWBA organized a game against the crew. The *Mariposa* team won 11–8. Only one more NSWBA club match was played between Sydney and Union before the association folded in 1891, marking the end of a five-year flirtation with the new American game. Baseball enthusiasts and managers soon learned, however, that A. G. Spalding, organizer of the first baseball world tour featuring American Major League players, intended to send two teams to the colony in 1888. This was to be the turning point in the development of Australian baseball.

The Spalding Baseball Tour of Australia introduced Australia to the American game. The tour was brash, expensive, and lavish—all of the things that other nations expected from Americans. Spalding, who had been a successful baseball player himself during the formative years of the sport in the United States, denied that he was trying to displace cricket as Australia's national pastime. Rather he hoped baseball would become "one of the kindred field sports of the country." A reporter, however, quoted Spalding as saying, "Baseball is a sport for the masses, cricket for the leisure classes. Baseball takes two to three hours. Cricket takes two to three days."[2] Spalding also expressed concern that the major English-speaking countries—Canada, the United States, Britain, Australia, and New Zealand—shared too few sports in common.

The Spalding tour was much more than just "the latest thing" from America. Bringing a new sport from a leading English-speaking nation to a group of prosperous British colonies was a unique occurrence in the Australian sporting and social calendar of the 1880s. The primary influence on Australia in the nineteenth century was Britain. This was reflected in virtually every aspect of Australian culture, but most directly in the ball game that Australia chose as its own. Cricket was British culture in Australia. It was the game of the average Australian, regardless of class or circumstances, and it was integral to both British and Australian nationalism. It was unthinkable that Spalding's tour in Australia could supplant British cricket with a new American game based on rounders. Spalding acknowledged this from the beginning and wisely promoted American baseball as a complement to rather than replacement for Australian/British cricket.

Spaulding's group of twenty players, several journalists, a cricket coach, a manager, two assistants, Spalding's mother, a few players' wives, and two professional entertainers—Professor Bartholomew, a daredevil balloonist and parachutist, and Clarence Duval, the Negro mascot of the tour—first toured the continental United States by rail before setting sail from San Francisco for Honolulu, New Zealand, and Australia. The tour reached Sydney on December 14, 1889. On December 24, 1888, the *Melbourne Age* had carried a long article on the rules of the game, accompanied by a diagram of the fielding positions. "The life and dash of baseball would make it popular with Australians. . . . [T]his will be the first link of a mutual friendship between the two continents." Sydney was the first port for the visiting Americans. Three well-attended games were played at the Sydney Cricket Ground. Two games played in Melbourne before Christmas drew 10,000 spectators. Chicago White Sox player John Tener commented to a local journalist that the crowd was "so enthusiastic that . . . they did not move until told that the game was over." Next the two Spalding teams traveled to Adelaide, where they played 3 games, each attracting about 2,000 spectators. On their return trip to Melbourne, they stopped in Ballarat and played a game before 4,500 people—a remarkably large crowd for an inland city.

When the Spalding tour sailed from Australia on January 7, they knew the tour had been a success. The tour went on to play in Colombo, Naples, Paris, London, Bristol, Birmingham, Glasgow, Manchester, Liverpool, Belfast, and Dublin. But none of these cities gave baseball the same reception and audience as did the cities in Australia. The Aussie press had given much space to covering the tour and were reasonably supportive, and they had received a warm welcome from both the cricket fraternity and local politicians. Spalding noted that the Australians were "the greatest sport loving people," and their temperate climate enabled them to play year-round. Spalding saw great potential for the game in Australia. Permanent baseball started in Australia in 1889 soon after the tour departed, and foundation clubs at St. Kilda in Victoria, Goodwood in South Australia, and East Melbourne still operate today.

The first teams of the New Victorian Baseball League were organized in March 1889 through the efforts of Harry Simpson of the Spalding tour, who stayed behind to develop baseball. The South Australian Baseball League came into existence just one month later. During 1889–90 Simpson moved among Adelaide, Broken Hill, and Melbourne helping to organize baseball clubs. Tragically, Simpson caught typhus and died in September 1891. With no family in Australia and having been in Sydney only that year, it must have been a lonely and painful death. Australian baseball's first development officer, the pioneer of several present clubs, lies in an unmarked grave in Sydney. Simpson's untimely death slowed Australian baseball development, especially in Sydney, though the sport did thrive in South Australia and Victoria; East Melbourne and Melbourne were competitive through the 1890s.

A Victorian proposal for an Australian baseball tour of America was met with great enthusiasm and a team was recruited from Victoria and South Australia. This team started with high expectations but was disappointed when their games either netted little financial reward or were canceled altogether. Worse, their manager, Harry Musgrove, abandoned the team in London as they prepared to return to Australia, taking most of the team funds with him. He reemerged months later in Australia with a new career as a theater entrepreneur. Nevertheless, the tour gave experience to many key Australian baseball players who became leaders in their local and state clubs.

The new millennium marked a new direction for Australian baseball as the state clubs that had started in the late 1890s in Victoria and New South Wales grew substantially, spawning other clubs. From 1900 to 1933, hundreds of teams in New South Wales, Victoria, and South Australia came and went, many of them affiliated with a parent cricket club. The baseball clubs of the twentieth century played their sport through the winter months.

This era of Australian baseball also marks the beginning of greater public and media interest in the game. Coverage of club and interstate games was now extensive, and baseball was considered a respectable game in its own right as well as the premier sport for cricketers in the off-season. Nevertheless, the stigma of being a "keep-fit-in-winter-for-cricket" sport relegated Australian baseball to second-class status. During the early 1900s Australian baseball teams played against teams from visiting American and Japanese ships and against professional American teams in 1914 and again in 1928–29. In addition an annual interstate carnival competition for adults and schoolboys was held, as well as a women's competition, and baseball teams started up in Queensland and western Australia.

Club and interstate baseball matches soon were played as pregames before Australian Rules football games in Victoria. This gave Melbourne baseball a distinct advantage, making the game better known on one hand but condemning it to live in the shadow of other sports on the other. By 1907 the matches were no longer called "interstate contests" and became known for the next sixty-five years as "carnivals."

Sixteen battleships of the touring American Great White Fleet visited Australia in August–September 1908. One hundred thousand people lined the harbor in Sydney to welcome them. They played five matches in Australia—two each against New South Wales and an "Australia" team in Sydney and another in Melbourne. The fleet won the series. Curiously, numerous Americans appeared soon after in the Sydney and Melbourne competitions as the American fleet later reported several hundred deserters in both cities.

Australia's first junior baseball was organized in 1907. It would be years, however, before a permanent junior system was in place. Eventually, junior baseball would develop high-quality players who would join the professional ranks in the United States, Japan, and Korea.

In October 1914 two Major League teams—the New York Giants and the Chicago White Sox, managed by John McGraw and Charles Comiskey, respectively—started a tour after the end of the Major League season, playing until the new season began in April. Both teams played their way across the U.S., and then sailed across the Pacific to Japan, Hong Kong, the Philippines, Australia, Ceylon, Egypt, Italy, France, and Britain. Upon arrival in Australia, the U.S. teams were feted and celebrated in an almost identical fashion to how the Spalding tour had been treated twenty-six years earlier. The Americans gave lots of instruction to Australian baseball players. Brisbane was the first port of call; on New Year's Day 1914 a large crowd saw the Giants beat the White Sox 2–1. This was probably the Queensland region's first serious look at the game they would later dominate. In Sydney the White Sox defeated the Giants 10–5. Games were also played against the Australian state teams of New South Wales and Victoria. Though beaten every time, the Aussies learned many valuable lessons about the game.

The Great War interrupted interstate play until 1919, and the war toll included many ballplayers. In the postwar years all three state baseball-governing bodies (South Wales, Victoria, and South Australia) made efforts to increase the profile of their sport. The Australian Baseball Council (ABC) was reformed in 1926 in the hopes that it would prevent misunderstandings and foster better communication and competition between the state teams. Never a national governing body before the 1950s, it nevertheless helped in a number of organizational ways. In the 1920s the three state bodies had been far too parochial to envisage anything much beyond "Will New South Wales win the Interstate Baseball Carnival again this year?" After a successful tour by the American fleet in 1926, the ABC, capitalizing on the fleet series' success, organized a visit of teams from Stanford University of California and Multnomah Athletics Club of Portland, Oregon. These two tours in the late 1920s had a significant impact, and are remembered by many Australians as the first baseball they ever saw. Many new players joined junior and senior club baseball.

This period of Australian baseball saw the game come of age and develop into a high-standard Australian sporting competition in which homegrown players developed from juniors in state and local clubs around the country. The national competition or carnival became known as the Claxton Shield in 1934, after sportsman Norrie Claxton donated the shield with his patronage. Australia's first Claxton Shield was held in Adelaide in August 1934 and was won by the hosts, South Australia. A few weeks after the 1939 Claxton Shield was played, Australia was at war with Germany. State clubs managed to keep local competitions going, though at times they had only a small number of players. All Claxton Shield play was abandoned during the war but the states agreed that New South Wales would host the first carnival when the war was over.

With the entry of the United States into the war in the Pacific, Australia found not only a powerful ally but also a new major consumer

18. *The 1937 New South Wales Championship team.* (Photo courtesy of the National Baseball Hall of Fame.)

visiting Australian cities. Visiting American servicemen were surprised to find lively baseball club competitions across the Australian state capital cities, albeit only in winter. The American visitors presented a great opportunity for the five Australian state baseball clubs to observe, play against, and entertain legions of men who had grown up playing baseball and loved it as an expression of their athleticism and nationalism. Throughout the war baseball thrived, and the participation of visiting American troops in Australian leagues was an impetus for a postwar baseball boom.

The postwar years of Claxton Shield produced quality competition worthy of the thousands of new players who were coming to the sport. All six mainland states participated in the series between 1946 and 1988, with the Northern Territory even fielding a team in the 1980s. Winter weather, especially rain, brought a push for a switch to summer baseball, and by 1970 all states were running a summer as well as a winter competition.

Many cricketers playing winter baseball had a difficult decision to make when their state changed to summer baseball. For some, it was easy as baseball had always been a way to stay fit for cricket, and now that it was a summer sport they would find something else. For others, the decision was agonizing. Not only were families and friendships affected but there were also club traditions. For a few there were career and economic concerns as well, as cricket offered the best players some hope of professional careers. Now, whether to continue with cricket in the summer or abandon it for baseball became, for the leading players, a decision as to how best to advance their potential for a professional career. Most of the top players stayed with cricket. Those who chose summer baseball gave up any chance of becoming a professional cricketer.

There was no denying the special relationship Australian baseball always had with cricket, but the basis of this relationship had always been that baseball was the subservient, junior partner to cricket. Cricket would get the first options on players, grounds, and funding. As Australian baseball players traveled overseas and entertained overseas players in Australia, there were always the questions: "Why does Australia play baseball in their winter? Is the appeal of Australian baseball so low that it can only be played when it doesn't conflict with cricket?" Today winter baseball continues to be popular in Australian club baseball not only for cricketers, who play baseball to stay in shape, but for many others who simply want to play a sport between August and April.

By 1960 Australian baseball was competing in the international arena with other leading baseball nations, and its junior clubs were training and supplying quality players such as Sid Thompson and Neil Page, the first Australians signed (1968) by the American Major Leagues. The Australian Baseball Federation now governed the sport and gave year-round guidance and administration. The question remained, however, as to whether the federation could go the next step and organize a new national competition to replace the Claxton Shield, which had become expensive and only offered a once-every-five-years opportunity for capital cities to host it.

In 1989 the Australian Baseball League (ABL) had eight teams: the Sydney Metros, Parramatta Patriots, Melbourne Monarchs, Waverley Reds, Gold Coast Clippers, Brisbane Bandits, Adelaide Giants, and Perth

Heat. The crowds and publicity were less than what was hoped for, but it was a start. The total ABL attendance was 376,000, with an average game attendance of 1,600, respectable for the first year of operation. At the end of year, though, the hapless Sydney Metros disbanded and the Melbourne Monarchs were expelled. The Metros were a curious, one-year wonder of a team with some bizarre adventures, such as being stranded in western Australia on their way to a series in Perth. They caught a commercial bus for the rest of the trip, were dropped a kilometer from the field, and climbed over the outfield fence to get into the ballpark. The first ABL grand final saw the two Melbourne teams, the Monarchs and Reds, play for the championship. This was fortunate because it saved the new league thousands of dollars in travel expenses. Even so, all clubs ran at a loss. Gate receipts averaged $40,000–$90,000, with sponsorships kicking in another $70,000 per team. About $500,000 was required to start a new team. Despite the financial woes, there was great optimism about the future of the new national league.

For the 1990 season, Pepsi paid $500,000 to become the naming sponsor of the league and remained so until 1994, when Pepsi withdrew, owing to poor results according to Pepsi, and poor commitment according to the ABL. The 1990 season saw limited television coverage, with Channel 9 covering the playoffs. Recorded attendance was 475,000. Two new teams, the Sydney Wave and Melbourne Bushrangers, joined the league. Entry into the competition by new teams in cities with ABL franchises was risky, but in the heady, early days of the league, expansion seemed a reasonable risk. Teams were eager to get into the league, despite the poor fortunes of some in the first year. Some did not have the financial means, which set precedents for the "deadbeat owner" syndrome of the future. As Baseball Victoria President Peter Dihm remarked,

Almost everybody except Perth and Sydney went into the ABL without enough money. And tried to cut each other's throats. That was crazy. That happened because they couldn't lie straight in bed. They were too fearful of telling their true financial position because people would take advantage of them.[3]

In the 1991 season, the costs of running an ABL team kept rising. Operating costs were now between $200,000 and $400,000 per team, with gate proceeds and sponsorships recouping only a fraction of that amount.

One of the highlights of the season was the record-breaking attendance of 11,444 at a heavily promoted Waverley Reds game. The Perth Heat, Adelaide Giants, Daikyo Dolphins, and Brisbane Bandits all managed to have regular television coverage. The Parramatta Patriots ended their season with a heavy loss and were sold, and became the Sydney Blues.

ABL's glamor team of the early 1990s was the Daikyo Dolphins. The Dolphins were put together from the core of the old Gold Coast Clippers, and with a prominent corporate sponsor there was ample funding. Not only did Daikyo put up lots of money, but they also attracted leading players from Australia and overseas, such as Dave Nilsson and John Jaha, to play for the Dolphins. The Daikyo Dolphins won the championship back to back in 1991 and 1992, but it was a bittersweet victory as the company pulled out of their commitment to the ABL that winter. The Dolphins would become the Gold Coast Cougars.

After a two-season absence, the Melbourne Monarchs rejoined the league in 1992, when the Footscray (Australian) Football Club purchased their license. This seemed to promise a stable future for the club. The Sydney Wave did not compete in 1992 because it lacked a lighted venue. The Sydney Blues emerged over the defunct Parramatta Patriots to claim the lighted stadium at Auburn. Televised games were shown every week and included a highlight show on Sunday mornings.

The 1993 season, the fifth for the ABL, enjoyed weekly television coverage including an ABL Game of the Week. The Melbourne Bushrangers moved to Canberra, while the Sydney Blues moved from Auburn to Parramatta Stadium, with its odd-shaped field. Originally a rugby field, it was converted to a baseball field but with a deep center field and a short left field, though a high net atop the left-field fence made it harder to hit a home run. The field dimensions brought criticism and derision from many sections of the league and baseball community.

The 1995 ABL season started without television coverage or a naming sponsor. Several weeks into the season, Channel 10 announced it would cover selected games on TV; Foxtel became the sponsor, and Coke was the official drink. The Sydney Blues beat the odds and won several spectacular games in the playoffs and took the championship.

By the beginning of the 1998 season, cracks in the ABL's financial management were visible everywhere. Reputedly $250,000 in debt, there were serious doubts the league would survive. The 1998 final between the Gold Coast Cougars and the Melbourne Reds, played at Altona, drew only 500 fans for the final and perhaps 1,000 for the grand final. The Cougars' Peter Hartas remarked on the dismal turnout.

Ten years down the track with the ABL, where are we? Lots of teams have gone broke. They gotta do somethin' to get people back to the game. It helps if you win. You saw what it was like at the '98 finals. I was embarrassed for the league. I didn't care if they were against us or with us as long as there were people there. I'd rather have people cheering against us than no one cheering at all. We Cougars couldn't believe the poor Melbourne crowd.[4]

The last ABL season was in 1999 and it was another dismal financial failure. Attendance was low, debts increased, and there was much doubt whether the league could continue. Throughout its ten-year history, the ABL suffered constant financial difficulties: owners refusing to pay, players demanding more money, high prices for equipment, stadium rental, and traveling expenses. While the ABL was deliberately established on the basis of autonomy for owners and a decentralized administration, it was clear after several years that there were flaws in this system. But the league did develop some top Australian baseball talent, some of whom won overseas professional contracts.

In 2000 the ailing Australian Baseball League was bailed out of certain liquidation by Australian-developed Major Leaguer Dave Nilsson and its name was changed to the International Baseball League (IBLA) of Australia. Nilsson had succored the embattled Gold Coast Cougars in 1998 and now rescued the entire league. Nilsson was confident from his years of experience in Claxton Shield and ABL competitions that his investment would keep the highest level of the Aussie game viable and perhaps attract international interest and sponsorships. Teams from Taiwan, Japan, Korea, and Hawaii were invited to join, making it an Asia/Pacific league, centered in Australia. The terms of the takeover of the ABL included Dave Nilsson paying $5,000,000 for the rights to an Australian national baseball competition for ninety-nine years. The team owners and Dave Nilsson believed that Australian baseball was entering a new era of security and prosperity. However, several weeks after the agreement and media releases, the ABL owners pulled out of the deal. This turn of events not only ended all the euphoria over the new national league but also killed any chance of another national league for Australian baseball. According to Nilsson the ABL wanted to go along with the new deal, but the owners were unhappy when they realized that Nilsson's $5,000,000 purchasing fee would not be used to assume their substantial debts.

Nilsson's IBLA operation began in early December 1999, but with small crowds and hefty expenses the teams soon floundered. Cost-cutting, lack of funds, and decreased services were apparent in all venues. Home runs were rare with the use of wooden bats. Media coverage was limited with few national radio or television stations even announcing results. For the IBLA and Dave Nilsson, it was a disappointing start.

On a positive note, Sydney's 2000 Olympics featured over 40 baseball games, enabling 25,000 to 50,000 to attend world-class baseball, thus proving Australians would pay to see good baseball. But following the Olympiad, IBLA's 2000-2001 season was made up of only a national series between Christmas and New Year's in major cities, and one international series based on the Gold Coast. These two series represented fewer than half of the baseball games that had previously been scheduled by the ABL. And then three weeks before the national Claxton Shield series was to be played, it was canceled, ostensibly because the grounds were not ready. There was speculation that the series was canceled because of political differences, dithering, and lack of funds. For the first time in over one hundred years (excluding wartime), Australian baseball would not have a national series.

While some might prematurely signal the beginning of the end of baseball in Australia following these woeful events, the game has survived in every corner of the country. At the club level, baseball is thriving. Hundreds of thousands of Australians compete in local leagues. Local clubs always have, and always will, own the real baseball game played in Australia. At the national level, the IBLA's performance in its first two years has left little confidence in building a true national competition.

Still, while the national league is in limbo, the increased memberships in club baseball all over the nation show that Australian club baseball will continue to give enjoyment to thousands of Australians who love the game. For me, as a fan and an amateur player, being involved in Australian baseball is to follow the sport with passion while knowing that it will never compete equally with other Australian sports such as cricket, rugby, and Australian Rules football.

The Australian style of baseball is similar to that in North America, notwithstanding the batting style and throwing, which are reminiscent of cricket. Pitching and fielding are the same, although some former cricketers find it strange that all fielders (not just the catcher-wicket-keeper) wear a mitt. Umpires are both respected and reviled—with disputes and ejections common at all levels. Spectators can be knowledgeable or "just in from the bush," not knowing anything about the game. Most local baseball clubs have a canteen that sells soft drinks, lollies, and some food, such as Australian meat pies, sausage rolls, and red-dye hot dogs. Whether American-style mustard is available for hot dogs depends on the individual club, but copious quantities of tomato sauce or ketchup are always available at any Australian baseball club canteen.

Finally, Australian baseball has received an enormous boost since winning the silver medal in the 2004 Olympics. Enjoying a national prominence absent since the 1999 Intercontinental Cup, Australian baseball was featured in the news and on every Olympic highlight show. With an Olympic medal, Australian baseball has won not only respect but also much needed financial support to develop the game at the junior level and hopefully to revive a national league.

Notes

1. *Sydney Mail*, July 13, 1878.
2. *The Spalding Official Base Ball Guide, 1890*, 93, courtesy the National Base ball Hall of Fame Library, Cooperstown NY.
3. Peter Dihm, interview by the author, April 1995, Melbourne.
4. Peter Hartas, interview by the author, October 1998, Sydney.

Bibliography

Dabscheck, Braham. "Australian Baseballers Form a Team of Their Own." *Sporting Traditions: Journal of the Australian Society for Sports History* 12, no. 1 (November 1995): 61–101.

Mitchell, Bruce. "A National Game Goes International: Baseball in Australia." *International Journal of the History of Sport* 9, no. 2 (August 1992).

———. "Two Tours and the Beginnings of Baseball in Australia." *Sporting Traditions: Journal of the Australian Society for Sports History* 7, no. 1 (November 1990): 3–24.

Palmer, Henry Clay, and Henray Chadwick. *Athletic Sports in America, England and Australia.* Philadelphia: Hubbard Brothers, 1889.

GEORGE GMELCH

Afterword

Is Baseball Really Global?

If we treat the fourteen baseball-playing nations in this volume as individual case studies and compare them, do any general patterns emerge in the history and development of baseball globally? The answer is yes, although how much we can say is limited by the diverse backgrounds and interests of the authors. With this in mind let's start with baseball's diffusion from its birthplace. The game arrived in the latter half of the nineteenth century to all the countries discussed in this book. The common belief, however, that Americans are responsible for spreading the game around the world is clearly wrong. As we have learned, the Japanese took the game to other countries in Asia, while the Cubans spread the game to neighboring Caribbean islands, notably Puerto Rico and the Dominican Republic.

Sometimes a single individual was responsible for introducing the game (or at least was given the credit). Examples include the American teacher Horace Wilson in Japan, lumber mill worker Albert Adlesberg in Nicaragua, and missionary Philip Gillett in Korea. More often, however, a group of people or an institution, such as the U.S. military in Latin America or Japanese colonial officials in Asia, brought the game. Local people watching soldiers and sailors playing baseball, for example, sometimes took up the game themselves. Locals were often invited to play and form their own teams. In other cases, as in Korea, colonial government policy aimed to encourage the local population to play. Returning students also have been baseball emissaries, bringing back the game after studying in the United States or Japan.

Deliberately attempting to introduce the game is quite different from being an inadvertent catalyst for its growth. In many cases (e.g., Australia, Brazil, Cuba, Puerto Rico) barnstorming foreign teams played an important role in exposing the new sport to the populace. The most heralded barnstormer was Albert Spalding and his 1888-89 world tour, which incited interest in baseball in Australia and Britain.[1] Korean players, returning home from Japan, traveled around Korea playing baseball and developing local interest. The influence of visiting American Negro League players who barnstormed through the Caribbean was a critical force in spreading the game there. These touring teams introduced the sport to many islanders who had never seen a baseball game before. The 1934 tour of Japan by U.S. Major League players, including Babe Ruth, led directly to the organization of the first Japanese professional league. This wasn't always the case. Of the eight nations visited by Spalding's world tour, Sri Lanka and Egypt never took up the game, and France didn't until after World War II, and then only minimally.

In most of our sample, baseball's growth as a sport has been glacially slow and spotty, characterized by periods of sound organization interrupted by stagnation, internal strife, and national events such as war and economic crises. The development of baseball in our three European cases—Italy, Holland, and Britain—has been particularly stunted. In recent years Major League Baseball International (MLBI) has spent lots of money trying to promote baseball in Europe with little to show for it. True, most European nations have a national team that competes in a continent-wide competition for the European Cup and for a spot in the Olympics once every four years, but beyond this there is still only spotty organization.[2] Alan Klein argues in *Growing the Game* that MLBI should forget about Western Europe and put its money into developing baseball in less developed nations, including those in Eastern Europe, where natural athletes would be attracted by the chance to make money playing professional baseball, similar to the way in which poor inner-city American blacks are drawn to basketball.[3]

In Britain and its former colonies, baseball faced stiff competition from the entrenched British game of cricket. Even today cricket has a much larger world following than baseball; eleven nations participate in cricket's international test match competition, and ninety-seven nations belong to the International Cricket Council. In the places where baseball did catch on, it did so primarily as an activity to keep cricketers and other athletes fit during their off-season. In Holland, Italy, and Brazil, among others, baseball has also had difficulty competing against soccer. I am reminded of baseball's marginal status in these nations when I meet their international students on my campus and ask what they know about baseball. Usually they know very little. Recently I had a conversation with two young men from England and China; neither one had an inkling that baseball existed in their homelands. The Chinese scholar thought I must be confusing his country with some other place like Taiwan.

In a number of instances, however, a nation's success in international baseball competitions, such as Taiwan's Little League Championships, Korea's winning the Asian Amateur Baseball Championship and being co-champions with Japan at the World Baseball Championships, and Australia's better than expected silver medal in the 2004 Olympics, has increased popular interest in the sport and been a source of national pride. Baseball sometimes becomes a vehicle for promoting nationalism. The Taiwanese, for example, used baseball to assert their identity over their Japanese colonizers, and later, in the 1970s, their Little League Championships fed the country's independence movement and activists used the game to challenge Chinese nationalist hegemony. In Korea baseball played a significant role in constructing an overarching national identity and in integrating the country's disgruntled minorities. For patriots in Cuba during Spanish rule, shunning the Spanish-style bullfights in favor of the radical new game of baseball was a bold political statement. That baseball became an official Olympic sport during the Olympic Games in Barcelona in 1992 has also boosted interest and government funding in Australia, China, Taiwan, and Korea. China is now working to build a strong team in order to compete in the 2008 Beijing games. But government support for baseball is precarious and could easily disappear now that baseball has been dropped from the 2012 games in London.[4]

One of the benefits of the diffusion of baseball to other nations is that it gives local people greater choice in the sports they can play and watch. Many people in Asia, in particular, no longer want only traditional sports but yearn for "modern" ones played by Western nations. For many, sports such as basketball and baseball have come to symbolize modernity.

In only five of the nations examined in this collection (Cuba, Japan, the Dominican Republic, Puerto Rico, and Canada), however, has baseball developed into a major national sport. If we add Venezuela and the United States to this list, we are talking about fewer than ten nations in the world where baseball is a national pastime. In only three of these—Cuba, the Dominican Republic, and the United States—can we genuinely talk about baseball as embodying the character of a nation. Nevertheless, baseball today is played in many more nations than ever before; the International Baseball Federation (IBF) claims to have ninety-seven members. Realistically, however, many of the countries the IBF counts, such as American Samoa, Armenia, Cameroon, Guyana, Iran, Israel, Micronesia, and Papua New Guinea, have nothing more than a correspondent and a few club teams in the capital city, and sometimes most of the players are expatriate Americans.

The status of baseball in our fourteen countries hardly adds up to a sport that has become truly global, certainly nothing like basketball. Ever since the NBA's Dream Team appeared at the 1992 Olympics in Barcelona, basketball has become, in the words of Sports Illustrated's Alexander Wolff, a global lingua franca.[5] NBA league games are now shown on television in 212 countries; the Los Angeles Lakers even have commentators who broadcast in Farsi. A 1997 survey of Western European youth found that 93 percent recognized the Chicago Bulls logo.[6] The Web site NBA.com draws over one-third of its hits from outside the United States. The NBA now has eleven offices outside North America, and 15 percent of the NBA's merchandising revenue comes from abroad. Among teenagers worldwide, the NBA is part of American popular culture, along with fashion, music, films, McDonald's, Coca Cola, and Nike.

There is little if any evidence that baseball will ever achieve this kind of international success. In most of our nations, baseball's growth is modest at best, while in Australia, Britain, and Nicaragua popular interest in baseball has waned. In England and Australia professional baseball leagues have folded. And in 2012 there will be no baseball played at the Olympics.

If we compare professional baseball's development in our sample nations with its development in the United States, the differences are staggering. With 30 major, 170 affiliated minor, and 44 independent professional league teams, the United States dwarfs its competition. Japan, the nation with the next most highly developed level of professional play, has only twelve teams in its Major League with a single minor league affiliate for each. Korea has eight Major League teams, China and Taiwan each have six, and the Dominican Republic has only five. The talent level of baseball players in most of the nations that have a professional league—China, Taiwan, Korea, the Dominican Republic, Nicaragua, Italy, Holland—rarely equals that of a low-level minor league in the United States. Except for Japan, where teams play 140 league games, no other professional league even approaches the 162 regular season game schedule played by MLB and the 144-game schedule of most American minor leagues. (In Taiwan they play 100 games, in Cuba 90, in the Dominican Republic 72, in Italy 54, in England 32, and in China 30.)

The average attendance at baseball games in all the professional leagues outside the United States, except for Japan, rarely equals the 3,200 spectators that the average American Class A minor league team draws on a typical night. Nowhere do the players' salaries approach the average MLB salary of $2.5 million per season; nowhere are foreign ball clubs worth anything close to the $300 to $900 million dollars MLB franchises bring. Only in the United States do both the majors and minors place no limit on the number of foreign or "import" players.

On the other hand, baseball in our sample nations is producing some very talented players, enough that MLB teams are sending scouts. All but Brazil have already contributed players to the U.S. Major Leagues. Indeed, on opening day of the 2005 season there were 242 foreign-born players on the MLB club rosters, representing 15 foreign countries, Puerto Rico, and the Virgin Islands. In total, the foreign born made up 29 percent of baseball's 829 players (750 active and 79 disabled) listed on opening day rosters. The largest contingent of foreign players (88 percent) came from the Caribbean and Latin America. The Dominican Republic led all countries with 91 players, followed by Venezuela with 46, and Puerto Rico with 34. The Washington Nationals alone had 16 foreign-born players from six nations (Cuba, the Dominican Republic, Japan, Mexico, Puerto Rico, and Venezuela), leading all other MLB teams. Three other teams (the Orioles, Dodgers, and Mets) each had thirteen foreign-born players. The real form baseball "globalization" has taken is not the export of the game from the United States to foreign countries but the migration of baseball labor to the United States. Welcome to the international pastime.

The presence of so many international players is changing the face of American baseball. For one, the game is becoming noticeably Latinized. When you walk into a clubhouse today you are as likely to hear Spanish as English; clubhouse music is often salsa or merengue; the food on the clubhouse training table and in spring training cafeterias often includes Latin dishes. Latin influence is also evident on the field, as Latin players bring a looser and more flamboyant style to the game. Think of Sammy Sosa hopping down the line or David Ortiz pointing to the heavens after hitting a home run. Players show exuberance when making a good play or getting an important hit. Such behavior was called "hot-dogging" in the 1960s when there were far fewer Latinos, and it could result in the pitcher knocking the offender down the next time he came to the plate. Today Latinos have reached the critical mass where such behavior is now an accepted part of the game. I believe that Latinos may also influence how today's players deal with losing. In my experience, Latinos more than Anglos tend to leave the game—win or lose—on the field. While they may be "emotional" immediately after making an error or blowing a lead, they are inclined to get over it more quickly than Anglo players. Latino players sulk less in the clubhouse and on the team bus. Not long ago, baseball managers expected their players to be subdued and quiet after a loss and would question a player's devotion to his team if he wasn't. I believe that is slowly changing toward the more relaxed Latino way.

Latinos are also influencing how positions are played. Having grown up playing on rocky fields, where bad hops made it prudent to protect oneself, Hispanic middle infielders sometimes field ground balls off to the side instead of getting their bodies directly in front of the ball as American players are taught to do. Latino infielders will often throw to first base while their bodies are off balance or on the run; an Anglo player would be more likely to plant his feet and then throw. This style is now becoming accepted and is rubbing off on Anglo players. Most baseball people now think that Latin American players have improved the game defensively and made it quicker. The influx of Hispanic players into MLB and their dominance at the top of most statistical categories has shattered the notion for mainstream American fans that their baseball players are the best in the world.[7]

Many Anglo players who never learned Spanish in school now know some of the language, and they've learned something about Latin American geography and customs. International players, whether from Latin America or Asia, inevitably also introduce American baseball fans to their countries and cultures, whether it is the customs mentioned by TV color commentators or cultural geography introduced through ESPN specials like those that followed Sammy Sosa and Pedro Martinez around their hometowns in the Dominican Republic.

What about Asian players? Might they also be agents of change? Because there are far fewer of them (22 on MLB's 2005 opening day rosters; less than one-tenth the number of Latinos), and because they are scattered widely around the two leagues, their influence is certain to be much less than that of Latinos. When I asked some of my baseball contacts (i.e., scouts and players) what influence Asian players (14 of the 22 are Japanese) might have, no one was sure. Several thought, however, that the Asians' highly disciplined approach to the game, healthier diet, rigorous training, and greater respect many have for their equipment is observed by their teammates. Japanese equipment—bats and gloves—have already found their way into American baseball (and most stadiums now have Diamondvision, which was developed in Japan). The unusual hitting style (when swinging the weight is transferred to the front side of the body more quickly than is true for most American players) has, largely because of Ichirō's success, been noted and analyzed by many. But it is too soon to say whether any of this will ever be mimicked by many American players.

The essays in this volume raise several interesting questions for future research. Will the transnational movement of players (e.g., Latinos and Asians playing in the United States, Americans playing in Japan and the Caribbean) homogenize baseball, flattening out local versions of the game into a globalized hybrid? We have already seen how the infusion of foreign talent into the U.S. Major Leagues is producing a hybridized form of baseball, one that exhibits many characteristics of the Latin American game. What is the appeal of baseball for fans in different cultures? The essays on Japan, Puerto Rico, and Cuba give some clues. How does the experience of being a spectator vary cross-culturally?

There is still much that we do not know about how baseball is transformed abroad, whether it is Korean professional baseball or pickup ball in a Dominican village. The diffusion of baseball is no different than the flow of knowledge, ideas, information, or technology, in that when it arrives in a new society it is changed as local people adapt the game to fit their own needs and values. While the essays in this volume give us some insight into the ways in which local people put their own stamp on the American game, there is much more to learn.

Notes

1. The underlying purpose of the first expedition/tour, which was limited to locations under European control, was to market Spalding's sporting goods.
2. MLBI is trying to rectify this by sponsoring teams and exposing schoolchildren to the sport through its curriculum-based Play Ball program. See Alan Klein's *Growing the Game: Globalization and Major League Baseball* (New Haven: Yale University Press, 2006), for an excellent discussion of MLBI's international efforts to promote baseball abroad, such as the envoy and coach-in-residence programs. The latter sends ten to fifteen American coaches to Europe for six to eight weeks during the summer to instruct local youth.
3. Klein, *Growing the Game*.
4. In 1981 baseball was granted the status of a demonstration sport for the 1984 Olympic Games in Los Angeles. Another demonstration tournament was held in 1988 at the Olympic Games in Seoul. At the International Olympic Committee congress, it was decided that the first official Olympic baseball tournament would be held in Barcelona in 1992.
5. Alexander Wolff, *Big Game, Small World* (New York: Warner Books, 2002), xvii.
6. Toby Miller et al., *Globalization and Sport: Playing the World* (London: Sage, 2001), 15.

7. At the end of the 2004 season, Ichirō Suzuki of Japan had the record for most hits in a single season. Johan Santana of Venezuela was the American League Cy Young winner. Dominicans owned the World Series MVP award (Manny Ramirez) the AL MVP award (Vladimir Guerrero), both League Championship Series MVP awards (Albert Pujols and David Ortiz), the Major League home run title (Adrian Beltre), and the RBI title (Miguel Tejada). Carlos Beltran of Puerto Rico emerged as arguably the best all-around player in the game and became the prize of the free agent crop.

The Contributors

CARLOS AZZONI, one of Brazil's leading economists, is the associate dean of the Faculdade de Economia, Administração e Contabilidade, University of São Paulo. He is the author of many scholarly articles, and this is his first publication on baseball. Like most Brazilians, his first love is *futebol* (soccer).

TALES AZZONI is a journalist and photographer with the Associated Press in São Paulo. He writes extensively on sports. While attending high school in the United States (while his father Carlos was teaching at Ohio State University), he played high school baseball. He later worked as a journalist at a daily newspaper in Florida before returning to Brazil. He follows Major League Baseball closely from São Paulo.

PETER CARINO is a professor of English at Indiana State University. His research interests include baseball in literature and culture. He coordinates the annual Indiana State Conference on Baseball and Literature, and is the editor of *Baseball/Culture: Selected Essays: 1995–2001*. He suffers the affliction of being a lifelong fan of the New York Mets.

THOMAS CARTER teaches at the Caerlon campus of the University of Wales. He spent the summers of his youth on Minnesota's small-town diamonds. Having traveled to Latin America while attending St. Cloud State University, he became interested in Cuban baseball. Later, while a PhD student at the University of New Mexico, he did his dissertation research on Cuban politics and baseball. He now specializes in the cross-cultural study of sport and is finishing a book on Cuban baseball since the end of the cold war.

JOSH CHETWYND was born in London but grew up in Los Angeles. In 1996 he discovered that Great Britain had a national baseball team; he has been a member of the squad ever since. He also played Division I college baseball at Northwestern University and played professionally in the independent Frontier League and in Sweden's Elite Series. He has worked as a journalist for *USA Today* and *U.S. News & World Report* and as an on-air TV broadcaster of British telecasts of Major League Baseball games. He holds two degrees in journalism from Northwestern and recently finished a law degree at the University of Arizona.

JOSEPH CLARK was raised in the United States but immigrated to Australia as a young man. During his second year in Australia he joined the Baulkham Hills baseball club in Sydney, which he still plays for twenty-five years later. While teaching history at a private secondary school, Joe's baseball coach suggested he investigate the history of Australian baseball. Unable to find any literature, Joe began doing research of his own, which ten years later has led to a PhD dissertation and a book, *The History of Australian Baseball.*

GEORGE GMELCH is Roger Thayer Stone Professor of Anthropology at Union College in upstate New York. He played minor league baseball in the 1960s while studying anthropology at Stanford University in the off-season. He has studied nomads, return migrants, commercial fishermen, Alaskan natives, and Caribbean villagers. Two of his most recent books have been on baseball: *In the Ballpark: The Working Lives of Baseball People* and *Inside Pitch: Life in Professional Baseball.* He is currently doing research on wine tourism in California's Napa Valley.

DAN GORDON is a freelance journalist who has published extensively on international aspects of baseball. He has followed the Red Sox since his father took him to his first baseball game at Fenway Park in the summer of 1975. His interest in global baseball grew out of his love affair with the ballpark atmosphere; he has long been fascinated with the subtle differences in how fans take in a game in other cultural settings. With a Thomas J. Watson Fellowship, Gordon studied baseball culture in Japan, the Dominican Republic, Cuba, and Nicaragua. He is the co-author of *Cape Encounters*.

COLIN HOWELL is a professor of history and director of the Gorsebrook Research Institute and the Center for the Study of Sport and Community Health at Saint Mary's University in Halifax, Nova Scotia. He is the author and editor of a number of books on sport history, including *Northern Sandlots: A Social History of Maritime Baseball* and *Blood, Sweat and Cheers: Sport and the Making of Modern Canada*.

WILLIAM W. KELLY is a professor of anthropology and Sumitomo Professor of Japanese Studies at Yale University. He is a leading authority on Japanese culture and sport. While doing fieldwork in rural Japan in the 1970s and 1980s, he occasionally played in a local farmers' baseball league, whose games began at 5:30 a.m. so team members could get to the rice fields afterward. He is the editor of *Fanning the Flames: Fandoms and Consumer Culture in Contemporary Japan*, and the author of *This Sporting Life: Sports and Body Culture in Modern Japan*. He is finishing a book about the Hanshin Tigers, a professional team in Osaka.

ALAN KLEIN is a professor of sociology-anthropology at Northeastern University. His academic interest in baseball research grew out of his love of the game. The convergence of the adult social scientist and the child who played the game came about in his reading a newspaper account of why the Dominican Republic was producing so many fine Major Leaguers. He says, "I was struck by the oversimplicity of the argument, and the shallow presentation of life and culture, and my research was launched. The idea that something I was so blinded by could be such a 'serious' field of study still intrigues me and informs my work." He is the author of *Sugarball: The American Game, the Dominican Dream*; *Baseball on the Border: A Tale of Two Laredos*; and *Growing the Game: Globalization and Major League Baseball*.

ANDREW MORRIS is an associate professor of history at California Polytechnic State University, San Luis Obispo. He is the author of *Marrow of the Nation: A History of Sport and Physical Culture in Republican China*, and he is currently working on a book on the history of Taiwanese baseball. In the early 1990s he lived two blocks from the baseball stadium in Taizhong, Taiwan, and became a die-hard fan of the President Lions, which led to an interest in questions of colonialism, nationalism, and ethnic identity in Taiwan's national game.

FRANKLIN OTTO was born and raised Puerto Rico. He taught in the U.S. Virgin Islands public schools in St. Croix from 1970 to 1973 and worked for the New York State Education Department's Office of Bilingual Education from 1977 to 2003. He has published articles on aspects of Puerto Rican baseball and on the experiences of Puerto Ricans living and playing in the United States.

WAYNE PATTERSON is a professor of computer science and associate vice provost for research at Howard University. He directs a U.S.–Brazil student exchange program with Carlos Azzoni, which is how he was introduced to *beisebol* in Brazil. He holds a PhD in mathematics from the University of Michigan and does research on computer security and cryptology. He first became interested in Brazilian baseball on his first trip to the country when he turned on the television set in his hotel room and found a live broadcast of a baseball game from Japan. Curious as to why a Japanese game would be broadcast in Brazil, he began his inquiry into *beisebol*.

JOSEPH A. REAVES is the national baseball writer for the *Arizona Republic*. For many years he covered Asia for the *Chicago Tribune, Reader's Digest*, and UPI. Upon returning to the United States, he worked for the *Chicago Tribune* covering the Chicago Cubs. He is the author of *Warsaw to Wrigley: A Foreign Correspondent's Tale of Coming Home from Communism to the Cubs* and *Taking in a Game: A History of Baseball in Asia*, which won the Jerry Malloy Prize for the best book in baseball in 2001.

HARVEY SHAPIRO has coached U.S. college baseball for over thirty years, notably at Springfield College, Bowdoin College, and the University of Hartford. He was hired to coach a club team (Amstel Tigers) in Holland, and several years later became the coach of the Dutch National Team. He has given baseball clinics in Zimbabwe, South Africa, Holland, Germany, and the Netherlands Antilles. He has also coached in the Cape

Cod Baseball League, the premier summer collegiate league, and in 1996 was named Manager of the Year.

THOMAS E. VAN HYNING was the U.S. correspondent for the Puerto Rico Baseball Hall of Fame from 1991 to 1996. He has written two books on the Puerto Rico Winter League. He has worked as an economist, city planner, and management consultant in Puerto Rico; a tourism and leisure studies researcher at Southern Illinois University; and as an assistant professor of tourism at Pennsylvania's Keystone College. Since 1994 he has been the research manager of the Mississippi Division of Tourism.

TIM WENDEL teaches writing at Johns Hopkins University and is the author of *Castro's Curveball* and *The New Face of Baseball: The One-Hundred-Year Rise and Triumph of Latinos in America's Favorite Sport.* He was one of the founders of USA *Today Baseball Weekly*, where he served as an editor and writer. He became interested in Cuban baseball when accompanying the 1992 U.S. Olympic team to Cuba for a series of exhibition games before the Barcelona Olympics. He said, "Not only was the level of play in Cuba far better than I expected, but the people's passion for the game was what it used to be in this country. I've been hooked ever since."

Index

Aaron, Hank, 166
Abe, Yusuke, 17, 19
Adlesberg, Albert, 177, 305
Albrook Field (Panama), 185
All-American Girls Professional
    Baseball League (AAGPBL), 219
Allen, Jim, 14
Alou, Felipe, 122
Amador, Julian, 178
Amateur Baseball World Champion-
    ship, 256–57, 260–61, 277
Archer, Jeff, 280–81
Armas, Enrique, 182, 183
Atlantic Series, 176
Australian baseball: Australian Base-
    ball League (ABL), 298–302; Clax-
    ton Shield, 296, 302; club matches,
    295; effects of World War I on,
    296; impact of American service-
    men on, 296–97; International
    Baseball League, 301–2; and in-
    ternational competition, 298, 302,
    303; New South Wales Baseball As-
    sociation, 291–92; origins of, 291–
    95; and relationship with cricket,
    298; tour of, 318

Barney, Bob, 213

barnstorming, 137, 162, 178, 185, 217,
    218, 306
Barrio Jonathan Gonzalez, 172
baseball academies, 123–25, 132; at
    Houston Astros, 180; for Nica-
    raguan prospects, 179; in Puerto
    Rico, 170
Baseball Hall of Fame: in Canada,
    218, 219; in Japan, 67; in U.S., 138,
    162, 223, 252
Baseball News, 280
basketball, 307
Beaufort, Duke of, 266
Best, Cal, 222
Bianchi, Roberto, 234–35
bird dogs, 181
Bithorn Stadium (San Juan), 160, 161,
    169, 170
Boucheir, Nancy, 213
Brazilian baseball: academies, 203;
    and attendance at games, 207; and
    Brazilian Olympic Committee,
    206; Confederation of Baseball
    and Softball, 201, 203, 206, 207;
    contrasted to U.S. baseball, 204;
    exhibition series against Colum-
    bia University by, 200; face of, 207;
    future of, 206–9; growth of, 203,

Brazilian baseball (*cont.*)
206; influence of Japanese community on, 197, 198–99; and international competition, 203, 205, 206; National team, 203, 205, 208; origins of, 198–99; vs. popularity of soccer, 196, 198, 206, 208, 209; post–World War II development of, 199; professionals playing in U.S. and Japan, 201–2; São Paulo Federation of Baseball and Softball, 199; series with Waseda University, 200; training methods in, 206–7; uniqueness of, 196

British baseball: Americanism of, 280; American tour with, 270; attendance at, 274, 275; cooperation with MLB by, 283–84; controversy within, 283; and exhibitions with Americans, 264, 265–67; fan behavior in, 275; foreign players in, 276, 283–84; future of, 282–85; Great Britain National Team, 263; leagues, 272–77, 280; media and, 267–68; origins of, 264; postwar, 278; regional issues in, 281–82; rules of, 273; vs. soccer, 263, 264, 267, 268, 269, 270, 272, 273, 275, 280; sportsmanship in, 264; U.S. Olympic team and, 275, 277; during wartime, 271, 277–78

buscón, 127–32, 180
Bush, George W., 197
Bushido, 9, 10

Canadian baseball: American influence on, 212, 213, 215, 216, 224; barnstorming in, 218; Baseball Canada, 223–24; color barrier in, 221–22; and concerns over respectability, 216–17; development of, 213; effects of World War II on, 220–21; future of, 224; Hall of Fame, 218, 219; minor leagues in, 217; and Negro Leaguers, 218–19; and players in early U.S. leagues, 214–15; players in MLB and, 212; Quebec Provincial League, 222; social classes within, 216, 217, 224; spread of, 215–16; women's, 219

Cardenal, Jose, 141
Castelli, Giorgio, 234
Castro, Fidel, 31, 122, 137–39, 140, 143, 144, 145, 149, 150, 153
Cayasso, Jorge, 178, 179
Central American Games, 179
Chappas, Harry, 237
cheering section. *See* Japanese baseball
Chinese baseball: Chinese Baseball Association, 59, 60; Chinese Baseball League (CBL), 44, 60; Chinese Educational Mission, 46–49, 50, 52, 53, 61; cultural revolution and, 56–57; foreigners in, 77–79; foreign scouting of, 83; gambling within, 82; origins of, 49–50; training in, 53–54, 59, 60
Choi, Heep Sop, 89, 91
Crane, Newton, 265, 266
cricket, 177, 263, 268, 306–7
Cuadra, Bayardo, 179
Cuban baseball: and attitudes toward Castro, 140; effects of embargo on, 136; equipment of, 139; exhibition series against Baltimore Orioles by, 144–45; exhibition series with U.S. by, 143–44;

fans of, 153–58; impact of revolution on, 139; nationalism and, 149; origins of, 147–49; popularity of, 143; as social event, 148

Dennis Martinez Stadium (Managua), 176
DePosada, Jorge L., 167–68
Di Gesu, Enzo, 232
diffusion of baseball, 305
Dominican baseball: academies, 123–25, 132; contemporary, 125–26; origins of, 118–22; and players in MLB, 118, 122; winter league of, 126–27
Dutch baseball (honkbal): baseball system in, 248; contrasted to U.S. baseball, 249, 251; Dutch Baseball Federation, 248, 251; Dutch National Team, 247, 249, 250, 251, 253–54; fans of, 259; fighting in, 256; future of, 261; and Harlaam Honkbal week, 254–55; media and, 252–53, 260; origins of, 247; player development in, 251–52; practice habits in, 250; Royal Dutch Baseball and Softball Association, 247, 253; vs. soccer, 247; umpiring in, 252; and visiting American teams, 248

Echevarría, Roberto González, 138
Escambrón Stadium (San Juan), 162
Espinoza, Lester Hernandez, 180
Espolita, Andres, 186
Esquina Caliente, 141
Estádio do Bom Retiro (São Paulo), 200
ethics in baseball, 10, 37
European Championship, 249, 259, 263, 281

Falcone, Pete, 238
Fowler, Dick, 220
Funderberk, Mark, 239

Garcia, Carlos, 188–91
Gasteazoro, Enrique, 183
Genovese, George, 140–41
Gillet, Phillip Loring, 92, 94, 95
Glorioso, Giulio, 233
Gould, Stephen, 213
Guillermon Moncada Stadium (Santiago), 257

Hanshin Tigers, 23, 24, 27, 30
He Long, Marshall, 54, 56, 57, 61
Herb Huton All-Americans, 98
Hernandez, Gerald, 191–93
Hernandez, J. J., 181
Hoak, Don, 138, 139
hockey, 215
Hong, Rong, 45–46, 61
Horikawa, Takahiro, 15–16
Humber, Bill, 215

International Baseball Federation, 308
international competition, 307; American, 258; Asian, 258–59; Cuban, 257, growth of, 307–8
Italian baseball: attendance at, 242; ballparks of, 243–44; corporate sponsorship of, 235–36; fans, 242–43, 244–45; Federazione Italiana Baseball and Softball, 229, 230–32; foreign players in, 236–39; hitters league in, 233–34; influence of U.S. Marines on, 235; international play by, 241–42, 260; Italians in minor leagues of, 241; lack of

as musicians, 179; beginnings of, 177–79; charity by, 181; effects of U.S. Marines on, 178; equipment in, 178; fans of, 175–76; food vendors and, 176; future of, 187; importation of players by, 186; and journalists, 190–91; Liga Profesional, 186; major leaguers in, 181; Mayor A Ball, 182, 188; National Guard team of, 186; Nicaraguan Federation of Amateur Baseball (FENIBA), 188–89; and players in U.S., 185; popularity of, 175; radio broadcasters of, 182; Sandanistas' impact on, 189, 191–92; scouting for, 181; teams, 175; and winterball, 175; street ball and, 177

Nichols, Kid, 215
Nilsson, Dave, 301–2

O'Malley, Peter, 44, 59, 123, 190
Oh, Sadaharu, 12
Oi, Celia Abe, 198
Ojima, Kleber, 205
Okazaki, Misuyoshi, 7, 16, 19
Oleksak, Michael and May, 197
Olympics, 40, 59, 60, 110, 261, 275, 285, 302, 303, 306, 307, 308, 309
Olympic Stadium (Montreal), 223
Orta, Jorge, 236, 237
Otsuka, Jorge, 201, 205–7
outlaw leagues, 220
Owen, Mickey, 166, 221

Padilla, Vincente, 181–82, 183, 187
Paquito Montaner Stadium (Ponce), 169
Pepitone, Joe, 90
PETCO Park (San Diego), 110

Pett, José, 201
Puerto Rican baseball: barnstorming tours by, 162; nicknames in, 164; origins of, 161–62; and players in U.S., 163–64; Semi-Pro League, 162–63; training in, 167
Puerto Rican Winter League: ballparks of, 168–69; fans of, 168; foreign players in, 165; future of, 170–71; salaries in, 166; training in 167–69
purity, 7–8, 13, 17; in Japanese high school baseball, 7–8; in Korea, 108

Randle, Lenny, 236–37
Rice, Grantland, 270
Roberto Clemente Stadium (Hato Rey), 175
Robinson, Jackie, 221–22
Rodriquez, Edgard, 192
Rondon, Tito, 183
Rosales, Efrain, 172–73, 174–75, 176, 186, 187, 188, 191
Roy, Jean Pierre, 221
Ruiz, Ivan, 182
Ruth, Babe, 23, 33, 55, 68, 69, 98, 108, 233, 234, 275, 306

São Paulo, 198, 200, 203
SARS, 43, 44, 59
Sasai, Yoshiko, 5, 6, 7, 10, 11, 12, 14
Sa Silva, Olimpio de, 199
senbazuru, 7
Shaw, George Bernard, 271
Sheldon, Dave, 239
Simontacchi, Jason, 237–38
Simpson, Harry, 294
Sixto Escobar Stadium (San Juan), 169

soccer, 5, 16, 19, 28, 35, 37, 40, 43, 57,
93, 172, 174, 175, 180, 184, 192, 193,
194, 196, 198, 199, 204, 206, 208, 213,
215, 230, 231, 232, 242, 243, 244, 245,
248, 250, 261, 263, 264, 267, 268,
269, 270, 272, 273, 275, 280, 307
Space Shuttle Discovery, 3
Spalding Official Baseball Guide, 267
Spalding World Tour, 264–65, 266,
292–94, 306
Springfield College, 246, 249
stickball, 183
Stimac, Craig, 239
Strohmayer, John, 168
Suzuki, Ichirō, 15, 18, 39, 208, 311, 313
Szulc, Tad, 138

Tener, John, 293
Tereharu, Hayato, 18
Tijerino, Edgard, 193
Tobita, Suishu, 9
Tokyo Giants, 18, 24, 32
Toronto Blue Jays, 224

Toronto Maple Leafs Club, 217
training: in China, 53–54, 59, 60; in
Japan, 4, 8, 9, 14, 15, 17, 27, 32, 36,
38, 52; in Korea, 102; in Puerto
Rico, 167; in Taiwan, 69, 75, 79–81

Urbanaz, Charlie, 250
USA Today Baseball Weekly, 141

Vargas, Calixto, 179, 180
violence in baseball: in Japan, 15;
in Korea, 92, 97, 110–11, 112; in Taiwan, 74
Vosberg, Ed, 238

Wakata, Koichi, 3, 19
Watanabe, Motonori, 17
Whiting, Robert, 7, 18, 36, 104
Wilson, Horace, 19, 306
Wilson, Willie, 190, 193
World Baseball Classic, 110

Yazawa, Kenichi, 14–15